HAW-HO-NOO;

OR,

RECORDS OF A TOURIST.

BY

CHARLES LANMAN,

AUTHOR OF "LETTERS FROM THE ALLEGHANY MOUNTAINS," ETC.

And without registering these things by the pen,
they will slide away unprofitably.
OWEN FELTHAM.

PHILADELPHIA:
LIPPINCOTT, GRAMBO AND CO.,
SUCCESSORS TO
GRIGG, ELLIOT AND CO.,
14 NORTH FOURTH STREET.
1850.

Entered according to the Act of Congress, in the year 1850, by

LIPPINCOTT, GRAMBO AND CO.,

in the Clerk's Office of the District Court of the Eastern District of Pennsylvania.

PHILADELPHIA:
T. K. AND P. G. COLLINS, PRINTERS.

TO

WILLIAM CULLEN BRYANT, ESQ.,

IN WHOM ARE BLENDED

ALL THE MORE EXALTED ATTRIBUTES OF

THE POET AND THE MAN,

This Volume

IS AFFECTIONATELY INSCRIBED,

BY

THE AUTHOR.

TO THE PUBLIC.

THE title and table of contents of this volume contain all that I have to say in regard to its character. My only apology for again appearing before the public is to be found in the treatment which I have heretofore experienced from the critics. With *one* exception, the more prominent periodicals of England and the United States have spoken of my former productions in the most kindly manner, and I sincerely thank them for their friendship. With regard to the exception alluded to—the *"North American Review"*—I have only to say that its assault upon me was cruel, prompted by an unworthy motive, and wholly undeserved. I write from impulse and for the pleasure which the employment affords. That my books are popular is indeed a matter of rejoicing; but I make no pretensions whatsoever in the literary line, and only desire the approbation of those who are willing to believe me a lover of truth, of nature, and my friends.

The word HAW-HO-NOO was originally applied to America by the Iroquois Indians, and signifies *the country upheld on the back of a turtle;* and my reasons for employing it on the present occasion are simply these—a portion of the volume is devoted to the traditionary lore of the Aborigines, and the whole has reference to my native land.

C. L

WASHINGTON, *Summer of* 1850.

CONTENTS.

RECORDS OF A TOURIST.

THE SUGAR CAMP.

Among our more agreeable recollections of the wilderness are those associated with the making of *maple sugar*. Our first taste of this sweetest of woodland luxuries was received from the hands of an Indian, into whose wigwam we had wandered from our father's dwelling on one of the Saturday afternoons of our boyhood. It was many years ago, and long before the frontier of Michigan was transformed into a flourishing member of the national confederacy. Since that time we have not only eaten our full proportion of the luxury in question, both in wigwam and cabin, but we have seen it extensively manufactured by the Indian, as well as the white man; and we now purpose to discourse upon the article itself, and upon a few incidents connected with its manufacture.

Maple sugar is made from the sap of a tree, known by the several names of rock maple, hard maple, and sugar maple, which is found in great abundance in various portions of the Union, but chiefly in the northern States. It is a lofty and elegantly proportioned tree, and its foliage is particularly luxuriant; and, when touched by the frosts of autumn, is pre-eminently brilliant. The wood is also highly esteemed for the beauty of its fibre, which consists of concentrical circles, resembling the eye of a bird; and hence the term *birds*-eye maple.

Generally speaking, the sugar-making season commences early in April, is universally considered as one of festivity, and seldom continues more than about four weeks. The sudden transition of the temperature from winter to spring is essential to its production, for at this season alone does the vital principle of the tree pass in large quantities from the roots into its branches. Hence it is that, while making this passage, the sap has to be withdrawn; and this is accomplished by making an incision in the tree some three feet from the ground, and receiving the liquid in a vessel prepared for the purpose. And it has been observed that, when a frosty night is followed by a dry and sunny day, the sap flows abundantly, at which times three or four gallons are obtained from a single tree in twenty-four hours. The process employed for converting the sap into sugar is perfectly simple, and consists in boiling it first into a sirup and then into a more tangible substance. Of this sugar there are two kinds, viz., the hard or cake sugar, and that of a friable character, which is produced by constantly stirring the thick sirup when it is becoming cool. The taste of the sap or juice, when taken from the tree, is just sweet enough to be noticed; and though we have never ascertained the quantity commonly obtained from a single tree, we have been told that a very fruitful tree, in a good season, may be made to yield five pounds of the best sugar. To the human palate this juice is not generally agreeable, but wild and domestic animals are said to be inordinately fond of it, and slake their thirst with it whenever they can. Although a sufficient quantity of maple sugar has never been manufactured in this country to rank it among our articles of exportation, it has, for many years past, been about the only sugar used by a large number of people—especially those who live in the more thickly-wooded districts of the States, and those inhabiting the northern and western frontiers of the United States and Canada. In the opinion of all who manufacture the article it is held in high estimation, both as a luxury and on account of its nutrition. In regard to this last quality, we believe it is superior to all other sugars; for we know, from personal observations, that when eaten by the Indian children, during the manufacturing season, they become particularly hearty, though exclusively confined to it as an article of food for weeks at a time.

From the very nature of the business, the making of maple sugar is commonly carried on in an encampment, and we now purpose to describe the various kinds with which we are acquainted, beginning, as a matter of course, with an Indian camp. We are speaking of the remote past, and of an encampment of Ottawa Indians, in one of the maple forests skirting the western shore of Green Bay. It is in the month of April, and the hunting season is at an end. Albeit, the ground is covered with snow, the noonday sun has become quite powerful, and the annual offering has been made to the Great Spirit, by the medicine men, of the first product of one of the earliest trees in the district. This being the preparatory signal for extensive business, the women of the encampment proceed to make a large number of wooden troughs (to receive the liquid treasure), and, after these are finished, the various trees in the neighborhood are tapped, and the juice begins to run. In the mean time, the men of the party have built the necessary fires, and suspended over them their earthen, brass, or iron kettles. The sap is now flowing in copious streams, and from one end of the camp to the other is at once presented an animated and romantic scene, which continues, without interruption, day and night until the end of the sugar season. The principal employment to which the men devote themselves is that of lounging about the encampment, shooting at marks, and playing the moccasin game; while the main part of the labor is performed by the women, who not only attend to the kettles, but employ all their leisure time in making the beautiful birchen mocucks, for the preservation and transportation of the sugar when made; the sap being brought from the troughs to the kettles by the boys and girls. Less attention than usual is paid by the Indians at such times to their meals, and, unless game is very easily obtained, they are quite content to depend upon the sugar alone. If an Indian happens to return from the river with a fish, he throws it without any ceremony into the boiling sap, dipping it out, when cooked, with a ladle or stick; and therefore it is that we often find in the maple sugar of Indian manufacture the bones of a trout, or some more unworthy fish. That even a bird, a rabbit, or an opossum, is sometimes thrown into the kettle instead of a fish is beyond a doubt; and we are not positively certain that the civilized fashion of eating jelly with roast lamb may not be traced to the barbarous custom of cooking animals in hot sap. That this sap itself, when known to be clear and reduced to the consistency of molasses, is a palatable article, we are ready to maintain against the world; and we confess that, when not quite so fastidious as now, we have often eaten it in truly dangerous quantities, even in the cabin of an Indian. As we have already intimated, the sugar season is dependent upon the weather; but, even when it is prolonged to four or five weeks, it continues from beginning to end to be one of hilarity and gladness. At such times, even the wolfish-looking dogs seem to consider themselves as entitled to the privilege of sticking their noses into the vessels of sap not yet placed over the fire. And in this manner does the poor Indian welcome returning spring.

It is now about the middle of June, and some fifty birchen canoes have just been launched upon the waters of Green Bay. They are occupied by our Ottawa sugar-makers, who have started upon a pilgrimage to Mackinaw. The distance is near two hundred miles, and as the canoes are heavily laden, not only with mocucks of sugar, but with furs collected by the hunters during the past winter, and the Indians are traveling at their leisure, the party will probably reach their desired haven in the course of ten days. Well content with their accumulated treasures, both the women and the men are in a particularly happy mood, and many a wild song is heard to echo over the placid lake. As the evening approaches, day after day they seek out some convenient landing-place, and, pitching the wigwams on the beach, spend a goodly portion of the night carousing and telling stories around their camp fires, resuming their voyage after a morning sleep, long after the sun has risen above the blue waters of the east. Another sunset hour, and the cavalcade of canoes is quietly gliding into the crescent bay of Mackinaw, and, reaching a beautiful beach at the foot of a lofty bluff, the Indians again draw up their canoes, again erect their wigwams. And, as the Indian traders have assembled on the spot, the more improvident of the party immediately proceed to exhibit their sugar and furs, which are usually disposed of for flour and pork, blankets and knives, guns, ammunition, and a great variety of trinkets, long before the hour of midnight. That the remainder of this night is devoted to feasting and dancing, and tumultuous recreation, is a matter of course. But the trader who would obtain from the Indians their more unique articles of merchandize, usually visits the encampment on the following morning, when he is always certain of obtaining from the young women, on the most reasonable terms, their fancy mocucks of sugar, all worked over with porcupine quills; and a great variety of beautifully worked moccasins, and fancy bags, made of the sweet-smelling deer skin. In about a week after their arrival at Mackinaw, the Ottawa Indians begin to sigh for the freedom of the wilderness; and, before the trader has left his bed on some pleasant morning, there is nothing to be seen on the beach at Mackinaw but the smoking embers of a score or two of watch-fires.

We would now conduct our readers into the sugar camp of a Frenchman. It is situated in one of the maple forests of Michigan, on the banks of the river Raisin, and within half a mile of the rude comfortable dwelling of the proprietor. Very much the same process is here pursued in making the sugar that we have already described, only that a large proportion of the labor is performed by the men and boys, the women participating in the employment more for the purpose of carefully packing away the sugar when made, and having a little romantic sport in the way of eating hot sugar in the aisles of the church-like forest. The season of winter with our Frenchman has been devoted almost exclusively to the pleasures of life, and the making of sugar is the first and probably the only really lucrative business which he ever transacts. By the term lucrative we mean a business which allows him to lay aside a little spare money, for, generally speaking (like the class to which he belongs in the north-west), he is perfectly satisfied if the agricultural products of his small farm yield him a comfortable living. Maple sugar and maple molasses are considered by our friend and his family as among their greatest luxuries; and, while he makes a point of taking a goodly quantity to market, he never fails to keep a plentiful supply of both under his own roof. In transporting his sugar (as well as all other marketable articles) to the neighboring town, he employs a rude two-wheeled vehicle, made exclusively of wood, and drawn by a Canadian pony. On his first visit to the town after the sugar season is ended, he will be accompanied by his entire family, decked in their more tidy garments; and, before his return home, you may be certain that the Catholic priest, whose church he regularly attends, will receive a handsome present of the newly-made sugar, with perhaps a small keg of the delicious maple sirup or molasses. And thus does the Frenchman of the frontier welcome the return of spring.

But we have spent some pleasant days in the sugar camps of the Dutch yeomanry on the eastern and southern side of the Catskill Mountains, and we must not omit to pay our respects to them. The very best of sugar is made in this region, and much of it into solid cakes of various sizes, from one pound to twenty. It is manufactured here both for home consumption and the market, and the price which it has usually commanded during the last ten years has been about one York shilling per pound. The labor in this region is about equally divided between the women and the men, and considerable attention is devoted to the cultivation of the maple-tree. In cooling their sugar, or rather in performing the business called "sugaring off," the Dutch employ immense wrought-iron pans, which are undoubtedly a great improvement upon the Indian and French fashions, which are simply no fashions at all, since the kettle employed to boil the sugar are used to cool it off.

But the Dutch of whom we are speaking, those especially who are more wealthy than their neighbors, have a very sensible mode of winding up their sugar-making labors by giving what they term a "*Sugar-bee*," or party. The elements which go to make up one of these rustic entertainments it would be difficult to describe. We may mention, however, that everybody is invited, old men and their wives, young men and maidens; that the principal recreation is that of dancing to the music of a fiddle; that a most sumptuous and excessively miscellaneous feast is spread before the multitude; that the people assemble in the afternoon, and generally succeed in getting home an hour or two *after* the break of day. That an abundance of maple sugar is met with on these occasions will be readily imagined, and we may add that, in those districts where temperance societies are unpopular, the sugar is taken considerably adulterated in whisky.

The last sugar-bee to which we ever had the pleasure of being invited, while once sojourning among the Catskills, was given by an old Dutchman who resided on the side of a mountain, some *ten* miles from our temporary abode. We started for his house about sundown, in a large lumber-wagon, which was packed by no less than eight buxom damsels and four young men besides ourself. Although when stepping into the wagon we were a perfect stranger to nearly all the party, we were received as an old friend. The damsels were in high glee; we had a reckless driver and a span of capital horses, and of course the young men were not at all backwards in their deportment. The first five miles of the road was very good, and, as we rattled along, the songs, uncouth and shrill, which were sung awakened many a mountain echo. But while all this was going on, and other things which we have not time to mention, the sky became overcast, and in a short time it began to rain, and a most intense darkness settled upon the world. Our driver became bewildered, and the first that *we* knew was that *he* had lost the road, and that our horses had halted directly in front of a huge stump. Having thus unexpectedly been brought to a stand, the male members of the party proceeded to reconnoitre, and one of them fortunately discovered a light at the distance of half a mile. Towards this light did the entire party direct their march, and about twelve o'clock succeeded in reaching a log-cabin, which was inhabited by an old hunter; and as the guests of this man did the party, in a very disagreeable mood, spend the remainder of the night. Long before the mists had left the valleys on the following morning, the party had worked its way out of the woods, and for a week afterwards we were frequently complimented for the important part that we had taken in the last *sugar-bee.*

We cannot conclude this article without remarking that maple sugar of rare quality is manufactured in the States of Vermont, New Hampshire, and Maine; but as we have never visited that section of the Union in the spring we cannot, from personal observation, speak of the New England sugar camps. That the maple sugar usually offered for sale in the Boston and New York markets is chiefly brought from this section of country we know to be a fact, and it is one which forcibly illustrates the true idea of Yankee enterprise.

P. S.—Since writing the above, we have had the pleasure of reading an interesting description of *a maple sugar camp,* by the eminent ornithologist Mr. Audubon, from which we gather the following particulars, viz., that the juice of the sugar maple was to him a most refreshing and delicious beverage; that it takes ten gallons of this juice to make one pound of grained sugar; that the best of the sirup is made at the close of the sugar season; and that the sugar maple is found in abundance from Maine to Louisiana, invariably growing on rich and elevated grounds.

THE OLD ACADEMY.

"I feel like one who treads alone
Some banquet hall deserted."—MOORE.

THE iron bolted-door swings and creaks upon its hinges, and we are standing within the dilapidated walls of "the old academy." Fifteen years have elapsed since we last stood here, a wild and happy school-boy. Then, this building was the chief attraction of a little village, which was made up of a pretty church, one old store and post-office, and a cluster of some twenty rural dwellings, situated on a broad street, canopied with venerable elms. In coming up here this afternoon, we noticed that the various woodlands on the surrounding hills were much narrowed by the farmer's axe, and we thought of the armies of men which time is continually leveling with the earth. Near a large pool in which we were wont to bathe many years ago, now stands a railroad depot, where locomotive engines do congregate, to enjoy a brief rest from their labors. Upon the walls of the old academy there seemed to be brooding the spirit of desolation, and we approached it with a heavy heart.

What a throng of recollections is rushing upon us as our footsteps now echo in the silent and abandoned place! The past appears before us like an open and familiar volume.

Here we are in the vestibule, where we scholars used to hang our caps and coats, and which we remember as the scene of many a scrape and scuffle between hot-headed and unfledged lawyers, doctors and divines! Oh, how real does everything appear! We could almost believe that not even a week had elapsed since our own loud laugh resounded here, when our heart knew not the burden of a care. There is the same old rent in the ceiling, which was made by a stroke of lightning, during a severe storm, when the whole school were pale and breathless with mortal fear; and yonder is the identical peg which Billy Langdon, "the bully," tried to usurp from us, and whom it was our good luck to punish with a flogging, thereby securing to ourself a reputation for possessing genuine courage. Since then, we have been a dweller in the wilderness and pent-up city, and have ever found courage to be a valuable quality in our intercourse with men. But a man may have a stout heart and yet be poor, unloved and unknown.

With timid footsteps we move along, peering into each nook and corner with curious eye. The threshold of another door is passed and we are in the large general school-room, with its rows of desks for the boys, and the platform with the large old-fashioned chair in the centre for the master. There, upon the floor, lies a tattered copy of Virgil, another of Euclid, a few leaves out of the National Preceptor, and a chapter or two of Murray's Grammar. Having fulfilled their office, they have been thrown aside as of no farther avail, even as some of the *noble-hearted* in the world are wont to treat their most faithful friends. Here, at our side, resting upon its shattered frame, stands the identical globe over which we once pondered with a wondering heart. It is covered with dust, through which we can just discover that the uppermost country is England. True, England is indeed without a rival in her glory, but is there not a stain of something resting upon her domain? Look at the condition of her people, who are sorely oppressed by the mean ambition of her aristocracy.—But to return. How neglected and lonely is this place! The dust upon the floor is so thick that our footsteps are as distinctly visible as when we walk upon the snow. A sunbeam stealing through a western window points us to the wall where hangs the old forsaken clock. Its song of "Passing away" is ended, and has been for many a year; but the language of its familiar countenance seems to be, "They are all gone, the pleasant, old familiar faces!" Yes, they are gone—but where? We know not the destiny of a single one. The hour-hand is resting upon the figure four, the hour of all others which we boys loved. Stop, did we not see the waving hand of our master, and hear the bustle of dismission? Yes, we have caught our cap—we are the first one out. Now listen to the loud, clear, hearty shout of half a hundred boys.—'Tis only the vision of a heated brain, and we are sitting once again at the same desk and in the same seat which were ours fifteen years ago. Here is the same fantastic ink-blot which we made when we indited our first and only poem to the eyebrows of a charming little girl, with whom we fancied ourself in love; and there is the same square cavity in the desk, which we cut with our knife, and where we used to imprison the innocent flies, which remembered fact is a memorial of our rare genius. But look! are we not a trespasser? for here cometh an ancient-looking spider with vengeance in his very gait. In moving out of his way, we notice that his gossamer hammock is in prime order. How like a nabob liveth that old spider! Around his home, we see the carcasses of a hundred insects that have afforded him food; he is monarch of all he surveys; and if he desires to become a traveler, he has but to leap upon the slender threads leading to the remotest corners of the room, which are to him safer and better than a railroad. This seat, which hath been inherited from us by a poor solitary spider, we now look upon perhaps for the last time. But we cannot take our final leave without dwelling upon one incident with which it is associated. That is the spot where we plead our cause, when once arraigned by the masters of the academy for having been the ringleader of a conspiracy. It was the third day of July, and on dismissing the school, our master had informed us that we must celebrate the memorable Fourth by *attending school.* Surprise, and a shadow of disappointment fell upon every countenance, and we sought our respective rooms murmuring. That evening our marbles and balls were idle. At my suggestion, the wink was tipt to a chosen band of patriots. We met, and after discussing the outrageous conduct of our principal, unanimously resolved that we would spend the following day at the neighboring village of Brooklyn, where we knew there was to be a celebration. We went, had a glorious walk, saw revolutionary soldiers, enjoyed a sumptuous dinner, heard a smart oration, fired unnumbered cannon, saw lots of pretty girls, and were at home again a little after sunset. On the following morning, the patriots were changed into a band of culprits, standing before our compeers to be tried, condemned and punished. Having been proved to be the leader, we are the chief speaker, and, in our boyish estimation, "defender of the constitution." Then it was, and in the seat already mentioned, that we delivered our maiden speech. It was a powerful appeal, no doubt, but was of no avail. We were condemned, and our punishment was, to be expelled. The next day, however, the whole of us were readmitted as regular members, and thus ended the affair of our impeachment.

Walking in this room and thinking upon this incident has brought before us a troop of shadows, that have once had a material existence. Our principal was one H——, who had thin lips, a sharp nose, gray eyes, and a cold heart. He was a good schoolmaster, but nothing more. He knew not what it was to be loved, for he could not sympathize with a single one of his pupils. He seldom smiled, and when he did it seemed to be against his nature. He was a most cruel man, as a scar upon my poor back might testify even now. What has become of him we know not, but if he be among the living, we are sure he is a solitary being and a misanthrope. His assistant, named W——, we distinctly remember as the ugliest-looking man we ever saw; but he was a good-hearted soul, and merited the friendly feelings which were lavished upon him so abundantly. When we last heard of him he was a much respected and well-established clergyman. And so it is that time works its changes.

Dearly do we love the memory of our school-fellows! Charley Snow was a rattle-headed southerner, who hated books, loved a frolic, and spent his money, of which he had an abundance, like water. The poet of our academy was Edward Hunt, the son of a poor woman and a widow, who lived upon a neighboring farm. He was a beautiful boy, fond of being alone, and when with his playmates shy as a captured deer. All the manual labor of his home he performed himself, and yet he had but few superiors as a student. More than half of his time was spent with his mother, and for that reason my heart ever yearned towards the noble boy. Our metaphysical philosopher was one Henry Clare, who had been made decidedly mad by too much learning. A splendid landscape or a brilliant sunset he could not understand, but over a piece of gray stone, a homely little insect or a leaf of sorrel, he would be in perfect raptures. But the youth who exerted the most salutary influence upon us was William Vane, whom his Maker had formed a cripple, but gifted with a superb intellect and the disposition of an angel. How kindly did he endeavor to cheer up those boys who came out of school with blistered hands, or were suffering with other troubles! Seldom did we ever hear an oath in the presence of William Vane, for few could endure his manly frown and reprimand. Many a soul will enjoy, or is enjoying a happy immortality on account of that unfortunate—no, that thrice-blessed youth, for from very childhood he was a Christian. One queer fellow that we had with us was Joe Leroy. He thought more of performing an odd caper than of anything else; but his particular passion was for athletic feats, such as climbing, running, and jumping. Once, with the aid of a rope, we saw him ascend one side of the academy building, pass over the roof, and descend upon the opposite side. He could outrun the whole of us, and in the department of jumping he was equal to a kangaroo. Jack Harmer was another lad to whom books were a terror. He longed to be a sailor, and devoted all his leisure time to sailing a little brig on a sheet of water in a meadow, two hundred feet wide. And so we could go on for hours, mentioning the names of those who were the playmates of our later boyhood. Where they are, and what their destiny, we cannot tell. That our own name has long since been forgotten by them we do not doubt. Is it not foolish, then, to cherish their memories in our heart as we do? No, for they are linked with a portion of the past that we would have immortal—the spring of our existence. The power of recalling the sunny hours of life, we would not part with for the world; next to our dreams of heaven, do we value the dreams of our early days. But like a weaver's shuttle is our life, and it were unwise for us to forget the future in thinking of the past. If we are permitted to live, how soon will our body be like this crumbling edifice, in whose deserted chambers we are now a pilgrim. Years ago we came here to school our mind; now, we are a teacher ourself, and of ourself too, but a very poor one, for we cannot rule the unruly passions of our heart. Our only hope is in the fountain filled with blood.

But if we remember rightly, there is a room in this old building that we have not yet visited. Yes, here is the narrow stairway that led to the Exhibition Hall in the second story. Cautiously we enter it; but here also has the spirit of desolation a home. On these mutilated seats once thronged thousands of spectators; and yonder is the platform where the youthful orators were wont to "speak in public on the stage." The only breathing creature that meets our eye is a little mouse running to his hole, almost frightened to death by our appearance. When last we stood in this place, thousands of human hearts beat happily, for parents listened to the eloquence of their children, and those children gloried in the realization of their long-cherished hopes. How vivid are our recollections of that exhibition day! It concluded an exile of three years from our far distant home in the wilds of Michigan. The period of return our heart panted after continually, for we were away from the home of boyhood, from a mother, a father, and sisters; and though we often visited, and were under the care of kindred, we felt ourself to be alone and companionless. And with that day, too, are associated events that flattered our youthful ambition; and though we know them to be idle as a tale that is told, we cannot but cherish the memory of that day even for them. But with our last day at school are associated some clouds and shadows, the most prominent of which were our leave-takings with our schoolfellows. We parted for our widely separated homes, and where we all are, or what is our present condition are things known only to the Father of the world.—It is well—it is well. "Our sorrow voices itself to the stranger many; and all that in other days were gladdened by our song—if still living—stray scattered through the world." It is well.

But the hours of day are almost numbered, and it is time for us to be gone; and besides the glow upon yonder window tells us that "the sun hath made a glorious set," and that we should improve the hour to the gratification of our passion for the poetry of the sky. A few moments more, and we are on the green in front of the Old Academy. Forgetful of the unnumbered feelings it has inspired and the pictures it has recalled, we are wending our way to the home of a kind friend, wholly absorbed with the gorgeous appearance of the western sky and the solemn twilight by which we are surrounded. The hour is one that we have ever dearly loved, for it is the sabbath of the day, when a solemn stillness is around, and an unutterable joy is wont to take possession of the soul.

ACCOMAC.

UPWARDS of two hundred years ago the long peninsula, now divided into the counties of Accomac and Northamptom, in Virginia, was known by the Indian name of *Acohawmack*. An extensive tribe of aborigines who occupied the country bore the same title, and the meaning of the word is said to be *People who live upon shell fish.* Next to a scanty record embodied in Captain Smith's History of Virginia, the earliest printed account of this region may be found at the conclusion of a pamphlet written by one COLONEL NORWOOD, of England, wherein he describes "*A Voyage to Virginia in* 1649." At the conclusion of his perilous voyage across the Atlantic, it was the author's misfortune to be wrecked upon one of the islands on the eastern shore of Accomac, and that, too, in the stormy month of January. To comment upon Norwood's well written and very interesting pamphlet is not now our object; but we will remark, in passing, that this document, taken in connection with the county records of the peninsula, which extend as far back as the year 1632, and also with the ancient graveyards of the region, would furnish material for an exceedingly valuable and entertaining volume, and we are surprised that some enterprising antiquarian of Virginia has not, long before this, taken the matter in hand. It is our province to speak of *Accomac* (by which we mean the ancient dominion known by that name) as it appears to the traveler of the present day.

What the distance may be from Washington to the northern line of Accomac we cannot imagine, but we know that if the morning cars to Baltimore are punctual, and you are fortunate enough to meet the Whitehaven steamboat at Baltimore at 8 o'clock, you may enjoy your next breakfast at Horntown, a few miles south of the Maryland line, and within the limits of Accomac. On board of the steamer which brought us down the bay, there was rather a scarcity of passengers but among them were some intelligent gentlemen, from one of whom we gathered the following items of information. The entire length of Chesapeake Bay, from Havre de Grace to Norfolk, is two hundred miles; in width it varies from five to twenty-six miles, and in depth from four to twenty-four fathoms. Its shores are low and level, with occasional bluffs, however, and its waters clear and of a greenish hue. It contains a great number of islands, some of which are exceedingly fertile, but destitute of all picturesque beauty. During the autumn and winter its shallower waters are filled with almost every variety of waterfowl; it is said to yield a larger quantity of oysters than any other section of the globe of the same size; and it is also famous for the abundance and quality of its shad, striped basse or rock-fish, its drum, sheepshead, and a species of sea-trout. On approaching the Wicomoco river, an island of one thousand acres was pointed out to us called Bloodsworth Island, which is the property of two men, who reside upon their domain, a pair of veritable hermits, who live upon fish and waterfowl instead of cultivating their soil. Our attention was also directed to a neighboring island, which seemed to be in a state of high cultivation, and we were told that the owner thereof had refused the handsome price of one hundred dollars per acre for the entire island. With regard to Deal's Island and Dames Quarter, in this vicinity of the bay, we heard the following anecdote. The *original* name of the first was "Devil's Island," and that of the second "Damned Quarter," as any one may see by referring to some of the older maps. Once upon a time, as the story goes, a Connecticut skipper in his smack chanced to make his course up the Chesapeake, and as he was a stranger in this region, he hailed nearly every vessel or boat he met with a lot of questions. "What island is that?" inquired the Yankee of a downward bound brig. "*Devil's Island*," was the brief reply; whereupon the stranger's conscience was a little disturbed. About an hour afterwards "What island is that?" again vociferated the skipper; and a Chesapeake fisherman replied, "*Damned Quarter.*" At this intelligence, the Yankee was so much alarmed that he immediately made a sudden tack, and with his helm "hard up" started for the outlet of the bay, and was never heard of more in southern waters.

The peninsula of Accomac, as nearly as we can ascertain, varies in width from eight to twelve miles, and is not far from seventy miles long. Generally speaking, it is almost as level as the sea, the highest ground not attaining a greater elevation than some twenty feet. The soil is of a sandy character, and the forests, which are quite extensive, are composed chiefly of pine and oak. The country is almost entirely destitute of running streams, and nearly all the inlets, especially on the bay side, are lined with extensive marshes, where snakes turtles, and lizards are particularly abundant. Along the sea side of Accomac lie a successions of sandy islands, which render the navigation dangerous, and between which and the main shore the water is shallow and far from clear. Two of the above islands, Assateague and Chingoteague, are inhabited by a peculiar people, of whom I shall have something to say in another place. The only villages in this district, properly so called, are Drummontown and Eastville; they are the county seats, and though bearing an ancient appearance, they contain some good houses, and are well worth visiting. You can hardly travel eight miles in any direction without coming to a post-office, which glories in a village name, and therefore appears on paper to much better advantage than in reality. In some parts of the country, we frequently noticed houses which seemed to have been abandoned by their owners, as if the soil in the vicinity had been completely worn out, and could not be profitably cultivated. These household ruins, together with the apparent want of enterprise which one notices everywhere, conspire to throw a gloom over the traveler's mind, thereby preventing him, perhaps, from fully appreciating the happiness which really prevails among the people. And these (as is the case, in fact, with every nook and corner of the world) constitute the principal attraction of Accomac; for man by nature is a lover of his kind, and "we have all one human heart by which we live."

If we were called upon to classify the Accomacians, we would divide them into the gentry, the miscellaneous fraternity, and the slave population. The gentry are a comparatively small class, but the principal landholders of the district. They come of good old English families, and are highly intelligent and well educated. The houses they occupy are homely in appearance, but well supplied with all the substantials that can add to the pleasures of country life. They seem to think more of comfort than display, and are distinguished for their hospitality to strangers. The miscellaneous fraternity to which we have alluded is more extensive. A very large proportion of them obtain their living from the sea, annually bringing up from its bed an immense quantity of oysters and clams, which they sell to the fishermen of Philadelphia and New York; but these fishermen not only send to market large numbers of fish, but during the winter and autumn months they make a good deal of money by killing waterfowl, which abound on all the shores of the peninsula. The more legitimate fishermen of Accomac, who number between thirty and forty voters, reside on the neighboring islands of Chingoteague and Assateague. They are an exceedingly hardy, rude, and simple-hearted race, and a little more at home on the water than on the land. The dangers to which they wilfully expose themselves are truly astonishing, and almost lead one to suppose that they are web-footed. We have been told of one individual who, for the want of a boat, once swam a distance of three miles in midwinter merely for the purpose of examining the wreck of a brig which had been abandoned by its owners; and we have heard of others who had been upset at sea, a distance of ten miles from shore, but who have regained their mother earth with the ease and carelessness of wild geese. In the miscellaneous fraternity may also be included the mechanics of the country, and all such people as stage-drivers, dram-shop keepers, peddlers, and other kindred birds.

The slave population of this district is decidedly the most extensive, and, if we are to judge by their general deportment and by what they say, they are undoubtedly by far the happiest class on the peninsula. We questioned them occasionally with regard to what we have been educated to look upon as a hard lot, but we never saw but one individual who succeeded in rousing our sympathies, and before he finished talking to us we discovered that he was a scamp of the first water, and therefore not worthy of credit. Every negro in this section of country has the evening hours to himself, as well as the entire Sabbath, and, instead of being "lashed" into obedience, is constantly treated with the utmost kindness. Many of them, who choose to labor for themselves, have free permission to follow any employment they please; and we know of several individuals who earn thirty dollars per month by voluntary labor, and whose services are valued by their masters at only ten or fifteen dollars; so that the servant pockets fifty per cent. of his monthly earnings. But what proves more conclusively than anything else that the black man's bondage is not unbearable, is the fact that they are the most moral and religious people of the country. They are, at the same time, the most polite and the most kindly spoken people that we have met with in our wanderings; and we verily believe that they would not break the imaginary chain which now binds them to their masters. We confess that we have a natural repugnance to the word *bondage*, but our dread of a mere idea cannot make us deaf to the eloquence of what we have *seen*. It is true that our experience has not been extensive, but we cannot see that the slaves so called of this region are any more to be pitied than the children of any careful and affectionate parent. A goodly number of the blacks in this region are free; and we know of one individual who is not only free, but the owner of no less than three farms.

And now, with regard to those traits which the Accomacians possess in common. In religion they are Methodists and Baptists, and in politics they belong to the rank and file of the unterrified Democracy. Those who are at all educated are highly educated; but of the twenty-five thousand souls who inhabit the peninsula, we suppose that not more than one thousand could distinguish the difference between the English and the Chippewa alphabet. In the two counties of Accomac and Northamptom, the idea of even a weekly newspaper was never dreamed of. The people are fond of amusements, which consist principally of dancing and card-playing parties, and the Saturday of each week is usually appropriated as a holiday. Any event which can bring together a crowd is gladly welcomed, so that court days, training days, election days, the Fourth of July, Christimas day, New Year's day, and Thanksgiving day are among the white days of the unwritten calendar of the Accomacians. The roads of the country are all by nature very good, and the people exceedingly fond of going through the world as pleasantly as possible; so that each man who can own a horse is sure of owning a gig, and many of them are particularly unique and tottleish, something like a scow-boat in a gale of wind.

But the crowning peculiarity of this nook of the great world has reference to the custom of raising and taming wild horses. Like everything poetical connected with the habits of our people, this custom is rapidly becoming obsolete, and will soon be remembered merely as an idle and romantic tale. The very idea of having to do with wild horses excited our fancy the very moment we heard the custom alluded to; and we made every effort to collect reliable information upon it, as it existed half a century ago. As good fortune would have it, we found out an intelligent and venerable gentleman, who supplied us with many interesting particulars. The "oldest inhabitant" to whom we allude is the Rev. DAVID WATTS, of Horntown, who is now in the 82d year of his age, and the substance of his information is as follows:—

In the Atlantic Ocean, off the north-eastern shore of Accomac, lies a long and sandy island known by the name of Assateague. The distance from one extremity to the other is perhaps ten miles, and in reaching it you have to cross a bay that is perhaps eight miles wide. At the present time, there are only four families residing upon the island, one of them having charge of the lighthouse, the remaining three being devoted to the fishing business. From time immemorial it has been famous for its luxuriant grass, and from the period of the Revolution down to the year 1800 supplied an immense number of wild horses with food. When these animals were first introduced upon the island has not been ascertained, but it is said that they were the most abundant about half a century ago. At that period there was a kind of stock company in existence, composed principally of the wealthier planters residing on the main shore. The animals were of the pony breed, but generally beautifully formed and very fleet; of a deep black color, and with remarkably long tails and manes. They lived and multiplied upon the island without the least care from the hand of man, and, though feeding entirely on the grass of the salt meadows, they were in good condition throughout the year. They were employed by their owners, to a considerable extent, for purposes of agriculture, but the finer specimens were kept or disposed of as pets for the use of ladies and children. The prices which they commanded on the island varied from ten to twenty dollars, but by the time a handsome animal could reach New York or New Orleans, he was likely to command one hundred and fifty or two hundred dollars.

But by far the most interesting circumstance connected with the wild horses of Assateague had reference to the annual festival of penning the animals, for the purpose, not only of bringing them under subjection, but of selling them to any who might desire to purchase. The day in question was the 10th of June, on which occasion there was always an immense concourse of people assembled on the island from all parts of the surrounding country; not only men, but women and children; planters who came to make money, strangers who wished to purchase a beautiful animal for a present, together with the grooms or horse-tamers, who were noted at the time for their wonderful feats of horsemanship. But a large proportion of the multitude came together for the purpose of having a regular frolic; and feasting and dancing were carried on to a great extent, and that too upon the open sandy shore of the ocean, the people being exposed during the day to the scorching sunshine, and the scene being enlivened at night by immense bonfires, made of wrecked vessels or drift wood, and the light of the moon and stars. The staple business of these anniversaries, however, was to tame and brand the horses; but to give an account of all the particulars attending these exciting scenes would require more time than I can spare at the present moment. Suffice it to say that the horses were usually cornered in a pen, perhaps a hundred at a time, when, in the presence of the immense concourse of people, the tamers would rush into the midst of the herd, and not only noose and halter the wild and untamed creatures, but, mounting them, at times even without a bridle, would rush from the pen and perform a thousand fantastic and daring feats upon the sand. Few, if any, of these horsemen were ever killed or wounded while performing these exploits, though it is said that they frequently came in such close contact with the horses as to be compelled to wrestle with them, as man with man. But, what was still more remarkable, these men were never known to fail in completely subduing the horses they attempted to tame; and it was often the case that an animal which was as wild as a hawk in the morning could be safely ridden by a child at the sunset hour. But enough, until some future day, on this interesting theme.

SALMON FISHING.

I like the society of fish, and as they cannot with any convenience to themselves visit me on dry land, it becomes me in point of courtesy to pay my respects to them in their own element.

WILLIAM SCROPE.

OF the genuine salmon, we believe there is but one distinct species in the world; we are sure there is not in the United States. From its lithe beauty, its wonderful activity, and its value as an article of food, it unquestionably takes precedence of all the fish which swim in our waters. It is an ocean-born fish, but so constituted that it has to perform an annual pilgrimage into our fresh-water rivers for the purpose of depositing its spawn. Their running time usually occupies about two months, and that is the period when they are in season, and of course the only period when they are taken in great numbers.

The variety of which we speak is a slender fish, particularly solid in texture, and has a small head and delicate fins. The upper jaw is the larger, while the tip of the under jaw in the female has an upward turn. The back is usually of a bluish color, the sides of a silvery hue, and the belly pure white, while along the centre of its body runs a narrow black stripe. The scales are small, and the mouth is covered with small, but stout and pointed teeth. A few dark spots are dispersed over that part of the body above the lateral line, and the females usually exhibit a larger number of these spots than the males. The tail of the young salmon is commonly forked, while in the adult fish it is quite square. To speak of the salmon as a bold biter and a handsome fish, or of his wonderful leaping powers, would be but to repeat a thrice-told tale.

And now for a few words on some of the habits of the salmon. He is unquestionably the most active of all the finny tribes, but the wonderful leaps which he is reported to have made are all moonshine. We have seen them perform some superb somersets, but we never yet saw one which could scale a perpendicular waterfall of ten feet. That they have been taken above waterfalls three or four times as high we do not deny; but the wonder may be dispensed with, when we remember that a waterfall seldom occurs, which does not contain a number of resting-places for the salmon to take advantage of while on his upward journey.

Contrary to the prevailing opinion, we contend that the salmon is possessed of a short memory. While fishing in a small river on a certain occasion, owing to the bad position in which we were placed, we lost a favorite fly, and it so happened that in about one hour afterwards a fish was taken by a brother angler, in whose mouth was found the identical fly that we had lost.

This fish is a voracious feeder, and an epicure in his tastes, for his food is composed principally of small and delicate fish, and the sea-sand eel; but it is a fact that the *surest* bait to capture him with is the common red worm.

The salmon is a shy fish, and as he invariably inhabits the clearest of water, it is always important that the angler's movements should be particularly cautious; and in throwing the fly, he should throw it clear across the stream, if possible; and after letting it float down for a few yards he should gradually draw it back again, with an upward tendency.

Like all other fish that swim near the surface of the water, the salmon cannot be eaten in too fresh a condition; and, judging from our own experience, they may be eaten three times a-day, for a whole season, and at the end of their running time they will gratify the palate more effectually than when first brought upon the table.

The process of spawning has been described by various writers, and the general conclusion is as follows. On reaching a suitable spot for that purpose, the loving pair manage to dig a furrow some six feet long, in the sand or gravel, into which the male ejects his milt, and the female her spawn; this they cover with their tails, and leaving this deposit to the tender mercies of the liquid elements, betake themselves to the sea whence they came. This spawning operation usually occupies about ten days, and takes place in the autumn; and when the spring-time comes the salmon are born, and, under "their Creator's protection," are swept into the sea, where they come to their natural estate by the following spring, and ascend their native rivers to revisit the haunts of their minnowhood. And it is a singular fact, that the salmon leaves the sea in an emaciated condition, acquires his fatness while going up a river, and subsequently returns to the sea for the purpose of recruiting his wonted health and beauty.

The salmon is a restless fish, and seldom found a second time in exactly the same spot; but his principal traveling time is in the night, when the stars are shining brightly and all the world is wrapt in silence.

The salmon come up from the sea during a flood or a freshet, and in ascending a river, they invariably tarry for a short time in all the pools of the same. Their object in doing this has not been clearly defined; but is it unreasonable to suppose that they are influenced by the same motives which induce a human traveler to tarry in a pleasant valley? The only difference is, that when the man would resume his journey he waits for a sunny day, while the salmon prefers a rainy day to start upon his pilgrimage. The best places to fish for salmon are the shallows above the deep pools; and it is a settled fact, that after you have killed a fish, you are always sure to find in the course of a few hours another individual in the same place. It would thus seem that they are partial to certain localities. Another thing that should be remembered is, that salmon never take the natural fly while it is in a stationary position, or when floating down stream; hence the great importance of carrying the artificial fly directly across the stream, or in an upward oblique direction. When you have hooked a salmon, it is a bad plan to strain upon him in any degree, unless he is swimming towards a dangerous ground, and even then this is an unsafe experiment. The better plan is to throw a pebble in front of him, for the purpose of frightening him back, and you should manage to keep as near his royal person as practicable. Another peculiarity of the salmon is the fact that (excepting the shad) it is the only fish which seems to be perfectly at home in the salt sea, as well as in the fresh springs among the mountains. It is also singular in the color of its flesh, which is a deep pink, and the texture of its flesh is remarkably solid: the latter circumstance is proved by the fact that you cannot carry a salmon by the gills, as you can other fish, without tearing and mutilating him to an uncommon degree.

In olden times there was hardly a river on the eastern coast of the United States, north of Virginia, which was not annually visited by the salmon; but those days are for ever departed, and it is but seldom that we now hear of their being taken in any river south of Boston. They frequented, in considerable numbers, the Susquehanna, the Delaware, and North rivers, but were eminently abundant in the Connecticut and the Thames. On the former stream it used to be stipulated by the day-laborer, that he should have salmon placed upon his table only four times in the week; and we have been told by an old man residing on the latter stream, that the value of three salmon, forty years ago, was equal to one shad—the former were so much more abundant than the latter. But steamboats, and the din of cities, have long since frightened the salmon from their ancient haunts, and the beautiful aborigines of our rivers now seek for undisturbed homes in more northern waters. Once in a while, even at the present time, the shad fishermen of the Merrimac and Saco succeed in netting a small salmon; but in the Androscoggin, Kennebec, and Penobscot, they are yet somewhat abundant, and these are the rivers which chiefly supply our city markets with the fresh article.

As the ice melts away in the spring, says Dr. J. V. C. Smith, in his interesting little book on the Fishes of Massachusetts, they rush to the rivers from the ocean; and it is an undeniable fact, confirmed by successful experiments, that they visit, as far as possible, the very streams in which they were born. When undisturbed, they swim slowly in large schools near the surface; yet they are so timid, that if suddenly frightened, the whole column will turn directly back towards the sea. It has also been proven that a salmon can scud at the surprising velocity of thirty miles an hour. The young are about a foot long when they visit the rivers for the first time; and at the end of two years, according to Mr. Smith, they weigh five or six pounds, and attain their full growth in about six years. When running up the rivers they are in a fat condition; after that period, having deposited their spawn, they return to the sea, lean and emaciated. In extremely warm weather, and while yet in the salt water, they are often greatly annoyed by a black and flat-looking insect, which is apt to endanger their lives. As soon, however, as the salmon reaches the fresh water, this insect drops off, and the fish rapidly improves.

The streams which these fish ascend are invariably distinguished for their rocky and gravelly bottoms, for the coldness and purity of their water, and for their rapid currents. Those which afford the angler the most sport, are rather small and shallow, and empty into tide-water rivers; while in these they are chiefly taken with the net. The tributaries of the Androscoggin, Kennebec, and Penobscot, having all been blocked up with mill-dams, the salmon is only found in the principal estuaries; and as these are large and deep, they are of no value to the angler, and will not be many years longer even to the fishermen who capture them for the purpose of making money. So far as our own experience goes, we only know of one river, within the limits of the Union, which affords the angler good salmon fishing, and that is the Aroostook, in Maine. We have been informed, however, that the regular salmon is taken in many of those rivers, in the northern part of New York, which empty into Lake Ontario and the upper St. Lawrence, but we are compelled to doubt the truth of the statement. Such may have been the case in former times, but we think it is not so now. Salmon are not taken at Montreal, and it is therefore unreasonable to suppose that they ever reach the fountain-head of the St. Lawrence; this portion of the great river is too far from the ocean, and too extensively navigated, and the water is not sufficiently clear. That they once ascended to the Ottawa river and Lake Ontario we have not a doubt, but those were in the times of the days of old. Another prevailing opinion with regard to salmon, we have it in our power decidedly to contradict. Mr. John J. Brown, in his useful little book entitled the "American Angler's Guide," makes the remark, that salmon are found in great abundance in the Mississippi and its magnificent tributaries. Such is not the fact, and we are sure that if "our brother" had ever caught a glimpse of the muddy Mississippi, he would have known by intuition that such *could* not be the case. Nor is the salmon partial to any of the rivers of the far South, as many people suppose, not being known in any river emptying into the Gulf of Mexico; so that the conclusion of the whole matter is just this, that the salmon fisheries of the United States proper are of but little consequence when compared with many other countries on the globe. When we come to speak of our territories, however, we have a very different story to relate, for a finer river for salmon does not water any country than the mighty Columbia—that same Columbia where a certain navigator once purchased a ton of salmon for a jack-knife. But that river is somewhat too far off to expect an introduction in our present essay, and we will therefore take our reader, by his permission, into the neighboring Provinces of Canada, New Brunswick, and Nova Scotia.

Before proceeding another step, however, we must insert a paragraph about the various methods employed to capture the salmon. The Indians, and many white barbarians, spear them by torch-light; and the thousands sent to market in a smoked condition are taken in nets and seines of various kinds. But the only instruments used by the scientific angler are a rod and reel, three hundred feet of hair or silk line, and an assortment of artificial flies. Our books tell us that a gaudy fly is commonly the best killer, but our own experience inclines us to the belief that a large brown or black hackle, or any neatly-made gray fly, is much preferable to the finest fancy specimens. As to bait-fishing for salmon, we have never tried it—we care less about it than we know, and we know but precious little. Next to a delicately made fly, the most important thing to consider is the leader of the line, which should be made of the best material (a twisted gut), and at least five feet in length. But if the angler is afraid of wading in a cold and even a deep stream, the very best of tackle will avail him nothing. It is but seldom that a large salmon can be taken, without costing the captor a good deal of hard labor, and a number of duckings. And when the character of the fish is remembered, this assertion will not appear strange. Not only is the salmon a large fish, but he is remarkable for his strength and lightning quickness. Owing to his extreme carefulness in meddling with matters that may injure him, it is necessary to use the most delicate tackle, in the most cautious and expert manner. To pull a salmon in shore, immediately after he has been hooked, will never do; the expert way is to give him all the line he wants, never forgetting in the mean time that it must be kept perfectly taut. And this must be done continually, in spite of every obstacle, not only when the fish performs his splendid leaps out of the water, but also when he is stemming the current of the stream, trying to break the naughty hook against a rock, or when he has made a sudden wheel, and is gliding down the stream with the swiftness of a falling star. The last effort to get away, which I have mentioned, is usually the last that the salmon makes, and it is therefore of the highest importance that the angler should manage him correctly when going down. Narrow rifts, and even waterfalls, do not stop the salmon; and bushes, deep holes, slippery bottoms, and rocky shores must not impede the course of the angler who would secure a prize. And though the salmon is a powerful fish, he is not long-winded, and by his great impatience is apt to drown himself much sooner than one would suppose. The times most favorable for taking this fish are early in the morning and late in the afternoon; and when the angler reaches his fishing ground, and discovers the salmon leaping out of the water, as if too happy to remain quiet, he may then calculate upon rare sport. As to the pleasure of capturing a fine salmon, we conceive it to be more exquisite than any other sport in the world. We have killed a buffalo on the head waters of the St. Peter's river, but we had every advantage over the pursued, for we rode a well-trained horse, and carried a double-barreled gun. We have seen John Cheney bring to the earth a mighty bull moose, among the Adirondac mountains, but he was assisted by a pair of terrible dogs, and carried a heavy rifle. But neither of these exploits is to be compared with that of capturing a twenty pound salmon, with a line almost as fine as the flowing hair of a beautiful woman. When we offer a fly to a salmon, we take no undue advantage of him, but allow him to follow his own free will; and when he has hooked himself, we give him permission to match his strength against our skill. Does not this fact prove that salmon fishing is distinguished for its humanity, if not for its *fishanity?* We have set in a cariole and driven a Canadian pacer, at the rate of a mile in two minutes and a half, on the icy plains of Lake Erie, and as we held the reins, have thought we could not enjoy a more exquisite pleasure. That experience, however, was ours long before we had ever seen a genuine salmon; we are somewhat wiser now, for we have acquired the art of driving through the pure white foam even a superb salmon, and that, too, with only a silken line some hundred yards in length.

One of the most fruitful salmon regions for the angler to visit lies on the north shore of the Gulf of St. Lawrence, between the Saguenay and the North-west river in Labrador. A few years ago, however, there was good fishing to be had in Mal Bay River, above the Saguenay, and also in the Jacques Cartier, above Quebec, but good sport is seldom found in either of those streams at the present time. But the principal tributaries of the Saguenay itself (particularly the River St. Margaret), afford the rarest of sport, even now. The streams of this coast are rather small, but very numerous, and without a single exception, we believe, are rapid, cold, and clear. They abound in waterfalls, and though exceedingly wild, are usually quite convenient to angle in, for the reason that the spring freshets are apt to leave a gravelly margin on either side. The conveniences for getting to this out-of-the-way region are somewhat rude, but quite comfortable and very romantic. The angler has to go in a Quebec fishing smack, or if he is in the habit of trusting to fortune when he gets into a scrape, he can always obtain a passage down the St. Lawrence in a brig or ship, which will land him at any stated point. If he goes in a smack, he can always make use of her tiny cabin for his temporary home; but if he takes a ship, after she has spread her sails for Europe, he will have to depend upon the hospitality of the Esquimaux Indians. At the mouths of a few of the streams alluded to, he may chance to find the newly-built cabin of a lumberman, who will treat him with marked politeness; but he must not lay the "flattering unction" to his soul that he will receive any civilities from the agents of the Hudson's Bay Company whom he may happen to meet in that northern wilderness.

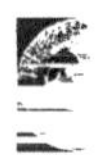

A large proportion of these streams run through an unknown mountain land, and are yet nameless; so that we cannot designate the precise localities where we have been particularly successful; and we might add that the few which have been named by the Jesuit Missionaries can never be remembered without a feeling of disgust. Not to attempt a pun, it can safely be remarked that those names are decidedly *beastly*; for they celebrate such creatures as the hog, the sheep, and the cow. The salmon taken on this coast vary from ten to forty pounds, though the average weight is perhaps fifteen pounds. They constitute an important article of commerce, and it is sometimes the case that a single fisherman will secure at least four hundred at one tide, in a single net. The cities of Montreal and Quebec are supplied with fresh salmon from this portion of the St. Lawrence, and the entire valley of that river, as well as portions of the Union, are supplied with smoked salmon from the same region. The rivers on the southern coast of the Gulf of St. Lawrence are generally well supplied with salmon, but those streams are few and far between, and difficult of access. But a visit to any portion of this great northern valley, during the pleasant summer time, is attended with many interesting circumstances. Generally speaking, the scenery is mountainous, and though the people are not very numerous, they are somewhat unique in their manners and customs, and always take pleasure in lavishing their attentions upon the stranger. The weeks that we spent voyaging upon the St. Lawrence we always remember with unalloyed pleasure; and if we thought that fortune would never again permit us to revisit those delightful scenes, we should indeed be quite unhappy.

The most agreeable of our pilgrimages were performed in a small sail-boat, commanded by an experienced and very intelligent pilot of Tadousac, named Ovington, and our companions were Charles Pentland, Esq., of Launce au Leau on the Saguenay, and George Price, Jr., Esq., of Quebec. We had everything we wanted in the way of "creature comforts;" and we went everywhere, saw everybody, caught lots of salmon, killed an occasional seal, and tried to harpoon an occasional white porpoise; now enjoying a glorious sunset, and then watching the stars and the strange aurora, as we lay becalmed at midnight far out upon the deep; at one time gazing with wonder upon a terrible storm, and then again happy, fearless, and free, dashing over the billows before a stiff gale.

Some of the peculiar charms of fly-fishing in this region are owing to the fact that you are not always sure of the genus of your fish even after you have hooked him, for it may be a forty or a twenty pound salmon, and then again it may be a salmon-trout or a four pound specimen of the common trout. The consequence is, that the expectations of the angler are always particularly excited. Another pleasure which might be mentioned is derived from the queer antics and laughable yells of the Indians, who are always hanging about your skirts for the express purpose of making themselves merry over any mishap which may befall you. The only drawback which we have found in fishing in these waters is caused by the immense number of musquitoes and sand-flies. Every new guest is received by them with particular and constant attention: their only desire, by night or day, seems to be to gorge themselves to death with the life-blood of those who "happen among them." It actually makes our blood run cold to think of the misery we endured from these winged tormentors.

Even with the Gulf of St. Lawrence before our mind, we are disposed to consider the Bay of Chaleur the most interesting salmon region in the British Possessions. This estuary divides Lower Canada from New Brunswick, and as the streams emptying into it are numerous and always clear, they are resorted to by the salmon in great numbers. The scenery of the bay is remarkably beautiful: the northern shore, being rugged and mountainous, presents an agreeable contrast to the southern shore, which is an extensive lowland, fertile, and somewhat cultivated. The principal inhabitants of this region are Scotch farmers, and the simplicity of their lives is only equaled by their hospitality; and upon this bay, also, reside the few survivors of a once powerful aboriginal nation, the Micmac Indians. But of all the rivers which empty into the Bay of Chaleur, there is not one that can be compared to the Restigouche, which is its principal tributary. It is a winding stream, unequal in width, and after running through a hilly country, it forces its way through a superb mountain gorge, and then begins to expand in width until it falls into its parent bay. The scenery is beautiful beyond compare, the eye being occasionally refreshed by the appearance of a neat farm, or a little Indian hamlet. The river is particularly famous for its salmon, which are very abundant and of a good size. But this is a region which the anglers of our country or the Provinces, with two or three exceptions, have not yet taken the trouble to visit, and many of the resident inhabitants are not even aware of the fact that the salmon may be taken with the fly. The regular fishermen catch them altogether with the net, and the Indians

with the spear; and it is a singular fact that the Indians are already complaining of the whites for destroying their fisheries, when it is known that a single individual will frequently capture in a single day a hundred splendid fellows, and that, too, with a spear of only one tine. It is reported of a Scotch clergyman who once angled in "these parts," that he killed three hundred salmon in one season, and with a single rod and reel. A pilgrimage to the Restigouche would afford the salmon fisher sufficient material to keep his thinkers busy for at least one year. The angler and lover of scenery who could spare a couple of months, would find it a glorious trip to go to the Bay of Chaleur in a vessel around Nova Scotia, returning in a canoe by the Restigouche, and the Spring River, which empties into the St. John. His most tedious portage would be only about three miles long (a mere nothing to the genuine angler), and soon after touching the latter river he could ship himself on board of a steamboat, and come home in less than a week, even if that home happened to be west of the Alleghany mountains.

Of all the large rivers of New Brunswick, we know not a single one which will not afford the fly fisherman an abundance of sport. Foremost among our favorites, we would mention the St. John, with the numerous beautiful tributaries which come into it below the Great Falls, not forgetting the magnificent pool below those falls, nor Salmon River and the Aroostook. The scenery of this valley is charming beyond compare, but the man who would spend a summer therein must have a remarkably long purse, for the half-civilized Indians, and the less than half-civilized white people, of the region, have a particular passion for imposing upon travelers and charging them the most exorbitant prices for the simple necessaries they may need. The salmon of the St. John are numerous, but rather small, seldom weighing more than fifteen pounds. The fisheries of the bay of Fundy, near the mouth of the St. John, constitute an important interest, in a commercial point of view. The fishermen here take the salmon with drag-nets, just before high water: the nets are about sixty fathoms long, and require three or four boats to manage them. The fish are all purchased, at this particular point, by one man, at the rate of eighty cents a-piece, large and small, during the entire season. The other New Brunswick rivers to which we have alluded are the Mirimichi and the St. Croix; but as we have never angled in either, we will leave them to their several reputations.

We now come to say a few words of Nova Scotia, which is not only famous for its salmon, but also for its scientific anglers. In this province the old English feeling for the "gentle art" is kept up, and we know of fly fisherman there, a record of whose piscatorial exploits would have overwhelmed even the renowned Walton and Davy with astonishment. The rivers of Nova Scotia are quite numerous, and usually well supplied with salmon. The great favorite among the Halifax anglers is Gold River, a cold and beautiful stream, which is about sixty miles distant from that city, in a westerly direction. The valley of the stream is somewhat settled, and by a frugal and hard-working Swiss and German population, who pitched their tents there in 1760. It is fifteen years since it was discovered by a strolling angler, and at the present time there is hardly a man residing on its banks who does not consider himself a faithful disciple of Walton. Even among the Micmac Indians, who pay the river an annual visit, may be occasionally found an expert fly fisher. But, after all, Nova Scotia is not exactly the province to which a Yankee angler would enjoy a visit, for cockney fishermen are a little too abundant, and the ways of the people in some ridiculous particulars smack too much of the mother country.

Having finished our geographical history of the salmon and his American haunts, we will take our leave of him by simply remarking (for the benefit of those who like to preserve what they capture), that there are three modes for preserving the salmon:—first, by putting them in salt for three days, and then smoking, which takes about twelve days; secondly, by regularly salting them down, as you would mackerel; and thirdly, by boiling and then pickling them in vinegar. The latter method is unquestionably the most troublesome, but at the same time the most expeditious; and what can tickle the palate more exquisitely than a choice bit of pickled salmon, with a bottle of Burgundy to float it to its legitimate home?

THE FUR TRAPPERS.

THE unique brotherhood of men to whom we now direct the attention of our readers have always depended upon the fur trade alone for their support, and as the various fur companies of North America have flourished and declined, so have the trappers multiplied or decreased in numbers. The French, who were the founders of the fur trade on this continent, established themselves here in 1606, and the trapping fraternity may therefore claim the honor of having existed nearly two centuries and a half. To estimate the precise number of individuals composing this class at the present time would be an impossibility. occupying as they do a section of country extending from the Pacific Ocean to Hudson's Bay.

By the laws of our country they have ever been looked upon as aliens from the commonwealth of civilization, and by the Indian tribes as trespassers upon their natural and inherited privileges. The blood of the white man, though frequently considerably adulterated, invariably runs through their veins, and the great majority trace their origin to a French, Scottish, or Irish ancestry, it being an established and singular fact that trappers of pure American blood are exceedingly rare. Those of the far north commonly have the dark eyes and hair of the Canadian Frenchman, and those of the south-west the flaxen hair and broad brogue of the Scotchman or Irishman. The motives generally found to have influenced them in entering upon their peculiar life are of course exceedingly various, but among the more common ones may be mentioned a deeply-rooted love for the works of Nature in their primeval luxuriance, want of sufficient intelligence to prosecute a more respectable business, and a desire to keep out of the way of certain laws which they may have transgressed in their earlier days. They are usually men with families, their wives being pure Indian, and their children, as a matter of course, half breeds. They have what may be termed fixed habitations, but they are rude log cabins, located on the extreme frontiers of the civilized world. In religion, as a class, they are behind their red brethren of the wilderness, and their knowledge of books is quite as limited. Generally speaking, they spend about nine months roaming alone through the solitude of the forests and prairies, and the remaining three months of the year with their families or at the trading posts of the fur companies. As their harvest time is the winter, they are necessarily men of iron constitutions, and frequently endure the severest hardships and privations. Understanding as they do the science of trapping and the use of the gun more thoroughly than the Indian, they eclipse him in the business of acquiring furs, and from their superior knowledge of the civilized world, limited though it be, they realize much greater profits, and hence it is that they are not only hated by the Indian but also by the traders. Their manner of dressing is ordinarily about half civilized, their buckskin hunting shirts and fur caps, of their own manufacture, appearing almost as picturesque as the blankets and plumes of the Indian himself. Like the Indians, too, they prefer richly-fringed leggins to pantaloons, and embroidered moccasins to shoes. To be perfectly free from every restraint both of body and mind, is their chief ambition, and to enjoy the freedom of the wilderness is their utmost happiness. Those who follow their trade among the mountains are commonly banded together in parties of half a dozen. They perform their long journey altogether upon horseback, and when among the mountains are as expert in scaling precipices, surmounting waterfalls, and buffeting snowstorms as the more hardy of the Indian tribes. They are expert horsemen, ride the best of animals, and take great pleasure not only in decking themselves with ornaments, but also in caparisoning their horses in the most grotesque yet picturesque manner. As to the animals which all of them make it their business to capture, it may be mentioned that chiefest among them all is the beaver; but a goodly portion of their income is derived from the furs and peltries of the martin, otter, muskrat, bear, fox, mink, lynx, wolverine, raccoon, wolf, elk, and deer, and the robes of the huge buffalo.

But let us describe the life of the trapping fraternity somewhat more minutely, in doing which we shall give an illustrative sketch of the career of a single individual, describing his departure from home, his sojourn in the wilderness, his return home, and his manner of spending his brief summer furlough.

It is a bright October morning, and about the threshold of the trapper's cabin there is an unusual stir. While the trapper himself is busily engaged in examining and putting in order his traps, packing away his powder and lead, with a number of good flints, giving the lock of his old rifle a thorough oiling, and sharpening his knives, his wife is stowing away in his knapsack a few simple cooking utensils, a small bag of tea and a little sugar, several pairs of moccasins and coarse woolen socks, and a goodly quantity of the sinewy material used in making snow-shoes. The fact that our friend is about to separate from his family for the most part of a year, makes him particularly kind to those about him; and, by way of manifesting his feelings, he gives into his wife's possession what little spare money he may have left in his pocket out of his earnings of the previous year, and allows his children to make as much noise as they please, even refraining from scolding them when they kick and abuse his favorite hunting dogs. All things being ready, night comes, and the trapper permits himself to enjoy another sleep in the midst of his household, but long before the break of day he has whistled to his dogs, and, with his knapsack on his back, has taken his departure for a stream that rises among the Rocky Mountains. If his course lies through a forest land he continues to travel on foot, taking his own leisure, killing a sufficient quantity of game to satisfy his wants, and sleeping at night upon his skins, under a canopy of leaves. If extensive water courses lie within his range, he purchases a canoe of some wandering Indians and plays the part of a navigator; and if he finds it necessary to cross extensive prairies, he obtains a pony, and, packing himself and plunder upon the animal, plays the part of an equestrian. When the first blast of December, accompanied by a shower of snow, sweeps over the land, it finds our trapper friend snugly domiciled in a log shanty at the mouth of the river where he purposes to spend the winter trapping for beaver.

And now all things are ready, and the trapper has actually entered upon his winter avocation. He has reconnoitered the valley in which he finds himself, and having ascertained the localities of the beaver, with their houses and dams, he forthwith manages to shoot a single male beaver, and having obtained from his glandulous pouch a substance called *castoreum*, he mixes it with a number of aromatics, and in three or four days he is supplied with a suitable bait and proceeds to set his traps. As the senses of the beaver are exceedingly keen, the business of the trapper requires experience and great caution, and he glides through the forests almost with the silence of a ghost; but, when a master of his calling, he seldom leaves a beaver village until, by his cunning arts, it has become depopulated. The war of extermination, as already intimated, begins at the mouth of the river, and with our friend will only cease when he has reached the fountain-head, or the season for trapping comes to an end. The coldest of winds may blow and the woods may be completely blocked with snow, but the trapper has mounted his snow-shoes, and day after day does he revisit and re-arrange his traps. If night overtake him when far removed from his shanty (which may be the case more than half the time), he digs himself a hole in some sheltered snow bank, and, wrapped up in his blanket by the side of his solitary fire, spends a strangely comfortable night. When not engaged with his traps, he employs his time in drying and dressing his furs; or, as fancy may dictate, he shoulders his gun and starts out for the purpose of capturing a deer, a bear, or some of the beasts which are wont to howl him to sleep at the midnight hour. Venison and bear meat constitute his principal food, but he is particularly partial to the tail of his favorite beaver. The only human beings with which he has any social intercourse during the long winter are the poor wandering Indians who chance to visit him in his cabin; and at such times many are the wild adventures and strange legends which they relate to each other around the huge fire of the trapper. And he now enjoys to perfection the companionship of his dogs. Companions, it is true, of another sort sometimes gather around his lonely habitation to relieve his solitude, for the snowy owl hoots and screams at night from the huge pine branch that reaches over his cabin, or perhaps an unmolested deer manifests its love of companionship by browsing the twigs in broad daylight almost at his very threshold. But now fair weather cometh out of the north, and the trapper begins to think that he has secured such a supply of furs as will guaranty him a comfortable support during the coming summer, and one by one he gathers in his traps. The crack of his rifle is now heard more frequently echoing through the woods, for he cares not to obtain more beaver skins even if he could, and he would obtain a sufficient number of miscellaneous furs to render his assortment complete. Heavy spring rains have set in, the water courses are nearly released from their icy fetters, and on issuing from his cabin, after a night of conflicting dreams, he finds that the neighboring stream has become unusually full. A single glance at its turbid waters is enough. He cuts down a suitable tree and builds him a canoe, and in this does he stow away his furs and all his other plunder; and, seizing his paddle, he jumps into his seat, and with a light heart starts for his distant home.

The rains are over and gone, and although our voyager has already been ten days upon the waters, he has yet at least a thousand additional miles to travel. Rapids without number are to be passed, many a laborious portage must be made around huge waterfalls, and at least two months must elapse before he can moor his little barge in the haven where he would be. Day follows day, and his course is onward. All along his route the forest trees are bursting their buds and decking themselves with the livery of the vernal season, while the grasses and flowers of the prairies are striving to overreach each other as they loom into the pleasant sunshine. And then, too, the heart of our voyager is cheered by the singing of birds. When night comes, and he has lain himself down by his watchfire on the shore, in some little cove, he is lulled to sleep by the murmuring music of the stream. If, on a pleasant day when he is fatigued, he happen upon an Indian encampment and finds that an extensive ball-play or an Indian horse-race, or any important medicine ceremony is about to occur, he tarries there for a few hours, and then, as his mind dwells upon the grotesque and laughable scenes he has witnessed, resumes his voyage in a more cheerful mood. Day follows day, and the stream upon which he is now floating is broad and deep, and sweeps onward as if rejoicing with pride for having triumphed over the obstacles of the wilderness, and is rapidly approaching the fields and the abodes of civilization. It is now the close of a day in the leafy month of June, and our voyager is gliding noiselessly into the quiet cove beside his cabin, and, uttering a loud whistle or whoop and firing his gun, his wife and children hasten to the shore, and—the trapper is at home!

The summer time, in the opinion of our trapper friend, is the season of unalloyed enjoyment, for it is then that he gives himself up to the gratification of all his desires. Having disposed of his furs and peltries at the nearest trading post for a few hundred dollars in cash, or its equivalent in merchandise, he deems himself independently rich, and conducts himself accordingly. In a fit of liberality, he orders his wife and children into his canoe and takes them upon a visit to the nearest frontier village or city, where he loads them with gewgaws, and the family spend a few days. The novelty of this visit soon passes away, and our trapper with his family are once more domiciled in their cabin. A week of inactivity then follows, and the trapper becomes as restless as a fish out of water. He is troubled with a kind of itching palm, and away he goes upon a vagabondizing tour among the hangers-on about the trading establishments, recounting to all who will listen to him his adventures in the wilderness, and spending the remainder of the summer after the manner of the idle and the dissipated. But the first frost brings him to his senses, and the trapper is himself again—for he is thinking of the wilderness.

THE CANADIAN RECLUSE.

Of the many singular characters which we have met with in our various travels, we remember none with more pleasure, and even wonder, than the hero of this chapter. In company with three friends, we were upon a fishing cruise along the northern shore of the river St. Lawrence, above the Saguenay, and having on a certain afternoon steered our little craft into a cove at the mouth of a brook, for the purpose of obtaining fresh water, we were surprised to find ourselves in the immediate neighborhood of a rude but comfortable log cabin. Curiosity, as a matter of course, led us to visit the cabin, and introduce ourselves to the proprietor. We did so, and were not only warmly welcomed, but were invited to tarry with our new acquaintance until the next day, and had we not accepted the invitation, the following particulars would not now be made known to the public.

The individual under consideration was a Frenchman, and a native of Quebec. He was above the medium height, about forty years of age, graceful in his manners, active in mind and body, and altogether just the character to rivet the attention of the most casual observer. He was wholly ignorant of the world, having never been out of his native city, excepting when he took up his abode in this out-of-the-way corner of the country, where, at the time we met with him, he had been secluded for nearly twenty years. He had a wife (but no children) who was as much like himself in appearance and character as nature could well allow her to be. He was totally illiterate, and yet possessed an attachment to the unwritten science of botany which was truly remarkable. His cabin had only two lower rooms and one garret, and yet the best of the three was exclusively appropriated to a collection of plants, gathered from the neighboring hills and mountains, and numbering several hundred varieties, together with large moose horns, furs, and other forest curiosities. He knew not the generic name of a single specimen, and yet he would expatiate upon their beauty in the most interesting manner, showing that he loved them with intense affection. To the hunting and cultivation of plants he told us he was in the habit of devoting more than half of his time, whereupon we asked him from what source he obtained his living. He informed us that having inherited the large tract of land upon which he resided, he had come here for the purpose of getting a living out of *that.* On casting our eyes about, and finding nothing for them to rest upon but mountains of solid rock, where even pine trees hardly had the courage to grow, we thought his reply somewhat mysterious. He smiled at our perplexity, and then told us that he had two or three profitable salmon fishing grounds within a mile of his house, which were rented out to Quebec fishermen, and yielded him all the necessaries of life, and that he obtained his fresh meats with his own hands from the forest.

Had we been inclined to doubt any of the assertions of our friend in regard to his good living, all such doubts would have been most assuredly dispelled by what we witnessed and enjoyed before closing our eyes on the night in question. Having taken us to the fishing ground lying nearest to his cabin, for the purpose of letting us see how the salmon were taken in the circular set nets (into which they swam on their way up stream when the tide was high, and from which they were taken by the hundred when the tide was low), he picked out a splendid twenty pound fish, and piloted us back again to his dwelling. He then excused himself from further waiting upon us, and, begging us to amuse ourselves by *examining his plants,* or doing anything else we pleased, he informed us that he must assist his wife in preparing our supper. We bowed our most willing assent, and as the sun was near his setting, we ascended a neighboring knoll for the purpose of enjoying the extensive prospect which presented itself to view.

We were looking towards the south, and across that portion of the noble St. Lawrence where it is without an island, and its shores are twenty-five miles apart. The retinue of clouds around the setting sun were brilliant to a marvelous degree, and were distinctly mirrored on the tranquil bosom of the superb river. In the distance we could barely discover the southern shore, forming a long narrow line of purple; about a dozen miles to the eastward one solitary ship lay floating at the mercy of the tide, and in the foreground was the cabin of our entertainer, partly hidden from our view by a few stunted trees, and apparently hemmed in by inaccessible mountains, while before the cabin lay extended some half dozen immense mongrel dogs, which were the only living creatures, besides ourselves, tending to animate the lonely scene. Silently communing with our own hearts, we watched with peculiar interest the coming forth, one after another, of the beautiful stars, and we could not but think of our distant homes, and of the ties which bound us to the absent and loved. One moment more, and we heard a loud hallo, which came from the lungs of our Canadian friend, who informed us that supper was ready, whereupon we descended to the cabin at a pace bordering upon a run.

And such a supper! Our host presided, and while two of his guests were seated on either side, the hostess occupied the opposite end of the table from her husband. She could not speak a word of English, and of course uttered all her apologies in French; and though the husband pretended to talk English, we begged him to remember that his guests all understood French, and that he had better converse as nature dictated. No objections were made, and we proceeded to business. The table was literally loaded; and, whilst the matron poured out a capital cup of coffee, the host overwhelmed the plates of his guests with various kinds of meat, most of which were fried or broiled almost to a crisp. We gave vent to our curiosity by inquiring the names of the dishes we were eating. From this moment, until the truly delicious feast was ended, the talking was all performed by the Canadian botanist, and the substance of his remarks may be stated as follows:

"That meat in the blue platter, gentlemen, was cut from the hind quarters of the biggest *black bear* ever seen among the mountains. He weighed over four hundred pounds, and was as savage as he was fat and big. I was climbing along the edge of a hill, about a week ago, for the purpose of securing a small yellow flower that I had discovered hanging from a rock, when the bear in question came running out of the mouth of his den, and saluting me with a long scratch on the back, I gave him a stab in the belly, and tumbled myself down the offset in the most hasty manner imaginable. I always take my gun with me when I go into the woods, and when I reached the bottom of the hill I looked out for the bear, and, discovering him on a stump some twenty yards off, I gave him a shot, and he made at me with the fires of revenge and rage in his eye. I climbed up a small tree, and while the rascal made an unsuccessful attempt to follow me, I reloaded my gun and sent another charge directly into his mouth, which gave him a bad cough, and in a short time he staggered a few paces from the tree and fell to the ground quite dead. *I then went back to the cliff to secure my yellow flower*, and during that afternoon, by the aid of my pony, dragged the bear to my cabin.

"In that dish, with a piece broken from the edge, gentlemen, you have a mixture of *moose tongue, moose lip*, and *moose brains.* I spent nearly a month moose-hunting, last winter, in company with a couple of Indians, and though the snow was deep, the crust hard, our snow-shoes in good order, our dogs brave and strong, and moose were numerous, we only killed about sixteen. I only brought home the heads (while the Indians were satisfied with the skins and haunches), but I was more than paid for all my trouble, in the way of hard traveling and cold sleeping, for in one of the moose-yards that we visited *I found a specimen of pine which I had never seen before.* It was very soft and beautiful, and I think the book-men of England would give a good deal of money if they could have it in their great gardens.

"As to that meat in the white dish, which you all seem to eat with such a relish, I think you will be surprised to learn that it is nothing but *beaver's tail.* To my taste it is the sweetest meat in the world, and I am only sorry that this valuable animal is becoming so very scarce in this section of country. My present stock of beaver's tail came from the shore of Hudson's Bay, and, though I bought it of an Indian, I had to pay him as much for the tails as the fur company paid him for the skins of his animals. I never trapped for beaver myself, but I have for otter, and often have great sport in killing seals, which are very abundant in the St. Lawrence, and afford to the Indians pretty good food during the hard winters. The only thing that I have against the beaver is, that he has a fashion, I am told, *of cutting down for his house such beautiful trees as the birch, mulberry, willow, and poplar before they are half grown.*

"As to the salmon upon which you have been feasting, gentlemen, you know as much about that particular individual as I do, since you saw him while yet in his native element. The men who hire my fishing grounds pay me so much for every fish they take, and sell them at a great profit in Quebec and even in Montreal. From the fisheries on this shore are the people of Canada exclusively supplied with the salmon, and when we have a good season our merchants manage to send over to the United States, in a smoked condition, a good many thousand. As to taking them with those pretty little flies, which you, gentlemen, always carry in your pocket-books, I never could understand how you manage to deceive so sensible a fish as the salmon. Of one thing I am certain: if you expect to take any of the salmon in this region with those little lines and hooks, you will be much mistaken. You will have to go down to the Saguenay, where I am told the fish do not know any better than to be deceived by your cunning arts. But, if I was ever to follow fishing as you do, it seems to me that instead of red, yellow, and blue feathers, I should cover my hooks *with the bright berries and buds which you may find upon some trees even during the fishing season.*"

This last remark of our host convinced us that he was indeed possessed with a ruling passion, and we of course gratified ourselves by humoring him to the length of our patience. He not only monopolized the conversation during supper, but he did most of the talking until bed-time. We spent the night under his roof, sleeping upon bear skins, spread on the floor; and, after an early breakfast, we bade him adieu, and pursued our course down the St. Lawrence.

TROUT FISHING.

It carries us into the most wild and beautiful scenery of nature; amongst the mountain lakes and the clear and lovely streams that gush from the higher ranges of elevated hills, or make their way through the cavities of calcareous rocks.

SIR HUMPHREY DAVY.

WERE it not for the salmon, we should pronounce the trout the most superb game-fish in the world. As the case now stands, however, we are inclined to believe that he has delighted a greater number of anglers than any other inhabitant of the "liquid plain." The characteristics of this charming fish are so well known that we shall not, on this occasion, enter upon a scientific description, either of his person or habits. In all the particulars of beauty, of color and form, of grace, of activity, of intelligence and flavor, as before intimated, he has but one rival. He always glories in the coldest and purest of water, and the regions of country to which he is partial are commonly distinguished for the wildness of their scenery; and therefore it is that to the lover of nature this imperial fish has ever been exceedingly dear. Their period of spawning is in the autumn, and they recover as early as February, thereby remaining in season a part of the winter, as well as the entire spring and summer—though the trouting months, *par excellence*, are May and June.

In weight, even when fully grown, the different varieties of trout run from four ounces to sixty pounds, and of the different distinct species found in the United States and Canada, we are acquainted only with the following:

The Common or Brook and River Trout.—There is hardly a cold and rocky stream in any of the New England or Northern States, or among the mountains of the Middle and Southern States, where this species is not found in abundance. In regard to weight, they ordinarily vary from three or four ounces to two pounds; and in color, according to the character of the brook or river which they inhabit. So apparent is the difference of color in this family, that, in the several sections of the country where they are found, they are designated by the names of Silver or Fall trout, as in Lake George; and the Black trout, as in many of the smaller lakes or ponds of New England. The only *civilized* mode employed by our people for taking them is with the hook; but, while the scientific angler prefers the artificial fly (with an appropriate reel), large numbers are annually destroyed by the farmers' boys with the common hook and red worm. As to the heathenish mode of netting this beautiful fish, we can only say that it merits the most earnest condemnation of every gentleman. The common trout is proverbially one of the most skittish of all the finny tribes; but, when he happens to be a little hungry, he is fearless as the hawk, and at such times often leaps into the air as if for the purpose of defying the cunning of his human enemies. According to our experience, the best bait for early spring fishing is the common worm, but for June, July, and August we prefer the fly. Sometimes, however, a minnow is preferable to either. The great charm of fly-fishing for trout is derived from the fact that you then see the movement of your fish, and if you are not an expert hand, the chances are that you will capture but one out of the hundred that may rise to your hook. You can seldom save a trout unless you strike the very instant that he leaps. But, even after this, a deal of care is required to land him in safety. If he is a half-pounder, you may pull him out directly; but if larger than that, after fairly hooking him, you should play him with your whole line, which, when well done, is a feat full of poetry. The swiftness with which a trout can dart from his hiding-place after a fly is truly astonishing; and we never see one perform this operation without feeling an indescribable thrill quivering through our frame. The fact that this is the only fish in the world which nature has designated by a row of scarlet spots along the sides, would seem to imply that she deemed it the perfection of her finny creations, and had, therefore, fixed upon it this distinguishing mark of her skill.

The Salmon Trout.—Under this head we include all those fish of the trout genus which are found only in those lakes of our country having no connection whatever with the sea. The fish now under consideration resembles, in its general appearance, the legitimate salmon, but is totally unlike it in several particulars. The salmon trout, for example, varies in weight from three to sixty pounds; and, if everybody is to be believed, they have been taken in some of our waters weighing upwards of one hundred pounds. They are also of much less value than the real salmon as an article of food, there being nothing at all delicate in the texture or flavor of a mammoth fish. As sporting fish, too, they are of little value, for they love the gloom of deep water, and are not distinguished for their activity. The names besides its own by which this fish is recognized, are the lake trout and the Mackinaw trout; and, by many people who ought to know better, they are often confounded with the genuine salmon. As is the case with the salmon, they are seldom or never found in any of our rivers, but chiefly in the lakes of the northern and northwestern States of the Union, being found in the greatest numbers at the Straits of Mackinaw, in Lake Superior, Lake George, and the other lakes of the Empire State, and in Moosehead Lake.

The Sea Trout.—Our idea of this fish is that it is quite at home in the "deep, deep sea," but rather partial to the brackish waters of large rivers and the inland bays of the American coast. And also that they vary in weight from three to fifteen pounds, and ought to be highly prized as a game-fish, their flesh being of a rosy hue, and excellent, and their courage and strength allied to those of their more aristocratic cousin—the salmon. Like the salmon and common trout, too, they scorn the more common baits of the fisherman, and possess a decided taste for the fly, albeit thousands of them are taken with the shrimp and minnow. The waters where they mostly abound are those of the lower St. Lawrence and its tributaries, the bay of Cape Cod, all along the southern shore of Barnstable, the entire shore of Martha's Vineyard, and the bays Delaware and Chesapeake. So much for the varieties of trout with which we are personally acquainted.

It now behooves us to record some of our experience in trout fishing, but we have already published in our books of travel, and elsewhere, quite as many *fish stories* as will be readily believed. We shall, therefore, content ourselves, on this occasion, with a brief description of our favorite localities.

As a matter of course, the first place that we mention in this connection is Saut St. Marie, which, for many reasons, is an exceedingly attractive place. In the first place, it is the outlet to Lake Superior, the largest body of fresh water on the globe. It is also the western terminating point of the lake navigation of the north. From the earliest periods of our history to the present time, it has been, as it were, the starting place for all the fur expeditions by land which have ever penetrated the immense wilderness bordering on Hudson's Bay and the Arctic ocean. The fall of the river St. Mary, at the spot called the Saut, is nearly twenty-five feet within the space of half a mile, so that from a canoe at the foot of the rapid it presents the appearance of a wall of foam. The width of it is reputed to be one mile, and on the British side are several beautiful islands, covered with hemlock, spruce, and pine, pleasingly intermingled with birch. The bed of the river at this point consists chiefly of colored sand-stones, the depth varies from ten to perhaps one hundred feet, and the water is perpetually cold, and as clear as it is possible for any element to be. But what makes the Saut particularly attractive to the angler, is the fact that the common trout is found here in good condition throughout the year. They are taken with the fly, and from boats anchored in the more shallow places of the river, as well as from the shore. We have known two fishermen to spend an entire day in a single reef, or at one anchorage, and, in spite of sunlight and east winds, have known them to capture more than a cart load of the spotted beauties, varying in weight from half a pound to three and four. How it is that the fish of this region always appear to be in season has never been explained, but we should imagine that either they have no particular time for spawning, or that each season brings with it a variety peculiar to itself. Those of the present day who visit Saut St. Marie for the purpose of throwing the fly, ought to be fully prepared with tackle, and that of the best quality. With regard to the *creature comforts* obtainable in the village of Saut St. Marie, they will be as well supplied as in any other place of the same size equally remote from the civilized centre of the world. And when the pleasures of trout fishing begin to subside they can relieve the monotony of a sojourn here by visiting the Indians in their wigwams, and seeing them capture (with nets, in the pure white foam) the beautiful white fish; they may also with little difficulty visit the copper mines of Lake Superior, or, if they would do their country service (provided they are Americans), they may indite long letters to members of Congress on the great necessity of a ship canal around the falls or rapids of St. Mary.

And now for the island of Mackinaw. For an elaborate description of this spot we refer our readers to any of the numerous travelers who have published its praises, not forgetting, by way of being *impartial*, an account from our own pen already before the public. The time is rapidly approaching, we believe, when this island will be universally considered one of the most healthful, interesting, convenient, and fashionable watering-places in the whole country. And the naturalists, not to say the angler, will find here the celebrated Mackinaw trout in its greatest perfection. And when the Detroit and Chicago steamer runs into the little crescent harbor of the island for the purpose of landing the traveler, and he discovers among the people on the dock some half-dozen wheelbarrows laden with fish four feet long and weighing fifty or sixty pounds, he must not be alarmed at finding those fish to be Mackinaw trout, and not sturgeon, as he might at first have imagined. The truth is, the very size of these fish is an objection to them, for, as they have to be taken in deep water, and with a large cord, there is far more of manual labor than sport in taking them. But when one of these monsters happens to stray towards the shore where the water is not over fifty feet, it is then, through the marvellously clear water, exceedingly pleasant to watch their movements as they swim about over the beds of pure white sand. As before intimated, the Mackinaw trout is far inferior to the common trout as an article of food, and to the white fish almost infinitely so.

The Mackinaw trout (as is the case with all salmon trout) is in fine condition throughout the winter months; and the Indians are very fond of taking them through the ice. Their manner of proceeding is to make a large hole in the ice, over which they erect a kind of wigwam, so as to keep out the light; and, stationing themselves above the hole, they lure the trout from the bottom by an artificial bait, and when he comes sufficiently near pick him out with a spear: and they are also taken with a hook. The voraciousness of the Mackinaw trout at this season is said to be astonishing; and it is recorded of a Canadian fisherman that, having lost all his artificial bait, by their being bitten to pieces, he finally resorted to a large jackknife attached to a hook which he had in his pocket, and which was swallowed by a thirty pound fish. Another anecdote that we have heard touching this mode of winter fishing is as follows, and shows the danger with which it is sometimes attended. An Indian fisherman, of renown among the tribes of Lake Superior, while fishing on this lake in the manner above mentioned, at a considerable distance from the shore, was once detached with a cake of ice from the shore and carried into the lake by the wind, and was never heard of more. Such a death as he must have met with it would be difficult to describe.

But we cannot leave Mackinaw without making a passing allusion to the fish whose Indian name is *ciscovet*. It is a beautiful fish, unquestionably of the trout family, a bold biter, richly flavored, and quite beautiful both in symmetry and color. They are not very abundant, and are altogether the greatest fishy delicacy in this region, excepting the white fish. They weigh from five to ten pounds, and are remarkable for their fatness. At the Island of Mackinaw the common trout are not found at all, but in all the streams upon the main shore of Lake Michigan, which is only a short distance off, they are very abundant and very large.

Another trouting region whose praises we are disposed to sing is that of northern New York, lying between Lake George and Long Lake. All the running waters of this section of country are abundantly supplied with common trout, and all the lakes (which are quite numerous) with salmon trout. The scenery everywhere is of the wildest and most imposing character. The two branches of the noble Hudson here take their rise, and almost every rood of their serpentine courses abounds in rapid and deep pools, yielding common trout of the largest size. But the angler who visits this region must not expect to be feasted with the fashionable delicacies of the land, or spend his nights in luxuriantly furnished rooms; he must be a lover of salt pork, and well acquainted with the yielding qualities of a pine floor. To those of our readers who would become better acquainted with the region alluded to, we would recommend the interesting descriptions of

Charles F. Hoffman, Esq., and the spirited though somewhat fantastic ones of J. T. Headley, Esq.

In the "times of old" we have enjoyed ourselves exceedingly in making piscatorial pilgrimages among the Catskill and Sharidaken Mountains, but their wilderness glory is rapidly departing. We can now only recommend this region as abounding in beautiful as well as magnificent scenery. Now, while we think of it, however, we have one little incident to record connected with Shaw's Lake, which beautifies the summit of one of the Catskills. Having once caught a large number of small common trout in a stream that ran out of this lake, we conceived the idea that the lake itself must of necessity contain a large number of full grown fish of the same species. With this idea in view, we obtained the services of a mountaineer named Hammel, and tried our luck at the lake, by the light of the moon, with set lines and live minnows. During the night we caught no less than forty-two trout, averaging in weight over a pound apiece. We were of course greatly elated at this success; and, having enjoyed quite a romantic expedition, we subsequently published an account of the particulars. A few days after this, a party of anglers residing in the town of Catskill saw what we had written, and immediately posted off to Shaw's Lake, for the purpose of spending a night there. They did so, and also fished after the same manner that we did, and yet did not capture a single trout. They of course returned home considerably disgusted, and reported that the lake in question was covered with dead eels, that the water was alive with lizards, that they saw the glaring eyes of a panther near their watch-fire, and that *we* had been guilty of publishing a falsehood. It now becomes us to deny, and in the most expressive tone, this rough impeachment, although we fully confess that there still hangs a mystery over our piscatorial good fortune.

If the anglers of New York city are to be believed, there is no region in the world like Long Island for common trout. We are informed, however, that the fish are here penned up in ponds, and that a stipulated sum per head has to be paid for all the fish captured. With this kind of business we have never had any patience, and we shall therefore refrain from commenting upon the exploits or trespassing upon the exclusive privileges of the cockney anglers of the empire city.

But another trouting region, of which we can safely speak in the most flattering terms, is that watered by the two principal tributaries of the river Thames, in Connecticut, viz., the Yantic and the Quinnebaug. It is, in our opinion, more nearly allied to that portion of England made famous by Walton in his *Complete Angler*, than any other in the United States. The country is generally highly cultivated, but along nearly all its very beautiful streams Nature has been permitted to have her own way, and the dark pools are everywhere overshadowed by the foliage of overhanging trees. Excepting in the immediate vicinity of the factories, trout are quite abundant, and the anglers are generally worthy members of the gentle brotherhood. When the angler is overtaken by night, he never finds himself at a loss for a place to sleep; and it has always seemed to us that the beds of this region have a "smell of lavender." The husbandmen whom you meet here are intelligent, and their wives neat, affable, and polite, understanding the art of preparing a frugal meal to perfection. Our trouting recollections of this section of New England are manifold, and we would part with them most unwillingly. Dearly do we cherish, not only recollections of scenery and fishing, but of wild legends and strange characters, bright skies, poetic conceptions, and soul-instructing lessons from the lips of Nature. Yes, and the secret of our attachment to the above-mentioned streams may be found in the character of these very associations. What intense enjoyment would not Father Walton have derived from their wild and superb scenery! The streams of England are mostly famous for the bloody battles and sieges which they witnessed for many centuries, and the turreted castles which they have only tell us eventful stories of a race of earth-born kings. But many of the streams of our country, even in these days, water a virgin wilderness, whose only human denizens are the poor but noble Indian tribes, who live, and love, and die in their peaceful valleys; and the unshorn forests, with the luxuriantly magnificent mountains, sing a perpetual hymn of praise to One who is above the sky and the King of kings.

Of all the New England States, however (albeit much might be written in praise of Vermont and New Hampshire, with their glorious Green and White Mountains), we believe that Maine is altogether the best supplied. In the head waters of the Penobscot and Kennebec, the common trout may be found by the thousand; and in Moosehead Lake, as before stated, salmon trout of the largest size and in great numbers. This is even a more perfect wilderness than that in the northern part of New York, and it is distinguished not only for its superb scenery, but its fine forests afford an abundance of large game, such as moose, deer, bears, and wolves, which constitute a most decided attraction to those disciples of the gentle art who have a little of the fire of Nimrod in their natures.

Another, and the last region towards which we would direct the attention of our readers, is that portion of Canada lying on the north shore of the St. Lawrence. At the mouth of all the streams here emptying into the great river, and especially at the mouth of the Saguenay, the sea trout is found in its greatest perfection. They vary from five to fifteen pounds, and are taken with the fly. But what makes the fishing for them particularly interesting, is the fact that when the angler strikes a fish it is impossible for him to tell, before he has seen his prize, whether he has captured a salmon trout, a mammoth trout, common trout (which are here found in brackish or salt water), or a magnificent salmon, glistening in his silver mail.

ROCK CREEK.

It was a delightful autumnal morning, and we had called upon a friend (who, like ourself, is a lover of nature), and proposed that we should spend a day in the woods; whereupon he whistled for his handsome greyhound, and with our sketch-books in hand, we departed. We turned our faces towards *Rock Creek*, which rises in the central portion of Montgomery county, Maryland, and after running a distance of some fifteen miles, finally empties into the Potomac, between Washington and Georgetown. And now, before going one step further, we wish to inform the reader that it is not our intention to give a complete description of this charming stream: to accomplish that task faithfully it would be necessary for us to write a thousand poems and paint at least a thousand pictures, every one of which should be a gem. We purpose only to record the more prominent impressions which have been left upon our mind by the excursions to which we allude.

We struck the creek just without the limits of the city, and the first object that attracted our attention was "Decatur's tomb." This memorial of a departed naval hero occupies the summit of a picturesque hill, and is shaded from the sun by a brotherhood of handsome oak trees. It is built of bricks (which are painted white), and resembles in shape a small Grecian temple without its columns, and is without any inscription. The remains of the commodore were originally deposited here, but his ashes have subsequently been removed to Philadelphia and deposited in his family vault. The land upon which this tomb is located is called Kalorama, and belongs to an estate originally owned by Joel Barlow, which fact is alone sufficient to give it a reputation; but it is somewhat more interesting to know that it was upon this spot of earth that Robert Fulton first tried his experiments while studying out the science of steam navigation. This was at the time when Barlow and Fulton were on the most intimate terms of friendship, and Kalorama was Fulton's principal home. A gentleman residing in Georgetown informs us that he can remember the time when an old wooden shed was standing in the vicinity of Rock Creek, where Fulton tried many of his experiments; and we are also informed that the parlor walls of Kalorama were once ornamented with fresco paintings executed by Fulton at the request of his friend Barlow. Subsequently to that period and while yet a member of Barlow's family, Fulton kept an account-book, in which he recorded all his business transactions, and that curious and valuable relic of the departed engineer is now in the possession of a citizen of Washington, by whose politeness we are privileged to gratify our antiquarian readers with a brief description of the account-book in question. It is of the size of an ordinary mercantile cash-book, and although only half filled with writing, it contains a record of business transactions occurring during the years 1809,–'10,–'11,–'12,–'13, and '14. It seems to have been kept with little regard to method, but nevertheless contains a great variety of items which are quite valuable in a historical point of view. On a fly leaf, for example, we have the following record :—

"1813. The dry-dock finished at the steamboat works in Jersey City on the 14th October. On that day, at 1 o'clock, the original North River steamboat entered for the first time, and I believe is the first vessel that has been in a dry-dock in the United States." :—

With regard to the name of the "original North River steamboat," I am not certain; but on the same leaf with the above, I find the following memorandum :—

"*Car of Neptune*—length of her bottom 157 feet; do. on deck 171 feet 6 inches; extreme width of the bottom 22 feet; do. on deck 26 feet."

With a view of showing the profitableness of the steam-boating business in the olden times, I append the following :—

"Total number of passengers in the Raritan for 1809:

202	to Elizabethtown Point, at 4s. each.		. . . . . .	101 00
1,480	to Amboy, at	8	do	1,480 50
692	to Brunswick, at	12	do	1,038 75
90	way			55 20
	Total receipts			2,675 45

"Of this sum one-sixth, equal 445 90, to patentees."

Of the various persons with whom Fulton seems to have had extensive dealings, the principal one was Robert R. Livingston, from whom large sums of money were frequently received. The principal items under the head of 1813 (which seems to have been a very busy year), give one an idea of the extent of FULTON'S business, and is as follows:—

"Steamboats building and engaged:

2	from New Orleans to Louisville and St Louis, Mississippi	$60,000
1	" Pittsburg to Louisville, Ohio	25,000
1	" Richmond to Norfolk, James River	35,000
1	" Washington to Malbourg, Potomac	20,000
1	on Long Island Sound, from New York to Hartford .	40,000
1	" East River ferry boat to Brooklyn	20,000
1,	Petersburg	25,000
1,	Elizabeth	30,000
1,	Robert Fulton	25,000
1,	Charleston	30,000
1,	Cape Fear	22,000
	Total	$332,000"

Another record which I find under the same head is this:—

"Waters under the direction of B. H. Latrobe, or such of them as he shall have a steamboat on and in actual operation by January, 1815. Such as shall not have the funds raised for one boat within one year from May 1, 1813, shall be at the disposal of Livingston and Fulton.

"1st, Potomac, from Georgetown to Potomac Creek.

"2d, for the sounds from Charleston to Savannah.

"3d, from Pittsburg to Louisville.

"4th, the Cumberland from Nashville to Louisville.

"5th, the Tennessee to Louisville.

"For raising companies, funds, and establishing these, he has to have of each one-third of the patentee's rights."

Under the head of 1812, we find a statement giving the expenses of a North River steamboat (what one we know not), which amounted to $610 per month, the boat making seventy-six trips. And as to wages, we gather that the captain received $50 per month; pilot, $35; engineer, $35; seamen and firemen, $20 each; cook, $16; servants, $14; and chambermaid, $8.

Another record readeth as follows:—

"*Gentlemen of influence in Cincinnati, Ohio.*—Jacob Burnet, Esq., Martin Baum, Esq., Jesse Hunt, General Findley, General Gano, Mr. Stanly."

The following I find under the head of "Notes on Steamboats:"—

"The Comet constructed at Pittsburg in the spring of 1813, for Mr. Smith, is 52 feet long and 8 feet beam, cylinder 6¼ inches diameter, 18 inches stroke, vibrating motion, no condenser or air-pump. The water wheel in the stern, 6 feet diameter, 8 paddles 2 feet 6 inches long and 11 inches wide. The boiler 14 feet long, 2 feet 6 inches wide, with a flue high, steam from 50 to 60 pounds to the inch square, 20 to 30 double stroke a minute. *This is Evans's idea of steam power by high steam. It was the Marquis of Worcester's* 120 *years ago; and Mr. Watts* 30 *years ago tried and abandoned it.*"

Another curious memorandum, which is without a caption, is as follows:—

"10,000 acres of pine land on Egg Harbor River, the property of Ebenezer Tucker, of Tuckerton, Burlington county, known by the name of Judge Tucker. Should this land produce only ten cords to an acre, it will be 1,000 to 100 acres, or 100,000 cords. The steamboats from New York will use 1,500 cords a year, or, for New York and Albany, 3,000 cords; thence 20 years would consume the wood of 6,000 acres, in which time, the first cut would grow up, and thus this 10,000 acres would perpetually supply the steamboats."

The longest record in this account book (like all the others) is in Fulton's own handwriting, and entitled "*Livingston and Fulton vs. Lake Champlain boat.*" It occupies four closely written pages, is dated October 12, 1810, and signed by Robert R. Livingston. It is an interesting document, but as the volume in question is about to be presented to the New York Historical Society, I will leave it with that honorable body to give it to the public in some of their interesting publications.

But enough of this episode. Though Rock Creek may have been the birthplace of Fulton's steamboat idea, yet it is certain that, with all his fiery monsters at our command, we could never ascend this beautiful stream without the use of our legs, and we will therefore rejoin our companion and continue our pedestrian pilgrimage.

Our next halting-place, after we left Kalorama, was at an old mill, located in the centre of a secluded glen. With the humming music of its wheels, with the polite attentions of the *floury* miller, and the rustic beauty of his cottage and children, we were well pleased, but with the natural loveliness of the place we were delighted. A greater variety of luxuriant foliage I never before witnessed in so limited a nook of the country. From one point of view a scene presented itself which was indeed exquisite. We were completely hemmed in from the great world, and, in addition to the mill and the cottage, we had a full view of the stream, which was spanned by a rustic foot bridge, upon which a couple of children were standing and throwing pebbles in the water, while a few paces beyond a man was pulling to the shore a small boat laden with wood. On either hand, a number of proud-looking oaks towered against the sky, and by the water's edge in the distance stood a stupendous silver willow, literally white with age; and, to complete the picture, we had in one place a mysterious brick ruin, and in the foreground a variety of mossy rocks, upon which, in a superb attitude, stood our beautiful greyhound, watching a little army of minnows sporting in a neighboring pool. And with what great name does our reader imagine this beautiful place is associated? None other than that of the late John Quincy Adams, who became its purchaser many years ago, and to whose estate (as I believe) it now belongs. And many a time, in other days, has that distinguished statesman spent his morning under the dome of the capitol in political debate, and the afternoon of the same day in this romantic glen, listening to the singing of a thousand birds, which had built their nests in the branches of his own trees.

The roads which cross the channel of Rock Creek, and frequently run for a long distance along its winding vale, are distinguished for their loneliness, and of course well adapted to please the poetic mind. Along many of them you might walk for miles without meeting a human being, but then you would be sure to frighten many a rabbit, and destroy the gossamery hammocks of unnumbered spiders. While passing along the road which took us from Adams' Mill further up the stream, we chanced to overtake a small negro boy (who was almost without any rags on his back, and whose straw hat looked as if the cows had feasted upon its brim), with whom our companion held the following dialogue:—

"Boy, where are you going?"

"I'm gwine down to Mr. Pierce's."

And here—taking out his pencil, holding up his sketch-book, and looking very fiercely at the darkie—our friend exclaimed, "I'll sketch you, you rascal."

Whereupon the poor boy uttered a most frightful yell, and ran away in the greatest consternation, as if we had been a pair of murderers.

Our next stopping-place was at a cider mill, where an old negro, with the assistance of a mule, was grinding apples, and another man was pressing the sweet juice into a mammoth tub. A lot of boys, who were out on a chestnut gathering excursion, had discovered the mill, and having initiated themselves into the good graces of the darkies, were evidently enjoying a portion of Mr. Horace Greeley's celebrated "good time."

But it is now about noon, and we have reached that spot upon Rock Creek known as Pierce's Plantation. Here we found the ruins of an old saw-mill, and while transferring a portrait of it to our sketch-book, with its half decayed dam, and two or three hoary sycamores and elms, we discovered a boy in the act of fishing. We bowed to him as to a brother angler, and looking into his basket, we found snugly lying there no less than half a dozen handsome fall* fish, weighing from six ounces to a pound each. These we of course purchased, and then inquired of the boy if he knew of a house in that vicinity where we could likely have the fish cooked. He replied in the affirmative, whereupon we sent him to the dwelling he mentioned for the purpose of warning the inmates of our approach. On our arrival there we were warmly welcomed, and in due time we had the satisfaction of enjoying as finely cooked fish as ever tickled the palate of Izaak Walton or Sir Humphrey Davy. Not only were we waited upon with marked politeness, but were treated with an abundance of delicious currant wine and new cider, and for all this truly southern hospitality we could make no return, excepting in the way of gratitude.

But, pleasant as was our reception and repast at this Rock Creek cottage, our own mind was more deeply impressed with the exquisitely charming appearance of the cottage itself and surrounding buildings. It struck us as one of the most comfortable and poetical nooks that we ever beheld. It seemed to have everything about it calculated to win the heart of a lover of nature and rural life. Though situated on the side of a hill and embowered in trees, it commands a pleasing landscape; and as it was built upwards of one hundred years ago, it is interesting for its antiquity. Surmounted as it is with a pointed roof, green with the moss of years, and flanked by a vine-covered porch, the vegetation which clusters around it is so abundant that you can hardly discover its real proportions. And all the out-buildings are in strict keeping with the cottage itself. It is, upon the whole, one of the most interesting nooks to be found anywhere within an hour's ride of the capitol; and we can fully understand what a certain wealthy gentleman *felt* when he made the remark that this Rock Creek cottage was the only place he had ever seen which he would prefer to his own, albeit

* The Fall Fish of Rock Creek is evidently identical with the Dace of Walton; it is really a beautiful and sweet fish, and well deserves its local reputation.

his own residence is one of the most costly and beautiful in the District of Columbia.

The scenery of Rock Creek for several miles above the Pierce Plantation is chiefly distinguished for its simple and quiet beauty. The whole vale in fact is remarkably luxuriant, and probably contains as great a variety of foliage as can be found in the same space in any section of the country. For miles and miles do the trees come together as if for the purpose of protecting the murmuring stream from the kisses of the sunlight, and even in September birds and flowers are quite abundant; for here it is (it would seem) that summer lingers longest in the lap of autumn. And such vines, too, as cluster along the margin of this stream! The graceful net-work which they have formed over the tiny waterfalls and the deep dark pools, with all their tendrils, are graceful beyond compare; and while happy children go there at times to gather the luscious grapes, we are certain that the little people of fairyland are well content with their allotted privilege of using the swing of the vine, while in the enjoyment of their midnight revels.

But we find that we are getting to be decidedly too poetical for our own safety and the comfort of our readers, and as the sun has long since passed the meridian, it is time that we should think of returning home. And, besides, as we shall return to the city by a different route from the one we came, we purpose to introduce to our readers one or two more "places of note" which are identified with Rock Creek.

And first as to the Rock Creek church, which lies somewhere between one and two miles eastward of the stream from which it derives its name. The original Rock Creek chapel was founded in the year 1719, and the bricks employed in its construction were brought from England. It became a parish church in 1726, at which time the glebe land (as at the present time, I believe) amounted to one hundred acres. It was rebuilt in the year 1768, and many improvements added in the year 1808. The first rector of the church was the Rev. George Murdock, who officiated for thirty-four years; his successors were Rev. Alexander Williamson, Rev. Thomas Read, Rev. Alfred Henry Dashields, Rev. Thomas G. Allen, Rev. Henry C. Knight, Rev. Levin I. Gills, Rev. Edward Waylen, and the present incumbent, Rev. William A. Harris. Of Mr. Read it is recorded that he presided over the church for forty years, during the whole of which time he was absent only *thirty* months; and with regard to Mr. Waylen, it may be stated that he compiled an interesting history of the Parish, which was published in 1845.

The appearance of Rock Creek church as it now stands is simply that of an old-fashioned but very comfortable brick church. It occupies the summit of a gentle hill, and is completely surrounded with a brotherhood of fine oak and chestnut-trees. On every side of it tombs and grave-stones are quite abundant, and some of them are so very old as to be almost entirely hidden in the earth. Although we spent nearly an hour in this city of the dead deciphering the various epitaphs, we only stumbled upon one which attracted our particular attention; it was a simple stone slab, covered with moss, upon which was this touching record:—

"*Grant, Lord, when I from death do wake,*
I may of endless life partake.
J. R.
1802."

And now, by way of variety, suppose our readers tarry with us for a few moments at the residence of a certain retired banker, which lies only a short distance from the Rock Creek church. With the elegant mansion and highly cultivated grounds, everybody must of necessity be pleased, for we believe that a more tasteful and superb place is not to be found in the country. It caps the summit of the loftiest hill in the vicinity of Washington, and while in one direction it commands a view of the Allegheny Mountains, in another lies spread out a complete panoramic view of the metropolis of the land, with a magnificent reach of the Potomac extending a distance of at least forty miles. To comment upon the spirits who preside over the mansion to which we have alluded is not our purpose, but we may mention in passing that among the numerous productions of art which adorn the interior are two capital pictures by Morland, and a very fine landscape by Gainsborough. But enough. The sun is already near the horizon, and even now the latter half of our walk home must be by the light of the moon. And so much for a vagabondizing day on Rock Creek.

LILLY LARNARD.

All that life can rate
Worth name of life, in her hath estimate;
Youth, beauty, wisdom, courage, virtue, all
That happiness and prime can happy call.

SHAKSPEARE.

LILLY LARNARD is an only child, the pride of her mother, and the delight of her father, who is the clergyman of a secluded and beautiful New England village. We desire to make our reader acquainted with this dear girl, but what can we find to say which hath not been anticipated by the poet? Her character is already revealed. Well, then, since we happen to be an intimate acquaintance and are in the mood, we will say something about her by way of illustration.

As we passed by her cottage this afternoon, which stands on the southern extremity of the green, about a hundred paces from the meeting-house, we noticed an almost startling stillness about the premises, as if the place were deserted; but this was owing to the heat and natural silence of the hour. The closed window-blinds, half hidden by woodbine and honeysuckle; the open doors, with a kitten sunning itself upon the sill of one of them, bespoke it not only inhabited, but the abode of peace and contentment. In a green grape-vine arbor beside the house sat our little heroine, engaged in drawing some curious flowers, which she had gathered in the meadow during her morning walk. At this moment two of her female cousins stopped at the front gate, and called her to go with them on a ramble through the woodlands. We had just time to change from one hand to the other our heavy string of trout, for we were returning home from angling, when out she came, bounding like a fawn, robed in white muslin, her gipsy bonnet awry, and a crimson scarf thrown carelessly over her shoulders. This simple dress is a specimen of her taste in such matters, and the very thing to correspond with her dark-brown curling hair, regular pearly teeth, blue, Madonna-like eyes, and blooming cheeks. A snow-white terrier, her constant playmate and companion, soon came following after, and having licked the hands of the two friends, as a token of recognition, leaped a neighboring fence, and led the way across a clover-field. When we turned to look again, the happy group were crossing a rude bridge at the foot of a hill; and following the path a short distance, they were lost to view.

Lilly Larnard is now in her sixteenth year. She is passionately fond of the country; and we do believe, could she obtain permission, would spend half her time in the open air. If she has but one summer hour to spare, she goes no farther than her favorite brook, half a mile from home, where she will angle away her time, wandering up the stream to where the overhanging trees throw a soft twilight upon her path; and, if *necessity* requires it, will off with her slippers, and wade in after a bunch of lilies or some golden pebbles. The neighboring farmer, as he comes to the post-office early in the morning, if he chances to pass the parsonage, will most likely be saluted by a sweet smile and bow. And from whom, do you think? From Lilly Larnard, to be sure, who is airing the parlor, dusting the furniture, or arranging some creeping flowers beside the door with her pretty face almost hidden in a "kerchief white." And it may be, when mowing in one of his fields in the afternoon, he will be surprised by a hearty laugh in an adjoining copse, and on looking around behold a party of girls returning from the strawberry hills, with Lilly as their leader. She is a pure-hearted lover of nature, and everything, from the nameless flower to the cloud-capt mountain, hath a language which causes her to feel that the attributes of God are infinite. For her gayer hours, Nature "hath a tale of gladness, and a smile and eloquence of beauty, and glides into her darker musings, with a mild and gentle sympathy, which steals away their sharpness ere she is aware."

But how does she busy herself at home? it will be asked. She is an early riser; and the first thing she does in the morning, after she has left her room, is to put everything in its place which is out of place. She kindly directs and helps Betty, the servant, to perform those numerous little household duties, such as feeding the chickens and straining the milk, not forgetting to give pussy a saucer full of the warm, sweet liquid. She sets the breakfast table, prepares the toast, and all those kindred delicacies, and pours out the coffee, sitting like a fairy queen in the old high-backed chair, with her parents on either side. And when her father clasps his hands to implore a blessing, she meekly bows her head, sweetly responding to the solemn Amen. If anything is wanted from the kitchen, she is up and away, and back again almost in a minute, so sprightly is she in all her movements. During the forenoon, she is generally helping her mother to sew or knit, or do anything else which is required to be done; or, if her father wants her to read one of his chaste and deeply religious sermons, the sweetness of her eloquent voice makes it doubly impressive. In the afternoon, she is generally engaged in some benevolent duty. Not one in a hundred is so well acquainted with the poor of the parish.

She enters the abode of the poor widow, and, besides administering to her temporal wants, gives her the overflowing sympathy of her own warm heart, administering at the same time the consolations of religion. It is a common sight to see her tripping along the street, with a basket on her arm; and the clerk, or more stately merchant, as he sees her pass his door, takes particular pains to make a bow, inwardly exclaiming—"Who now is to become the debtor of Lilly Larnard?" And the stranger who may have met her in his walk, fails not to inquire of his host, at evening, the name of the lovely creature who wears a white dress and gipsy bonnet.

Lilly is a Christian, not only a church-going Christian, but her life is one continued round of charitable deeds and pious duties, almost worthy of an angel. She has a class of little boys in the Sabbath school, and they are all so fond of their amiable teacher that I do believe they would undergo almost any trial for her sake. She *loves* her Bible too, and would be unhappy were she deprived of the privilege of reading it every day. When she rises from her pillow at dawn, she kneels beside her couch, and breathes her offering of prayer; and so, too, when the day is closed and she retires to repose.

Her father is a clergyman of easy fortune. The prayer of his youth seems to have been kindly answered by the Most High. About one year ago he bought a beautiful chestnut pony, and, all saddled and bridled, presented it to Lilly on her fifteenth birthday. As might be expected, she was perfectly transported with the gift. "Oh! father," she exclaimed, "how I will try to merit your approbation in every action of my life."

A colored boy, named Tommy, is Lilly's groom and page, and he seems to love the pony and his mistress above everything else in the world. A smarter and better-hearted page did not follow a high-born lady of the feudal times. Lilly has now become a first-rate rider; and often, when with her friends, takes pleasure in boasting of her noble accomplishment, and the speed of her horse. When she has been out riding, she almost always manages to canter through the middle street of the village on her return. Sometimes she is alone with her dog, and sometimes with a female friend; but the forelock of her pony is always surmounted by a few flowers, or a cluster of green leaves, for she has a queer notion of ransacking the most secluded corners of the field and wood. Only a week ago (the very day we caught that two-pound trout), while standing upon a hill, we saw her trying to leap a narrow but deep brook, and she did not give up trying until she had accomplished the deed. We thought that if her pony had been gifted with the power of speech, he would have exclaimed, "Well done, you courageous girl, you possess a wonderful deal of spunk!"

Lilly left school about two years ago, because her father chose to superintend her education himself. She is a good scholar in everything requisite for a lady. You could hardly puzzle her with questions in history, geography, or mathematics. Her modesty and simplicity of character are so great that you would be surprised at the extent of her book-information and practical knowledge. She has a wonderful talent for making herself agreeable under all circumstances. If she meets a beggar woman in the street, she will talk familiarly with her about her sorrows, instructing her to bear up under every trial. She is the universal favorite of the whole village. All who know her, the poor and the rich, from the child of three years to the hoary head, all love her with the affection felt toward a sister or daughter. She smiles with those who smile, and weeps with those who weep. Servant-girls consult with her about purchasing a new dress, and little children invite her to participate with them in their pastimes.

Lilly Larnard is a lover of poetry. Yes, whether she sees it in the primrose and the evening cloud; or hears it in the laughing rivulet and the song of birds; or reads it in the pages of Spenser, Milton, Shakspeare, Wordsworth, or Coleridge. And she is a *writer*, too, of sweet and soothing poetry, just such as should always emanate from the pure-hearted. To give the reader an idea of her poetic powers, we will here quote her last effort, which was written with a pencil on a fly-leaf of Dana's Poems while walking on the sea-shore; for, be it known that the village of her birth is within sound of the never-ceasing roar of the Atlantic. The title of it is—

A SEA-SHORE ECHO.

"Alone! and on the smooth, hard, sandy shore of the boundless sea! A lovelier morning never dawned upon the world of waters. O! how balmy, how clear, how soul-subduing, how invigorating is the air! Calmness sits throned upon the unmoving clouds, whose colors are like the sky, only of a brighter hue. One of them, more ambitious than its fellows, is swimming onward, a wanderer, and companionless. O that I could rest upon its 'unrolling skirts,' and take an aerial pilgrimage around the globe—now looking down upon its humming cities, and fruitful and cultivated plains; and again, upon some unpeopled wilderness or ocean solitude! But alas! the peerless beauty of that light cloud will be extinguished, when the sun shall have withdrawn his influence, and, if not entirely dispersed, will take another shape, and make its home in darkness. And so have I seen a man, when wandering from the heavenly sunshine of religion, passing from his cradle to the grave.

"As I gaze upward into yon blue dome, the anxieties of life are all forgotten, and my heart throbs with a quicker pulse, and beats with an increasing thrill of joy. How holy and serene those azure depths of air! Strange, that aught so beautiful should canopy a world of tears, decay, and death! Yonder sky is the everlasting home of countless worlds; the vast ethereal chamber, where are displayed the wonders of the thunder, and lightning, and rainbow; and a mirror, too, reflecting the glorious majesty, the wisdom and power of the Omnipotent. Lo! across my vision there is floating another cloud, whiter than the driven snow! Rearward, there trails along another, and still another, until pile on pile they reach upward to the very zenith; and oh, how gorgeous the scenes which my fancy conjures up, delighted with their changing loveliness! One moment, I behold a group of angels reclining at ease upon the summit of a pearly battlement; and now, summoned by a celestial strain of melody, they spread their pinions for a higher flight—a flight into the diamond portals of the New Jerusalem. Again, a river of pure white foam rolls swift but noiseless through unpeopled valleys, hemmed in by airy mountains of wondrous height, until its waters empty into a tranquil sea, boundless and 'beautiful exceedingly;' and on this, a myriad of swanlike barges are gliding to and fro, without a breeze, while the voyagers are striking their golden harps, and singing hymns of sweetest strain and holiest import, whose echoes die away on the shadowy waves. There! all these, like the dreams of youth, are melting into nothingness; and my eyes now rest only upon the dark blue ocean.

"The green waves of the Atlantic, with their undulating swell, come rolling in upon the sand, making a plaintive music, sweeter than the blended harmonies of a thousand instruments. Would that I might leap in and wrestle with them, and, when overcome by fatigue, lay my heated brow upon those cool watery pillows, rocked to sleep as in a cradle, while my lullaby would be the moaning of the sea. The mists of morning are all dispelled, and the glorious sunshine, emblem of God's love, is bathing with effulgent light the ocean before me, and behind me the mountains and valleys of my own loved country. Look! how the white caps chase each other along the watery plain, like the milk-white steeds, striving in their freedom to outstrip the breeze. Whence comes this breeze, and whither is it going? Three days ago, at set of sun, it spread its wing near to a sandy desert of Africa, where a caravan of camels, and horses, and men, had halted for the night; and at the dawning of to-morrow, it will be sporting with the forest-trees of the western wilderness!

"Far as the eye can reach, the sea is 'sprinkled o'er with ships,' their white sails gleaming in the sunlight. One of them has just returned from India, another from the Pacific, and another from the Arctic Sea. Years have elapsed since they departed hence. They have been exposed to a thousand dangers; but the great God, who holds the ocean in the hollow of his hand, has conducted them back to their desired homes. How many silent prayers of thanksgiving, and what a thrilling and joyous shout, will echo to the shore, as those storm-beaten mariners drop anchor in their native waters! Yonder, too, are other ships, bound to the remotest corners of the earth. They seem to rejoice in their beauty and speed, and proud is their bearing; but will they ever return? Alas! the shadowy future alone can answer. Farewell, a long farewell, ye snowy daughters of the ocean."

But to return. Lilly Larnard is fond of music, too, and plays delightfully on the harp. Her voice is sweeter than the fall of waters when heard at a distance in the stillness of the twilight hour. She knows nothing of fashion; and if she did, would consider it beneath her dignity to be incommoded or swayed by it. Instead of decking herself with gew-gaws for a brilliant appearance in the gay saloon, within sound of the rude jest and foolish flattery, she strives by watchfulness and care to purify her daily conduct; for hers is not less prone to sin than all other human hearts. "Necklaces does she sometimes wear, in her playful glee, made of the purple fruit that feeds the small birds in the moors, and beautiful is the gentle stain then visible over the blue veins of her swan-like bosom." Beautiful as she is, a feeling of vanity never yet entered the heart of the rector's daughter. She feels too deeply the truth, that personal charms, which are the only pride of weak-minded persons, time will eventually transform into wrinkled homeliness; and that an affectionate heart and good understanding will endure, and become more perfect, until the pilgrimage of life is ended.

Never has Lilly Larnard been more than thirty miles away from the village of her birth. She has read of cities, and the busy multitudes that throng them; of armies and navies; of politics and war; but all these things to her are but as the visions of a dream. She is ignorant of the real condition and character of the great world, for naught but the echo of its din has ever fallen upon her ear. She listens with wonder to the deeds of which we sometimes tell her we have been an unwilling witness in the wilderness of men. She thinks it strange, that the inhabitants of cities think so much of the present life, and so little of the future. Her days have been spent in innocence beneath the blue dome of the illimitable sky, inhaling the pure unadulterated air of the country, now sporting in the sunshine, and now sprinkled by a refreshing shower; while the loveliest of flowers and birds, and holy and tender affections, have been her hourly companions; and her nights have passed away in pleasant dreams of that bright world beyond the stars.

BASSE FISHING.

"We delight, as all the world has long well known, in every kind of fishing, from the whale to the minnow."

CHRISTOPHER NORTH.

THE beautiful fish now chosen for our "subject theme" is a genuine *native American*, and ranks high among the game fish of the country. When fully grown, he is commonly about fifteen inches long, two inches in thickness, and some five inches broad, weighing perhaps five or six pounds. He belongs to the perch family, has a thick oval head, a swallow tail, sharp teeth, and small scales. In color, he is deep black along the back and sides, growing lighter and somewhat yellowish towards the belly. He has a large mouth and is a bold biter, feeds upon minnows and insects, is strong and active, and when in season possesses a fine flavor. He spawns in the spring, recovers in July, and is in his prime in September.

The black basse is peculiarly a Western fish, and is not known in any of the rivers which connect immediately with the Atlantic Ocean. They are found in great abundance in the upper Mississippi and its tributaries, in all the great lakes excepting Superior, in the upper St. Lawrence, in Lake Champlain and Lake George, and nearly all the smaller lakes of New York. In portions of the last-named State they are called the Oswego basse, in the southwest the black perch, and in the northwest, where they are most abundant, the black basse. In nearly all the waters where they abound has it been our good fortune to angle for the fish, and his very name is associated with much of the most beautiful scenery in the land. Our own experience, however, in basse fishing is chiefly identified with Lake George, Lake Erie, Lake Michigan, and the upper Mississippi, and to these waters alone is it our purpose to devote a few paragraphs.

And, first, as to the beautiful "Horicon" of the North. Embosomed as it is among the wildest of mountains, and rivaling, as do its waters, the blue of heaven, it is indeed all that could be desired, and in every particular worthy of its fame. Although this lake is distinguished for the number and variety of its trout, I am inclined to believe that the black basse found here afford the angler the greatest amount of sport. They are taken during the entire summer, and by almost as great a variety of methods as there are anglers; trolling with a minnow, however, and fishing with a gaudy fly from the numerous islands in the lake, are unquestionably the two most successful methods. As before intimated, the basse is a very active fish, and, excepting the salmon, we know of none that perform, when hooked, such desperate leaps out of the water. They commonly frequent the immediate vicinity of the shores, especially those that are rocky, and are seldom taken where the water is more than twenty feet deep. They commonly lie close to the bottom, rise to the minnow or fly quite as quickly as the trout, and are not as easily frightened by the human form.

The late William Caldwell, who owned an extensive estate at the southern extremity of Lake George, was the gentleman who first introduced us to the basse of said lake, and we shall ever remember him as one of the most accomplished and gentlemanly anglers we have ever known. He was partial to the trolling method of fishing, however, and the manner in which he performed a piscatorial expedition was somewhat unique and romantic. His right hand man on all occasions was a worthy mountaineer, who lived in the vicinity of his mansion, and whose principal business was to take care of the angler's boat, and row him over the lake. For many years did this agreeable connection exist between Mr. Caldwell and his boatman, and, when their fishing days were over, was happily terminated by the deeding of a handsome farm to the latter by his munificent employer. But we intended to describe one of Mr. Caldwell's excursions.

It is a July morning, and our venerable angler, with his boatman, has embarked in his feathery skiff. The lake is thirty-three miles long, and it is his intention to perform its entire circuit, thereby voyaging at least seventy miles. He purposes to be absent about a week, and, having no less than half a dozen places on the lake shore where he can find a night's lodging, he is in no danger of being compelled to camp out. His little vessel is abundantly supplied with fishing tackle, as well as the substantials of life, and some of its liquid luxuries. He and *Care* have parted company, and his heart is now wholly open to the influences of nature, and therefore buoyant as the boat which bears him over the translucent waters. The first day his luck is bad, and he tarries at a certain point for the purpose of witnessing the concluding scene of a deer hunt, and hearing the successful hunter expatiate upon his exploits and the quality of his hounds. On the second day the wind is from the south, and he secures no less than twenty of the finest basse in the lake. On the third day he also has good luck, but is greatly annoyed by thunder showers, and must content himself with one of the late magazines which he has brought along for such emergencies. The fifth and sixth days he has some good fishing, and spends them at Garfield's Landing (for the reader must know that there is a tiny steamboat on Lake George), where he has an opportunity of meeting a brotherhood of anglers, who are baiting for the salmon trout; and the seventh day he probably spends quietly at Lyman's Tavern, in the companionship of an intelligent landscape painter (spending the summer there), arriving at home on the following morning.

As to our own experience in regard to basse fishing in Lake George, we remember one incident in particular which illustrates an interesting truth in natural history. We were on a trouting expedition, and happened to reach the lake early in June, before the basse were in season, and we were stopping with our friend Mr. Lyman, of Lyman's Point. The idea having occurred to us of spearing a few fish by torchlight, we secured the services of an experienced fisherman, and with a boat well supplied with *fat pine*, we launched ourselves on the quiet waters of the lake about an hour after sundown. Basse were very abundant, and we succeeded in killing some half dozen of a large size. We found them exceedingly tame, and noticed, when we approached, that they were invariably alone, occupying the centre of a circular and sandy place among the rocks and stones. We inquired the cause of this, and were told that the basse were casting their spawn, and that the circular places were the beds where the young were protected. On hearing this our conscience was somewhat troubled for what we had been doing, but we resolved to take one more fish and then go home. We now came to a large bed, around the edge of which we discovered a number of very small fish, and over the centre of the bed a very large and handsome basse was hovering. We darted our spear, and only wounded the poor fish. Our companion then told us that if we would go away for fifteen minutes, and then return to the same spot, we should have another chance at the same fish. We did so, and the prediction was realized. We threw the spear again, and again missed our game, though we succeeded in nearly cutting the fish in two pieces. "You will have the creature yet; let us go away again," said my companion. We did so, and lo! to our utter astonishment, we again saw the fish, all mutilated and torn, still hovering over its tender offspring! To relieve it of its pain we darted the spear once more, and the basse lay in our boat quite dead; and we returned to our lodgings on that night a decidedly unhappy man. We felt, with the *ancient mariner*, that we "*had done a hellish deed*," and most bitterly did we repent our folly. Ever since that time have we felt a desire to atone for our wickedness, and we trust that the shade of Izaak Walton will receive our humble confession as an atonement. The basse that we took on the night in question, owing to their being out of season, were not fit to eat, and we had not even the plea of palatable food to offer. The maternal affection of that black basse for its helpless offspring, which it protected even unto death, has ever seemed to us in strict keeping with the loveliness and holiness of universal nature.

And now with regard to Lake Erie. We know not of a single prominent river emptying into this lake in which the black basse is not found in considerable numbers. The sport which they yield to the disciples of Walton at the eastern extremity of the lake has been described by George W. Clinton, Esq., of Buffalo, in a series of piscatorial letters published in the journals of that city; and, as we would not interfere with him while throwing the fly in his company on the same stream, neither will we trespass upon that literary ground which he has so handsomely made his own. When, however, we hear the green waves of Lake Erie washing its western shores, we feel that we have a right to be heard, for in that region, when it was for the most a lonely wilderness, did we first behold the light of this beautiful world. With the windings of the Sandusky, the Maumee, the Huron, and the Detroit rivers we are quite familiar, and we know that they all yield an abundance of black basse; but with the river Raisin we are as well acquainted as a child could be with its mother's bosom. Upon this stream was the home of our boyhood, and at the bare mention of its name unnumbered recollections flit across the mind, which to our hearts are inexpressibly dear.

Even when a mere boy we esteemed the black basse as a peer among his fellows, and never can we forget our first prize. We had seated ourself at the foot of an old sycamore, directly on the margin of the river Raisin, and among its serpent-like roots we were fishing for a number of tiny rock basse that we had chanced to discover there. We baited with a worm, and while doing our utmost to capture a two-ounce fish, we were suddenly frightened by the appearance of a black basse, which took our hook and was soon dangling in the top of a neighboring bush. Our delight at this unexpected exploit was unbounded, and, after bothering our friends with an account of it until the night was far spent, we retired to bed, and in our dreams caught the same poor fish over and over again until morning. From that day to this, rivers and fish have haunted us like a passion.

Like the trout, the black basse seems to be partial to the more romantic and poetical places in the rivers which they frequent. On the river Raisin, for example, we used to enjoy the rarest of sport at an old and partly dilapidated mill-dam, which was covered with moss, and at the foot of which were some of the nicest "deep holes" imaginable. Wherever the timbers of the dam formed a "loop-hole of retreat," there we were always sure of finding a basse. And we also remember an old mill, in whose shadowy recesses, far down among the foundation timbers, the basse delighted to congregate, and where we were wont to spend many of our Saturday afternoons; but our favorite expeditions were those which occupied entire days, and led us along the banks of the Raisin, in the vicinity of its mouth, and far beyond the hearing of the mill-wheel or the clink of the blacksmith's anvil. At such times the discovery of old sunken logs was all that we cared for, for we knew that the basse delighted to spend the noontide hours in their shadow. And when we could borrow a canoe, and obtain a foothold on the extreme point of a wooded island, so as to angle in the deep and dark holes, we seldom failed in realizing all the enjoyment that we anticipated. And, if we chanced to come across a party of fishermen drawing the seine, we were sure to forget our promise to our parents to return home before sundown, and, far too often for a good boy, did we remain with them even until the moon had taken her station in the sky. To count the fish thus captured, and to hear the strange adventures and exploits talked over by these fishermen, was indeed a delightful species of vagabondizing; and we usually avoided a very severe scolding by returning home "with one of the largest basse ever caught in the river," which we may have taken with the hook or purchased of the fishermen. But we are talking of the "times of the days of old," and as we remember that the glories of the River Raisin, in regard to its scenery and its fish, are for ever departed, we hasten to other waters.

In fancy we have now crossed the peninsula of Michigan, or rather compassed it by means of the splendid steamers which navigate the waters of Huron and Michigan, and we are now on the banks of the river St. Joseph. This is a small river, and unquestionably one of the most beautiful in the western world. It runs through an exceedingly fertile country, abounds in luxuriant islands, is invariably as clear as crystal, and in its course winding to an uncommon degree. It is navigable for small steamboats to the village of Niles, fifty miles from its mouth, and for batteaux somewhere about fifty miles further, towards its source. Early in the spring it abounds in the more common varieties of fresh-water fish, but throughout the summer and autumn it yields the black basse in the greatest abundance.

Our piscatorial experience upon the St. Joseph has not been very extensive, but we deem it worthy of a passing notice. We were on our way to the "Far West," and had been waylaid in the beautiful village of Niles by one of the fevers of the country. The physician who attended us was a genuine angler, and we believe that our speedy recovery was owing almost entirely to the capital fish stories with which he regaled us during that uncomfortable period. Be that as it may, one thing we very clearly remember, which is this: that we enjoyed some of the most remarkable basse fishing in his company that we have ever experienced. It was in September, and we commenced fishing at three o'clock in the afternoon. We baited with live minnows, fished with hand lines, and from a boat which was firmly anchored at a bend of the river, and just above a long and very deep hole, two miles above the village of Niles. Our lines were upwards of a hundred feet long, and, as the current was very rapid, the pulling in of our minnows was performed with very little trouble. The sun was shining brightly, and the only sounds which floated in the air were the singing of birds, the rustling of the forest leaves, and the gentle murmuring of the waters as they glided swiftly along the luxuriant banks of the stream. We fished a little more than two hours, but in that time we caught no less than ninety-two basse, a dozen of which weighed over five pounds, and the great majority not less than two pounds. Such remarkable luck had never been heard of before in that vicinity, and of course for several days thereafter the river was covered with boats; but, strange to say, nearly all the anglers returned home disappointed. On a subsequent occasion, the doctor and his patient made another trial at their favorite spot, but succeeded in taking only a single fish, from which circumstance we came to the conclusion that we had actually cleared that portion of the river of its fishy inhabitants.

Before quitting the St. Joseph, we ought to state that its beautiful tributaries, the Pipe Stone and the Paw-Paw, afford a superior quality of basse, and that no pleasanter fishing-ground can anywhere be found than at the mouth of the parent river itself. With regard to the other principal rivers of western Michigan, we can only say that the Kalamazoo and the Grand River are not one whit behind the St. Joseph in any of those charms which win the affections of the angler and the lover of nature.

We come now to speak of the Upper Mississippi, in whose translucent waters, as before stated, the black basse is found in "numbers numberless." Not only do they abound in the river itself and its noble tributaries, but also in the lakes of the entire region. The only people who angle for them, however, are the travelers who occasionally penetrate into this beautiful wilderness of the Northwest. Generally speaking, the basse, as well as all other kinds of fish, are taken by the Indians with a wooden spear, and more to satisfy hunger than to enjoy the sport. The angler who would cast a fly above Fort Snelling must expect to spend his nights in an Indian lodge instead of a white-washed cottage, to repose upon a bear-skin instead of a bed (such as Walton loved) which "smells of lavender," and to hear the howl of the wolf instead of a "milk-maid's song."

As our piscatorial recollections of the section of country just named are not particularly interesting, and as it is attracting much attention at the present time (1849), under the new name of *Minesota*, or *Turbid Water*, we shall conclude our essay with the following general description.

According to the final provisions of the act of Congress which has lately transferred this extensive wilderness into a Territory of the United States, it is bounded on the north by the British possessions, on the east by Lake Superior and the State of Wisconsin, on the south by the State of Iowa, and on the west by the Missouri river and the extensive possessions of the Indians. The surface of the country is generally level, and it has been estimated that at least two-thirds of its area consists of prairie land, the remainder being forest. Much of the soil is fertile, and easy of cultivation. It is watered by no less than six of the most suberb rivers on the face of the earth—the Mississippi and Missouri, River Au Jacques, the St. Peters, or Minesota River, the Red River, emptying into Hudson's Bay, and the St. Louis, emptying into Lake Superior. Were it not for the Falls of St. Mary (a canal having been built around those of Niagara), a vessel sailing from the city of New York, by the St. Lawrence and the great lakes, might deposit her merchandise almost within its very heart; while it is a well-known fact that a New Orleans steamer may, by the Mississippi and Missouri rivers, transport the products of the South to its more remote extremities. The two facts, that Minesota is laved by the waters of the largest lake in the world, and that in its very centre are located at least a thousand lesser lakes, which constitute the fountain-head of the Father of Waters, are in themselves sufficient to give it a world-wide reputation. In addition to all this, the climate of this territory is all that could be desired. The winters are indeed somewhat long and cold, but they are regular; and, as to the summers, we have never witnessed any that were to us so bracing and delightful. The dreaded ague is a stranger in this region, and the very night-airs seem to increase the strength of the voyagers and Indian traders, who, for the most part, are the only civilized inhabitants of the domain. Game is found in the greatest abundance, from the buffalo to the deer and the grouse, and there is no region in the world where can be found a greater variety of fresh-water fish.

The Indian population is by far the most extensive now existing within its limits, but the nations are only two in number, the Chippeways and the Sioux. The wrongs which these unfortunate children of the wilderness have for many years past endured from the more unprincipled traders are among the blackest crimes of the white man, and it is to be most sincerely hoped that a new order of things will now be brought about which may in some slight degree atone for those wrongs. To us, who have been a devoted lover of the red man, even from childhood, the fact that the race is literally withering from the land of their fathers is indeed depressing and sickening. With all his faults, we dearly love the poor neglected and deeply-wronged Indian, and we verily believe that our beloved country can never prosper, as it might, until we have done something to atone for the unnumbered outrages committed against the race by our more unworthy citizens. But we are wandering.

With regard to the towns or villages existing at the present time in Minesota, we can offer but little. So far as we now remember, they consist of only three: Fond du Lac, on the St. Louis, a mere trading post; St. Peters, at the mouth of the river of that name, distinguished as the site of Fort Snelling, as being within five or six miles of the Falls of St. Anthony, and at the head of steamboat navigation; and the hamlet of St. Paul, which is on the west side of the Mississippi, only about six miles below the mouth of the St. Peter's. The fact that the last-named place has been selected as the seat of government of the new Territory renders it of some interest. It is situated on a bluff which rises some fifty feet above the Mississippi, and, though flanked by a thinly-wooded, or rather prairie country, the soil is fertile, and the scenery both up and down the Mississippi is exceedingly beautiful. Unlike that portion running south of the Missouri, this portion of the great river is invariably translucent, and for many reasons is interesting to an uncommon degree. Steamboats drawing only a few inches of water navigate this portion of the river during the whole summer. When we visited St. Paul (1846) the majority of its dwellings, if not all (numbering not more than half a dozen), were built of logs, and, though very comfortable, were not particularly showy. At that time, too, the only business carried on there was that of trading with the Indians. Our most vivid recollections of the place are associated with a supper that we enjoyed in the cabin of the principal trader. We had lost ourself in traveling by land from Lake St. Croix to the village, and for many hours before our arrival we had been in a particularly hungry mood. We entered St. Paul just as the sun was setting; and it so happened that, on the very outskirts of the place, we chanced to kill a couple of young coons. A portion of one of these animals, fried in its own fat, with a dish of tea, constituted our supper, and a more truly satisfactory supper we have hardly ever enjoyed, albeit we have been quite an extensive traveler in the wilderness. If the citizens of St. Paul only welcomed their newly-appointed governor by giving him a coon supper, we feel confident that he was well pleased with the reception.

With regard to the agricultural products, we cannot speak with much confidence. Wild rice, we know, grows in great abundance, and is the staple article of food with the Indians. For corn, the climate is considered rather cold; but potatoes and the more common vegetables grow to perfection. In many parts the maple-tree predominates, and a fine sugar is produced in considerable quantities. The principal timbers are pine and a dwarfish oak. The only Alpine region of Minesota is that which lies upon Lake Superior, and the beautiful mountains which here kiss the blue of heaven are invariably covered with a miscellaneous forest; and, if half the stories we have heard are true, they must abound in the valuable minerals of copper and silver.

Those of our readers who may desire further information in regard to the Territory of Minesota would do well to consult the following authorities, viz., Gen. Pike, who traveled through the region in 1806;

Henry R. Schoolcraft's Travels, both in 1820 and 1832; Major Long, who visited Leech Lake in 1823; and M. Nicolet, whose map of the region is exceedingly valuable; an occasional item of information may also be obtained from a little work entitled "A Summer in the Wilderness," published in 1846.

A VIRGINIA BARBECUE.

THE word *barbecue* is said to be derived from a combination of two French words, signifying *from the head to the tail*, or rather, "according to the moderns," *the whole figure, or the whole hog*. By some, this species of entertainment is thought to have originated in the West India Islands. However this may be, it is quite certain that it was first introduced into this country by the early settlers of Virginia; and though well known throughout all the Southern States, it is commonly looked upon as a "pleasant invention" of the Old Dominion. The idea was evidently conceived by a rural population, and in a district where villages and the ordinary public buildings of the present time were few and far between. For purposes of business or pleasure, the people found it necessary, or advisable, to meet together in masses, at stated periods; and as these meetings were made a kind of rural festival, and as the animals served up on such occasions were commonly roasted entire, it was not unnatural that the feast should eventually have become known as a barbecue.

Of the genus barbecue, as it exists at the present time, we believe there are only two varieties known to the people of Virginia, and these may be denominated as social and political. The social barbecue is sometimes given at the expense of a single individual, but more commonly by a party of gentleman, who desire to gratify their friends and neighbors by a social entertainment. At times, the ceremony of issuing written invitations is attended to; but, generally speaking, it is understood that all the yeomanry of the immediate neighborhood, with their wives and children, will be heartily welcomed, and a spirit of perfect equality invariably prevails. The spot ordinarily selected for the meeting is an oaken grove in some pleasant vale, and the first movement is to dispatch to the selected place a crowd of faithful negroes, for the purpose of making all the necessary arrangements. If the barbecue is given at the expense of half a dozen gentlemen, you may safely calculate that at least thirty servants will be employed in bringing together the good things. Those belonging to one of the entertainers will probably make their appearance on the ground with a wagon load of fine young pigs: others will bring two or three lambs, others some fine old whisky and a supply of wine, others the necessary table-cloths, plates, knives, and forks, others an abundance of bread, and others will make their appearance in the capacity of musicians. When the necessaries are thus collected, the servants all join hands and proceed with their important duties. They first dig a pit, four feet wide, two or three deep, and as long as they require, into which they throw a quantity of wood, for the purpose of obtaining therefrom a bed of burning coals. This done, the more expert kitchen negroes proceed to roast (by laying them upon sticks across the fires) the various animals prepared for the occasion. In the mean time, all the other arrangements are progressing, such as spreading the white cloths upon the temporary board tables, and clearing a place for dancing. The guests begin to assemble about ten o'clock, and by noon there is hardly a tree within hailing distance of the centre of attraction to which a horse is not fastened. The assembly is quite large; and white dresses and scarlet shawls are as numerous as the summer flowers upon the neighboring hills. Old men are here with their wives and daughters, in whose veins floweth the best of aristocratic blood; young husbands with their wives; unmarried gentlemen with a bevy of laughing girls under their charge; and children of every age, from the wild and boisterous boy to little girls just old enough to totter after a butterfly. One, or perhaps two hours, are then spent by the multitude in playing rural games, in social converse, in telling stories, or in discussing the news of the day. Finally, the pigs and lambs have all been roasted, and the feast is ready; whereupon there followeth as busy and satisfactory a scene as can well be imagined. After it is ended, the negroes come into rightful possession of all the tables and the abundance of good things left over; and, having quietly invited a number of their friends, with their families, they proceed to enjoy their portion of the entertainment, which is generally concluded by a regular negro frolic, with banjo and fiddle, in a neighboring grove.

In due time, after the more substantial feature of the barbecue has been enjoyed, the musicians are summoned to their allotted places, and the entire party of ladies and gentlemen proceed to trip the light fantastic toe. The exercise continues for whole hours, and white-haired men and little girls are seen wending their way through the intricate mazes of the country dance and the Virginia reel. As the sun nears the horizon, the more advanced members of the party quietly take their departure, leaving a cloud of dust behind them on the road. By the time the last day-flower has closed its petal, the young men and maidens have entire possession of the barbecue ground; and having wound up the last reel by the light of the newly risen moon, they dismiss the musicians, gather together their hats and shawls, and with many a song and jest return to their several homes.

With regard to the political barbecue, we have to remark that it differs from the one already described only in the following particulars: It is generally gotten up by the leaders of one of the political parties, and speeches take the place of dancing, although ladies in considerable numbers are invariably in attendance. Previous to the appointed day for the political barbecue, a placard is nailed to all the barn doors and blacksmith shops in the district or county where it occurs, to the effect that "several distinguished speakers will be present on the occasion," and that the people of all parties are invited to be present. If the entertainers on this occasion are of the Whig party, the first speech, as a matter of course, is delivered by a Whig orator, and it is no uncommon sight to see this gentleman standing literally *on the stump.* After he has taken his seat, he is usually followed by a brother orator of the Democratic party; and so, alternately, are the principles of the prevailing parties fully discussed. Generally speaking, the greatest decorum exists, not only among the speakers but among the listeners; and if severe remarks are dropped in the heat of debate, they are not commonly considered of sufficient consequence to create a breach between personal friends. There are times, however, when even the political barbecue is concluded by a dance; but as the crowd is then particularly miscellaneous, the hilarity which usually prevails is apt to be a little too boisterous. When given in the autumn, new cider usually takes the place of more stimulating drinks (so far as the multitude are concerned, at any rate), and when this is the case, it is very seldom that any improprieties occur. But, generally speaking, a genuine Virginia barbecue, whether of a political or social character, is a rural entertainment which deserves far more praise than censure, and we know of none which affords the stranger a better opportunitiy of studying the character of the yeomanry of the Southern States.

DEATH IN THE WILDERNESS.

MIDWAY between the St. Louis River and Sandy Lake, in the Territory of Minesota, is to be found one of the largest and most forbidding of tamarack swamps. From time immemorial it has been a thing of dread, not only to the Indians, but also to the traders and voyagers, for directly across its centre runs the portage train leading from the waters of Lake Superior to those of the Upper Mississippi. For a goodly portion of the year it is blocked up with snow, and during the summer is usually so far covered with water as only occasionally to afford a little island of coarse vegetation. It is so desolate a place as to be uninhabited even by wild animals, and hence the pleasures of traveling over it are far from being manifold. In fact, the only way in which it can be overcome during the vernal months is by employing a rude causeway of logs for the more dangerous places; and as it happens to be directly on the route of a portage over which canoes and packs of furs are annually transported to a considerable extent, we cannot wonder that it should frequently be the scene of mishaps and accidents. Evidences to prove this, we distinctly remember to have seen, when once crossing the swamp, for all along the trail were the skeletons of canoes, which had been abandoned by their owners, together with broken paddles and remnants of camp furniture. But the most interesting object that we witnessed in this remote corner of the wilderness was a rude wooden cross, surmounting a solitary grave. And connected with this grave is the following story, obtained from one who assisted at the burial.

It was a summer day, and many years ago, when a stranger made his appearance at the Sault St. Marie. He reported himself as coming from Montreal and anxious to obtain a canoe passage to the head waters of the Mississippi. He was a Frenchman, of elegant address, and in easy circumstances, so far as one could judge from his stock of

traveling comforts. His name and business, however, were alike unknown, and hence a mystery attended his every word and movement. Having purchased a new canoe and a comfortable tent, he secured the services of four stalwart Chippeways and started upon his western pilgrimage. He sailed along the southern shore of Lake Superior, and as its unique features developed themselves to his view one after another, he frequently manifested the gratification he experienced in the most enthusiastic manner, thereby increasing the mystery which surrounded him. Wholly unacquainted with the language spoken by his companions, he could only converse with them by signs; but though they could not relate to him the traditions associated with the sandstone cliffs, mountains, and beautiful islands which they witnessed, they did everything in their power to make him comfortable. They entered his tent and built his watch-fire at night, supplied him with game and fish, and during the long pleasant days, when skimming over the blue waters, entertained him with their romantic but uncouth songs. In due time, they reached the superb and most picturesque St. Louis River, surmounted by means of many portages its waterfalls, entered and ascended one of its tributaries, and finally drew up their canoe at the eastern extremity of the portage leading over the tamarack swamp.

The spot where the voyagers landed was distinguished for its beauty, and as they arrived there in the afternoon, they concluded that a better place could not be found to spend the night. The tent of the stranger was therefore erected, and while the Indians busied themselves in preparing the evening meal, the former amused himself by exploring the immediate vicinity of the encampment. He wandered into a neighboring swamp for the purpose of obtaining a few roots of the *sweet flag* of which he was particularly fond, and on his return to the tent ate an unreasonable quantity of what he had collected. On that night he was taken sick, and while endeavoring to account for heart-burning and severe pains that he experienced, he pulled out of his pocket a specimen of the root he had eaten and handed it to the Indians. They were surprised at this movement, but on examining the root they found it to be a deadly poison, whereupon they managed to inform the stranger that he had made a great mistake, and would

probably lose his life. This intelligence was of course received with amazement and horror, and the unhappy man spent a most agonizing night. At daybreak he was a little better, and insisted upon immediately continuing his journey. The voyagers obeyed, and packing up their plunder, started across the portage in single file. The excitement which filled the mind of the stranger seemed to give new energy to his sinews, and he traveled for about an hour with great rapidity; but by the time he reached the centre of the tamarack swamp his strength failed him, and he was compelled to call a halt. Upon one of the green islands, already mentioned the Indians erected his tent, and, with all the blankets and robes belonging to the company, made him as comfortable as possible. The hours of the day were nearly numbered; the stranger had endured the severest agony, and he knew that he was about to die! He divested himself of his clothes, and with all his papers and other personal property, motioned that they should be placed in a heap a few paces from the door of his tent. His request was obeyed. He then handed them all the money he had, and dispatched all his attendants upon imaginary errands into the neighboring woods, and when they returned they found the heap of clothes and other property changed into heaps of ashes. They supposed the sick man had lost his reason, and therefore did not deem his conduct inexplicable. They only increased their kind attentions, for they felt that the stream of life was almost dry. Again did the stranger summon the Indians to his side, and pulling from his breast a small silver crucifix, motioned to them that they should plant upon his grave a similar memento; and hiding it again in the folds of his shirt, cast a lingering and agonizing look upon the setting sun, and in this manner breathed his last.

By the light of the moon did the Indians dig a grave on the spot where the stranger died, into which they deposited his remains, with the crucifix upon his breast. At the head of the grave, they planted a rude cross made of the knotty tamarack wood, and after a night of troubled repose, started upon their return to the Sault St. Marie, where they finally recounted the catastrophe of their pilgrimage. And such is the story that we heard of the lonely cross on the northern wilderness surmounting the remains of the nameless exile.

ROCK FISHING.

Of recreations, there is none
So fine as fishing is alone;
All other pastimes do no less
Than mind and body both possess:
My hands alone my work can do,
So I can fish and study too.

ISAAK WALTON.

THE STRIPED BASSE, OR ROCK-FISH.

WE consider the rock-fish, striped basse, one of the finest game fish to be found in American waters. From all that we can learn, it is peculiar to this country, and to particular sections, not being found farther north than Maine, nor farther south than the Carolinas, where it is known as the Rock-Fish. It varies in weight from six ounces to one hundred pounds; and though a native of the ocean, it spends a portion of every year in the fresh water rivers—yet it seems to be partial to the mouths of our larger estuaries. Our naturalists have pronounced it a member of the perch family, and doubtless with scientific propriety; but we have seen a basse that would outweigh at least four score of the largest perch found in the country. The rock is a thick-set and solid fish, having a strong bony mouth, and sharp teeth. In color, it varies from a deep green on the back to a rich silvery hue on the belly, and its scales are large and of a metallic lustre. But the distinguishing feature of this fish consists in the striped appearance of its body. Running from the head nearly to the tail, there are no less than eight regularly marked lines, which in the healthy fish are of a deep black. Its eyes are white, head rather long, and the under jaw protrudes beyond the upper one, somewhat after the manner of the pike. The strength of the basse is equal to that of the salmon, but in activity it is undoubtedly inferior. As an article of food, it is highly valued, and in all the Atlantic cities invariably commands a good price.

The spawning time of this fish we have not positively ascertained, though we believe it to be in the spring or early summer. The New York markets are supplied with them throughout the year, but it is unquestionably true that they are in their prime in the autumn. The smaller individuals frequent the eddies of our rivers, while those of a larger growth seem to have a fancy for the reefs along the coast. On the approach of winter, they do not strike for the deep water, but find a residence in the bays and still arms of the sea, where they remain until the following spring. They begin to take the hook in April, and, generally speaking, afford the angler any quantity of sport until the middle of November. For the smaller fish at the North, the shrimp and minnow are the most successful baits; and for the larger individuals nothing can be better than the skin of an eel, neatly fastened upon a squid. The river fisherman requires a regular fit out of salmon tackle, while he who would capture the monsters of the ocean only needs a couple of stout Kirby hooks, a small sinker, a very long and heavy line, a gaff hook, and a surf boat. But those who capture the basse for lucrative purposes resort to the following more effectual methods—first by using set lines, and secondly by the employment of gill-nets and the seine. The sport of taking a twenty-pound basse in a convenient river is allied to that of capturing a salmon, but as the former is not a very skittish fish, the difficulties are not so great. As before intimated, all our Atlantic rivers, from the Penobscot to the Savannah, are regularly visited by the basse; but we are inclined to believe that they are found in the greatest abundance and perfection along the shores of Connecticut, Rhode Island, Massachusetts, and Maine. At any rate, our own experience has been confined to this region; and though we remember with unfeigned pleasure our success in taking the larger varieties along the shores of Martha's Vineyard, at Montauk Point, and in the vicinity of Watch Hill, yet we are disposed to yield the palm to Block Island. This out-of-the-way spot of the green earth belongs to Rhode Island, comprises a whole county of that State, and lies about forty miles from the main shore. It is nine miles in length, and varies in width from three to four miles. It is quite hilly, with an occasional rocky shore, contains a number of salt water ponds, and is covered with a scanty growth of trees and other vegetation. The male inhabitants, numbering only a few hundred souls, are devoted exclusively to the fishing business, and they are as amiable and honest at heart, as they are rude and isolated in their manner of life. Block Island sailors frequently find their way to the remotest quarters of the globe, though few who were born upon the island ever become entirely weaned from its ocean-girt shores. The Block Island fishermen build their own smacks, and as these are about the only things they do manufacture, they have acquired remarkable skill in building swift vessels, which are also distinguished for their strength and safety.

The pleasantest time to kill basse at Block Island is in the month of October, and immediately after a severe blow, for then it is that the larger fish seek a sheltering place between the reefs and the shore. And if the angler would be certain of success, he ought to be upon the water before sunrise, or at the break of day. He must have only one companion, a stalwart Block Islander, whose duty it shall be to steady the boat, as she dashes along upon the restless bosom of the ground swell, so that, with his legs carefully braced, he can throw his squid to a great distance, instead of being thrown himself into the sea. And if an occasional shark should stray into the vicinity of his boat, he must not suffer himself to be alarmed, for a single discharge from the fisherman's pistol (which he usually carries for that purpose) will be sure to frighten the monster out of his way. Gulls without number, large and small, of a dark gray and a pure white, will be sure to fly screaming above his head, and their wild chorus will mingle well with the monotonous war of the waves as they sweep upon the shore. The fatigue attendant upon this mode of fishing is uncommonly great; and if the angler should happen to strike a forty-pounder, he will be perfectly satisfied with that single prize; but if his luck should lie among the smaller varieties, he ought to be content with about half a dozen specimens, weighing from ten to fifteen pounds, which would probably be the result of the morning's expedition. On returning to the shore, the angler will find himself in a most impatient mood for breakfast; but with a view of enhancing the anticipated enjoyment, he should first throw aside his clothes and make a number of plunges in the pure white surf, which will cause him to feel as strong and supple as a leopard.

We did think of commenting upon Block Island as a most fitting place to study the mighty ocean, for the waves which wash its shores come from the four quarters of the globe. It so happens, however, that we have just been reading a passage in an admirable little volume entitled "*The Owl Creek Letters*" (the author is a man after our own heart), which was written at Block Island, and we are sure the passage in question would "take the wind out of any sail" that our pen might produce. The passage alluded to is as follows :—

"Men speak of our 'mother the earth.' But I never could appreciate the metaphor. A hard mother is old Terra. She refuses us food, save when compelled by hard struggling with her, and then yields it reluctantly. She deceives us too often, and finally takes us, when worn and weary, only by the difficult digging of a grave.

"But the ocean is mother-like, singing songs to us continually, and telling a thousand legends to our baby ears. She casts up toys to us on every shore, bright shells and pebbles. (What else do we live for?) True, maniac as she is, she sometimes raves madly and hurls her children from her arms, but see how instantly she clasps them again close, close to her heaving bosom, and how camly and quietly they sleep there—as she sings to them—nor wake again to sorrow."

As to basse fishing in the vicinity of New York, where scientific anglers are quite abundant, it affords us pleasure to give our readers the following account, written at our request by G. C. Scott, Esq., who is quite distinguished for his love and practical knowledge of the gentle art.

"The weather and the tide are in our favor, and the moon all right, for this planet, you must know, always gives the basse an excellent appetite and great activity. Speaking of its influence upon the appetite of fish, reminds me that those in the waters near the ocean bite best in the new of the moon; whilst salt water fish which are up the creeks and near to fresh water, are killed in the greatest number during high tides, and immediately after a hard 'nor'easter,' when the wind has shifted to the north-west. You may prove these facts without going half a dozen miles from old Gotham, and I have always noticed that it is better fishing in 'the Kills' and at the hedges of Newark Bay, as well as at those in the lower part of the Bay of New York, when the tide is high; while the fishing at King's Bridge and the mouth of Spiting Devil is always best at extreme low tides.

"As we are out after basse, suppose we 'make a day of it,' and first try the bridge at Haerlem Dam. Being an angler yourself, you know of course that much depends upon bait, and we will want to use the best. As it is the month of August, we will purchase a few shedder crabs in the market; and if we find shrimp necessary, we can procure enough of them at either of the fishing-grounds. During the spring, I use shad roes for basse bait; but in summer, and until the first of October, I prefer shedder crabs; after that, I use shrimp and soft-shell clams. Some anglers prefer shrimp at all seasons, as it is well known that small basse are more generally taken with them; but for my part, give me shedder crabs enough, and I will agree to forego the use of all other kinds of bait for basse. Next, you may want to know how to rig your tackle? Where we are going to-day, you want nothing but a good basse rod, reel and float, with a single gut leader, to which you fasten a hook and attach it to the line one-third of its length from the hook. Use your float only when the tide runs slowly, for bottom fishing is the best for large fish, unless you troll for them, when you use a squid and fish in the Bronx with a regular trolling tackle, of sufficient strength to land a fish weighing one hundred and fifty pounds, for they are sometimes caught there of that weight, but generally from thirty to eighty pounds.

"Well, having arrived at King's Bridge, and as it is about ebb tide, we will first see what we can kill from the east bridge. I like bridge fishing, for it is so fine to pay out line from; and then in striking a fish thirty yards off, there is so much sport in playing him, and your being such a distance above the water, you generally fasten him at the first bite. Reel off! reel off! you have struck him! There! give him play, but feel his weight and let him contend for every inch of line that you give him, or he will take the whole of it without exhausting himself, and you will lose him. Keep him in slack water, and after playing him until you kill him, land him on the shore, for he is too heavy to risk your tackle in raising him to the bridge. And now, having fished out the last of the ebb, and the turn until the tide runs too fast to use a float, just step into this punt and we will anchor out near the edge of the current, by the first island below the mill, and fish in the current without the float, until the tide turns, when we will make for the mouth of the Spiting Devil, and fish fifty rods below it in the Hudson.

"Now, my friend, this day's sport may be considered a fair criterion for these grounds. We have taken between twenty and thirty basse, but there is only one that weighs over five pounds, and their average weight will not vary much from half that. To-night we will troll in the Bronx, for if the sky be clear, the basse will bite sooner at a squid 'by the light of the moon' than in the day time; and there is very little use in stopping to try McComb's Dam, as the sport will not be first-rate there until the Croton Aqueduct is finished and the coffer dam is torn away, so that the fish may have a clear run and unobstructed passage between the East and Hudson rivers. It is supposed that this will be effected next year, when McComb's Dam will retrieve its lost honors and furnish one of the best places for sport in this vicinity, to those who prefer bridge fishing.

"Having given you a taste of the sport on the waters bounding this island on the north and east, let us to-day fasten our punt to the lower hedges of New York bay, and try the difference between 'bottom fishing,' and that 'with the float.' I will remark, in passing, that it is better to anchor your punt about a rod above the hedge and fish towards the hedge without a float, than to fasten your boat to the hedge, as commonly practiced, and fish with a float; for you will notice that while you, in the old way, are continually reeling up and making casts, I am feeling for them with a moving bait toward the bottom, and as near the hedge as I can venture without getting fast. And then when I strike, I am sure to fasten them as they turn from me for the shelter of the hedge. I can also better play my bait without the danger of too much slack. You will see also that I kill the largest fish.

"Let us now up anchor and away for the Kills and to the reef opposite Port Richmond. Here the fish are about as large as those at the hedges we just left. The tide is nearly full, and we will fish without the float until it is about to turn, when we will move over to the Jersey shore about fifty rods below the mouth of Newark Bay. Here, as the tide is just in the turn, we can fish an hour of the ebb with floats, when it will be best to try bottom-fishing again. Well, if you are tired of killing younglings varying from one to three pounds, let us put the punt about and prepare for a beautiful row up to the third, fourth, and fifth hedges in Newark Bay—trying each one—and we may strike some fish that will try our tackle. Change your leader for a heavier one and let go the anchor, for we are three rods above the hedge. The water is quite slack, and we will try the float until the tide ebbs a little more and the current becomes more rapid. There, sir, what think you of that? He feels heavy—see him spin! take care of your line or he'll get foul, as I cannot govern him, and it will be with great difficulty that I keep him out of the hedge. What a splendid leap! I'll see if I can turn him—here he comes—take the landing net—there! there, we have him, and I will bet the champagne that he weighs nearer twenty pounds than ten!

"Thus, my friend, having shown you the principal grounds and informed you of the bait and tackle to be used in killing basse in this vicinity, I hope that you will not be at loss for piscatorial sport when trying your skill in the waters of old Gotham."

It is now time that we should say something about basse or rock fishing in the South. The only streams frequented by this fish, of which we have any personal knowledge, are the Potomac, and Roanoke, though we have heard many wonderful stories related of the James River and the Great Pedee. In speaking of the Potomac we are sorely tempted to indite an episode upon the beautiful and magnificent sweeps which this river makes after it leaves the gorge of Harper's Ferry until it loses itself in Chesapeake Bay, and also upon its historical associations, among which the genius of Washington reigns supreme—but it is our duty to forbear, for we should occupy too much time.

Unquestionably, the finest rock-ground on the Potomac is the place known as the Little Falls, about four miles above Georgetown. At this point the river is only fifty yards wide, and as the water descends not more than about ten feet in running three hundred yards, the

place might be more appropriately termed a schute than a fall. The banks on either side are quite abrupt and picturesque; the bed of the stream is of solid rock, and below the rapids are a number of inviting pools, where the water varies from forty to sixty feet in depth. The tides of the ocean reach no further up the Potomac than this spot, and though the rock-fish are caught in considerable numbers at the Great Falls (which are ten miles further up the river, and exceedingly romantic), yet they seem to be partial to the Little Falls, where they are frequently found in very great numbers. They follow the shad and the herring in the spring, but afford an abundance of sport from the 1st of May until the 4th of July, though they are caught in certain portions of the Potomac through the year, but never above the Great Falls. The rock of this portion of the Potomac vary in weight from two to eighteen or twenty pounds, and it is recorded of the anglers and business fishermen that they frequently kill no less than five hundred fish in a single day. The favorite bait in this region is the belly part of the common herring, as well as the shiner and smelt; but it is frequently the case that a common yellow flannel fly will commit sad havoc among the striped beauties. A stout rod, a large reel, and a long line are important requisites to the better enjoyment of rock-fishing at this point; but as the good standing places are few in number, many anglers resort to boat-fishing, which is here practiced with pleasure and profit. Of the many scientific anglers who visit the Little Falls during the spring and summer, the more expert ones come from Washington; and of one of these the story is related that he once killed no less than eighty handsome rock-fish in a single afternoon. He occupied a dangerous position upon two pointed rocks in the river (one foot upon each rock and elevated some five feet above the water), and fished in a pool that was some seventy feet down the stream, while the fish were landed by an expert servant stationed on the shore about thirty feet below the spot occupied by the angler. The gentleman alluded to is acknowledged to be the most successful angler in this region, and in an occasional conversation with him, we have obtained a goodly number of piscatorial anecdotes. One or two of them are as follows:—

On one occasion, while playing a good-sized rock-fish, it unfortu-

nately ran around a sharp rock, and by cutting the line made its escape, carrying off the angler's float, and a favorite fly. On the third day after this event a boy who was playing on the river about half a mile below the Falls, happened to see a cork darting hither and thither across the surface of the water, and immediately went in pursuit of the life-like piece of wood. After many twistings and turnings and a long row, he finally overtook it, and to his utter astonishment he landed in his boat a very handsome five pound Basse. He recognized the fly as the one commonly employed by our angler, to whom the fly, the float and the fish were promptly delivered by the honest boy.

Another and a similar incident was as follows:

Our angling friend had lost another float, by the obstinacy of another fish. About a week after the mishap a fisherman who had a "trot line" set across the river at Georgetown, for the purpose of taking cat-fish, discovered a great splashing in the water near the middle of his line, and on hastening to the spot he had the pleasure of pulling up a very handsome twelve pound Basse. After faring sumptuously upon the fish, the fortunate individual took it into his head that the tackle belonged to *the* angler of the Falls, whereupon he delivered it to our friend, accompanied with a statement of the manner in which he made the discovery. The distance traveled by that fish, with a hook in his mouth, was four miles, and it was by the merest accident that his leading string had become entangled with the "trot line."

The angling ground at the Little Falls is annually rented by the proprietors to a couple of men named Joe Paine and Jim Collins, who are the presiding geniuses of the place, and have been such for upwards of twenty years. They pay a rent of seventy dollars per annum, and as they receive from fifty cents to five dollars from every angler who visits them, and as they are occasionally troubled with as many as thirty individuals per day, it may readily be imagined that their income is quite respectable. Some of Collins' friends allege that he has several thousand dollars stowed away in an old pocket book, which it is his intention to bequeath to a favorite nephew, he himself being a bachelor. The reputation of Jim Collins in this section of country is very extensive, and that this should be the case is not at all strange, for he is a decided original. He is about fifty years of age, measures six feet

10

five inches in height, and the offshoots from the four prongs of his body number *twenty-four* instead of twenty as in ordinary mortals; I mean by this, that his fingers and toes number no less than twenty-four. Notwithstanding this bountiful supply of fingers and toes, Jim Collins has a great antipathy to useful labor, and is as averse to walking as any other web-footed animal. Fishing and sleeping are his two principal employments; and that he is a judge of good whisky, none of his acquaintance would have the hardihood to doubt. The taking of small fish he considers a business beneath his dignity, and the consequence is that his tackle consists of a miniature bed cord, with a hook and cedar pole to match, and his bait a whole herring. He commonly fishes in a boat, and the dexterity with which he *"Kawallups"* the fish upon his lap is truly astonishing. But if you would see Jim Collins in his glory, wait until about the middle of a June afternoon, after he has pocketed some fifteen dollars, and he is sunning himself, with pipe in mouth, upon the rocks, absorbed in *fishy contemplations*. His appearance at such times is allied to that of a mammoth crane, watching (as he does his cockney brethren of the craft) the movements of a lot of half-fledged water birds.

During the fishing season he is generally actively employed, but the remainder of his time he spends about the Little Falls, as if his presence were indispensable to the safe passage of the waters of the Potomac through this narrow gorge. That Jim Collins should have met with many queer mishaps, during a residence of twenty years on the Potomac, may be readily imagined; but we believe, the most unique adventure of which he has ever been the victim, happened on this wise. The substance of the story is as follows:—

Our hero is a great lover of "sturgeon meat," and for many years past it has been a habit with him to fish for that huge leather mouthed monster with a large cord and sharp graffling hooks, sinking them to the bottom with a heavy weight and then dragging them across the bed of the stream; his sense of touch being so exquisite, that he can always tell the instant that his hooks have struck the body of a sturgeon, and when this occurs it is almost certain that the fish becomes a victim to the cruel art. In practising this mode of fishing, Jim Collins invariably occupies a boat alone, which he first anchors in the stream.

On one occasion he had been fishing in this manner for a long time without success, and for the want of something more exciting, he had resorted more frequently than usual to his junk bottle. In process of time, however, he found the exercise of fishing decidedly a bore, but as he was determined not to give up the sport and at the same time was determined to enjoy a quiet nap, he tied the cord to his right arm, and lounged over on his back for the purpose of taking a snooze. There was an unusual calmness in the air and upon the neighboring hills, and even the few anglers who were throwing the fly at the Falls, did so in the laziest manner imaginable. While matters were in this condition, a sudden splash broke the surrounding stillness, which was immediately followed by a deafening shout, for it was discovered that a sturgeon had pulled poor Collins out of his boat into the swift stream, and was in great danger of leading him off to the residence of *David Jones.* At one moment the fisherman seemed to have the upper hand, for he pulled upon his rope, and swore loudly, sprawling about the water like a huge devil fish; but in another instant the poor fellow would suddenly disappear, and an occasional bubble rising to the surface of the stream, was all the evidence that the fellow was not quite drowned. This contest lasted for some fifteen minutes, and had not the sturgeon finally made his escape, Jim Collins would have been no more. As it happened, however, he finally reached the shore, about two hundred yards below the Falls, and as he sat upon a rock, quite as near the river Styx as he was to the Potomac, he lavished some heavy curses upon the escaped sturgeon, and insisted upon it, that the best hooks that man ever made were now forever lost. Years have elapsed since this occurrence took place, and when the ancient Fisherman "hath his will," he recounts the story of this catastrophe with as brilliant a fire in his eye as that which distinguished the countenance of Coleridge's particular friend, the "Ancient Mariner."

Before closing this essay, it is "right and proper" that we should allude to the beautiful scenery that the angler will enjoy in going to and returning from the Little Falls. The entire region, in fact, known by the name of Cooney, and comprehending some fifteen miles of the Potomac, is particularly picturesque, but is at the same time said to be the most barren and useless portion of Virginia. In visiting the Falls you have to pass over a kind of wooded and rocky interval, and by an exceedingly rough road, which is annually submerged by the spring freshets. The water here sometimes rises to the height of fifty feet, and often makes a terrible display of its power; on one occasion the water came down the valley with such impetuosity that a certain wall composed of rocks six or eight feet square, and united together with iron, was removed to a distance of many rods from its original position. To the stranger who may visit the Little Falls, we would say forget not on your return to Washington, the superb prospect which may be seen from the Signal Tree on the Heights of Georgetown. From that point the eye comprehends at one glance, the church spires and elegant residences of Georgetown, the Metropolis of the land, with its capitol and numerous public buildings, and the more remote city of Alexandria, with a reach of the magnificent Potomac, extending a distance of at least thirty miles. The better time to look upon this prospect, is at the sunset hour, when the only sounds that fill the air are the shrieking of the swallows, and the faintly heard song of a lazy sailor far away upon the river, where perhaps a score or two of vessels are lying becalmed, while on the placid stream a retinue of crimson clouds are clearly and beautifully reflected. Scenes of more perfect loveliness are seldom found in any land.

RATTLESNAKES.

We believe that we have seen a greater number of these reptiles, in our various journeyings, and been more intensely frightened by them than any other scenery-loving tourist or angler in the country, and hence the idea of our present essay. We shall record our stock of information for the benefit of the general reader, rather than for the learned and scientific, beginning our remarks with what we know of the character of that really beautiful and magnanimous, but most deadly animal, which was adopted as the Revolutionary emblem of our country, as the eagle is now the emblem of the Republic.

The rattlesnake derives its name from an instrument attached to its tail, consisting of a series of hollow scaly pieces which, when shaken, make a rattling or rustling noise. The number of these pieces or rattles are said to correspond with the number of years which the animal has attained, and some travelers assert that they have been discovered with thirty rattles, though thirteen is a much more common number. It is one of the most venomous of serpents, and yet one that we cannot but respect, since it habitually makes the most honorable use of the singular appendage with which it is gifted. It never strikes a foe without first warning him of his danger. In form it is somewhat corpulent, has a flat heart-shaped head, and is supplied with fangs, varying from a half-inch to an inch in length, which lie hidden horizontally in the flesh of the upper jaw, and are capable of being thrown out like the blade of a knife. The venom emitted by it is so deadly that it has been known to cause the death of a human being in a very few hours, and to destroy a dog or cat in less than twenty minutes, and yet we have met with some half-dozen individuals in our travels who have been bitten by the rattlesnake without being seriously injured. Horses and cattle are known to become exceedingly terrified at its appearance, and generally speaking, when bitten, die in a short time, and yet we once saw a horse, which was only troubled in consequence of its bite, by a disease resembling the scurvy. The hair dropped from the skin of the quadruped, and he looked horribly if he did not feel so. As to the effect of this poison upon hogs, it has frequently been proven to be perfectly harmless, and we know it to be the custom in certain portions of the country for farmers to employ their swine for the express purpose of destroying the rattlesnakes infesting their land. The effect of the rattlesnake's bite upon itself is said to be generally fatal. In regard to the antidote of this poison we are acquainted with only one, which is the plant commonly called the rattlesnake weed. Both the leaf and the root are employed, and applied internally as well as externally. This plant grows to the height of six or eight inches, has one stock and a leaf resembling in shape the head of the rattlesnake, and is almost invariably found in those sections of the country where the reptile abounds.

The courage of the rattlesnake is by no means remarkable, and it is but seldom that they will dispute the right of way with a man who is not afraid of them. They are sluggish in their movements, and accomplish the most of their traveling during the nocturnal hours. They feed upon almost every variety of living creatures which they can overpower. They are not partial to water, but when compelled to cross a river or lake, they perform the feat in a most beautiful manner, holding their heads about one foot from the surface, and gliding along at a rapid rate. They are affectionate creatures, and it is alleged that when their offspring are very young, and they are disturbed by the presence of man, the mothers swallow their little ones until the danger is past, and then disgorge them alive and writhing.

Another of their peculiarities consists in the fact, that they may be entirely disarmed by brandishing over their heads the leaves of the white ash, which are so obnoxious to their nervous system as to produce the most painful contortions of the body. When traveling at night in search of food, or for purposes of recreation, as it may be, they have a fashion of visiting the encampments of hunters, and it has been ascertained that the only way of keeping them at a respectable distance is to encircle the camp with a rope, over which they are afraid to crawl;—and it has frequently happened to hunters, in a snake country, that on awaking after a night of repose, they have discovered on the outside of their magic circle as many as a dozen of the charming creatures, carefully coiled up and sound asleep. It is also related of this snake that it has the power of throwing off or suppressing a disagreeable effluvium, which is quite sickening to those who come within its range. If this be true it occurs chiefly in the month of August, when the weather is sultry and the snake is particularly fat. That this snake has the power of *charming*, as some writers maintain, may be true, but we know not of an authenticated instance. That it may have a very quiet way of stealing upon its prey seems to us much more plausible—but upon this fact we are non-committal. As to their power of *hissing*—that also is an undecided question. In regard to their manner of biting we can speak with more confidence. They never attack a man without first coiling themselves in a graceful manner, and instead of jumping they merely extend their bodies, with the quickness of thought, towards their mark, and if they do not reach it, they have to coil themselves again for a second effort, and when they hit a man at all, it is generally on his heel, for the bruising of which they have the authority of the Scriptures.

The rattlesnake is peculiar to the American continent. Four varieties alone are known to naturalists, three of which are found in the United States, and one in South America. In the States bordering on the Gulf of Mexico they attain the length of seven and eight feet and a diameter of three to four inches—the males having four fangs, and the females only two. These are characterized by a kind of diamond figure on the skin, and are partial to the low or bottom lands of the country. Those found in the Middle and Northern States are called the common or banded rattlesnakes, and are altogether the most abundant in the Union. They vary in length from two and a half to four feet, and are partial to mountainous and rocky districts. There is also a very small, but most dangerous variety, called the ground rattlesnakes, which are found on the sterile and sandy prairies of the West, and to a limited extent in the barren districts of the South. In Canada they are almost unknown, and even in the more thickly settled States of the Union they are rapidly becoming extinct. As to their value, it may be stated that their oil and gall are highly prized in all sections of the Union for medicinal purposes, and by the Indians and slave population of the South, their flesh is frequently employed as an article of food, and really considered sweet and nourishing.

The attachment of the Aborigines to this famous reptile is proverbial: among nearly all the tribes, even at the present day, it is seldom disturbed, but is designated by the endearing epithet of *grandfather*. It is recorded, however, by the early historians, that when one tribe desired to challenge another to combat, they were in the habit of sending into the midst of their enemy the skin of a rattlesnake, whereby it would appear to have been employed as an emblem of revenge. And as to the origin of the rattlesnake, the old men among the Cherokees relate a legend to the following effect, which, the reader will notice, bears a striking analogy to the history of our Saviour. A very beautiful young man, with a white face and wrapped in a white robe, once made his appearance in their nation, and commanded them to abandon all their old customs and festivals, and to adopt a new religion. He made use of the softest language, and everything that he did proved him to be a good man. It so happened, however, that he could make no friends among them, and the medicine men of the nation conspired to take away his life. In many ways did they try to do this—by lashing him with serpents and by giving him poison, but were always unsuccessful. But in process of time the deed was accomplished and in the following manner. It was known that the good stranger was in the habit of daily visiting a certain spring for the purpose of quenching his thirst, and bathing his body. In view of this fact, the magicians made a very beautiful war-club, inlaid with bone and shells, and decorated with rattles, and this club they offered to the Great Spirit, with the prayer that he would teach them how to destroy the stranger. In answer to the prayer, a venomous snake was created and carefully hidden under a leaf by the side of the spring. The stranger, as usual, came there to drink, was bitten by the snake, and perished. The Cherokee nation then fell in love with the snake, and having asked the Great Spirit to distinguish it, by some peculiar mark, from all the other snakes in the world, he complied by transferring to its body the rattles which had made the club of sacrifice so musical to the ear, and so beautiful to the eye. And from that rattlesnake are descended all the poisonous snakes now scattered through the world.

We commenced this article with the determination of not writing a single paragraph (for the above legend, after a fashion, is historical) which could be classed with the unbelievable things called "Snake Stories," but the following matter-of-fact, though disconnected anecdotes, may not be unacceptable to our readers.

We were once upon a fishing expedition among the mountains of North Carolina, with two other gentlemen, when it so happened that we concluded to spend the night in a deserted log cabin, belonging to one of the party. By the light of a large fire, we partook of a cold but comfortable supper, and after talking ourselves into a drowsy mood, we huddled together on the floor, directly in front of the fireplace, and were soon in a sound sleep. About midnight, when the fire was out, one of the party was awakened by a singular rattling noise, and having roused his companions, it was ascertained beyond a doubt that there were two rattlesnakes within the room where they were lying. We arose, of course, horrified at the idea, and as we were in total darkness, we were afraid even to move for fear of being bitten. We soon managed, however, to strike a light, and when we did so, we found one of our visitors on the hearth, and one in the remotest corner of the room. We killed them, as a matter of course, with a most hearty relish, and in the morning another of the same race, just without the threshold of the cabin. The reptiles had probably left the cabin just before our arrival, and on returning at midnight, had expressed their displeasure at our intrusion upon their abode, by sounding their rattles.

On another occasion we were of a party of anglers who killed a rattlesnake on one of the mountains overlooking Lake George (where this reptile is very abundant), and after its head had been cut off and buried, one of the party affirmed that there was not a person present who could take the dead snake in his hand, hold it out at arm's length, and give it a sudden squeeze, without dropping it to the ground. A wager was offered, and by the most curious and courageous of the party was accepted. He took the snake in his hand and obeyed the instructions, when the serpentine body suddenly sprang as if endowed with life, and the headless trunk struck the person holding it, with considerable force upon the arm. To add that the snake fell to the ground most suddenly is hardly necessary. We enjoyed a laugh at the expense of our ambitious friend, but the phenomenon which he made known, remains to this day entirely unexplained. Since that time we have been led to believe that there is not one man in a thousand who would have the fortitude to succeed in the experiment above mentioned.

A WESTERN PIONEER.

It was about twenty years ago, on a bright November morning, that a large covered wagon, drawn by four horses, came to a halt in front of the office of the Receiver of Money for the Public Lands in the village of Monroe, territory of Michigan. The wagon in question contained implements of husbandry, a plentiful stock of provisions, and all the household furniture of a family consisting of an old man and his wife, three sons, and two daughters; and their outside possessions were comprised in a small but miscellaneous herd of cows, oxen, sheep, and hogs. The head of this family was a New York farmer in indigent circumstances, who had conceived the idea of making himself a home in what was then the wilderness of Michigan. All the money he had in the world was one hundred dollars, and with this he purchased at the land-office a tract of eighty acres of uncultivated land, which he had never seen, but upon which he was about to locate with his family. The honest and independent deportment of this emigrant enlisted the feelings of the Receiver, and he accordingly extended an invitation to him and his party to spend the night under his roof. The invitation was accepted, and after a "lucid interval" of comfortable repose, and cheered by a warm breakfast, the emigrating party respectfully took their leave of their entertainer, and started upon their dreary pilgrimage.

The distance they had to travel was some hundred and eighty miles. As the roads were new and rough, they plodded along, day after day, at a slow rate, and with much difficulty; took their meals in the open air, and spent their nights under a tent, with only a few heavy quilts to protect them from the dampness of the ground. While upon this journey they were overtaken by cold weather, and, in fording one of the many streams which crossed their route, the venerable emigrant had one of his legs frost-bitten, which resulted, after much delay and trouble in sending for a physician, in its amputation. His life was spared, however, and in due time, in spite of the calamity which had befallen them, the emigrants were encamped upon their "land of promise."

Having thus reached the end of their journey, the first thing to be done was to erect a suitable dwelling wherein to spend the winter; and, the father of the family having been rendered almost helpless by his misfortune, the labor of building it devolved exclusively upon his sons, the youngest of whom was a mere boy. Animated by a most noble spirit, they fell to work without any delay, and in the course of ten days had accomplished their first task, and were the masters of a comfortable log-cabin. It stood on the sandy knoll of an "oak opening," and in the immediate vicinity of a sparkling rivulet. The only evidences of civilization which surrounded them were the stumps, and chips, and decaying branches which covered the site of their labors; but the emigrants had a home, and though a rude and apparently comfortless one, they were satisfied, if not happy.

The winter days passed rapidly away; and, while the disabled emigrant did little else than keep himself warm by his huge wood-fire, his sons were felling the trees on every side, and doing their utmost to enclose their domain. And at night, when gathered at the evening meal, or in a circle around their hearth, and the newly-cut wood was hissing under the influence of the bright flame, they would talk over the pleasures of other days, experienced in a distant portion of the land, and cherish the hope that the future had even more happiness in store. Within their cabin was to be found the spirit of genuine religion, and, as the hopeful music of woman's voice was there, and their hearts were bound together by the chords of a holy family love, they were indeed happy.

It was now the spring-time of the year, a warmer tint was in the sky, and all around the wilderness was beginning to blossom like the rose. The birds were building their nests, and their sweet minstrelsy was heard throughout the air; and there, too, was the tinkling of bells, for the cattle sought their food in the remote dells, and returned at the sunset hour, with their udders teeming full. The brush and waste wood of the "girdled clearings" were gathered into heaps and burnt—in the daytime forming fantastic columns of smoke, and at night making the midnight darkness, save where the flame was particularly brilliant, more profound. And then the plough was brought forth, and made to try its strength in turning up the virgin soil. Our emigrant friend has now entirely recovered from his late disaster, and, having manufactured for himself an artificial leg, he begins to think it time for him to lend a helping hand towards accelerating the improvements of his "farm." The smell of the ploughed field has given him a thrill of pleasure, and he determines to try what he can accomplish in the way of planting corn. This effort proves successful, and, as he becomes accustomed to the use of his new member, he takes the lead in most of the farming operations, and thinks no more of his past sufferings than of the fact that he is what many people are pleased to term a poor man.

As industry and virtue are almost invariably followed by prosperity, we must not wonder at the future career of our Western pioneer. Five years have passed away, and, as his crops have been abundant, we find him the possessor of half a thousand acres of valuable land instead of one hundred. He has also gathered the means to build himself a new frame house; and, as the "harvest is past and the summer ended," his barns are filled to overflowing. On every side are spread out extensive fields, and his hired men may be counted by the dozen. They have gathered in the crops, and, after a brief furlough, a portion of them will take possession of the barns, and devote themselves to the flail, while the remainder will enter some neighboring woodland with their axes, and proceed in their laborious work of destruction. Winter comes, and still the sounds of the flail and the axe are heard in the barn and in the forest. The coldest of winds may blow, and the snow may fall so as to bury the fences, but what matter? The genius of health reigns supreme. All the day long, and at night, huge fires are blazing in the dwelling of the pioneer; his larder is filled with an abundance of the good things of life, and his numerous cattle are more comfortably housed than himself when first he came into the wilderness. Spring has returned once more, and a new life has been instilled not only into the earth, but also into the blood of man.

It is now the delightful season of midsummer, and we see before us, basking in the sunshine, a domain of two thousand acres of land, in the highest state of cultivation. Capping the summit of a hill stands a spacious and elegant mansion, surrounded with outhouses, and bespeaking the possessor to be a man of opulence and taste. In one direction, fading away to a great distance, lie a succession of fields waving with golden grain; in another, hill beyond hill of the deep green and graceful corn; in another we see a magnificent meadow, with hundreds of cattle and horses and sheep quietly grazing or sporting in their glee; and in another direction an almost impenetrable forest, where the black-walnut, the white-wood, the oak, and the hickory strive to excel each other in the respective attributes of beauty and might. And this is the home and the domain of the Western pioneer. Less than a mile distant from his mansion stands a charming village, from which arises a single spire, pointing to the Christian's home. The pastor of that church is the youngest son of our friend the pioneer. Within said village, too, may be seen an "Eagle Hotel," and a "New York Store," which are both the property of his two elder sons. At their expense a public school has been established within the village. The country around is intersected with the best of roads, along which the heavily-laden wain pursues its snail-like course, and the mail coach rattles along with its panting horses, nine passengers on the inside, and a deep coating of dust on the boot and everything outside. Plenty and peace have taken possession of the land, and the pioneer of other days has become the nabob of the present time.

PIKE FISHING.

If so be the angler catch no fish yet hath he a wholesome walk to the brook-side, and pleasant shade by the sweet silver streams.

ROBERT BURTON.

THE Pike is a common fish in all the temperate, and some of the northern regions of the world; but in no country does he arrive at greater perfection than in the United States. For some unaccountable reason he is generally known in this country as the pickerel; and we would therefore intimate to our readers that our present discourse is to be of the legitimate pike. In England, he is known under the several names of pike, jack, pickerel and luce. His body is elongated and nearly of a uniform depth from the head to the tail; the head is also elongated, and resembles that of the duck; his mouth is very large and abundantly supplied with sharp teeth, and his scales are small and particularly adhesive; the color of his back is a dark brown, sides a mottled green or yellow, and belly a silvery white. The reputation of this fish for amiability is far from being enviable, for he is called not only the shark of the fresh waters, but also the tyrant of the liquid plain. He is a cunning and savage creature, and for these reasons even the most humane of fishermen are seldom troubled with conscientious scruples when they succeed in making him a captive. Pliny and Sir Francis Bacon both considered the pike to be the longest lived of any fresh water fish, and Gesner mentions a pike which he thought to be two hundred years old. Of these ancient fellows, Walton remarks, that they have more in them of state than goodness, the middle sized individuals being considered the best eating. The prominent peculiarity of this fish is his voraciousness. Edward Jesse relates that five large pike once devoured about eight hundred gudgeons in the course of three weeks. He swallows every animal he can subdue, and is so much of a cannibal that he will devour his own kind full as soon as a common minnow. Young ducks and even kittens have been found in his stomach, and it is said that he often contends with the otter for his prey. Gesner relates the story that a pike once attacked a mule while it was drinking on the margin of a pond, and his teeth having become fastened in the snout of the astonished beast, he was safely landed on the shore. James Wilson once killed a pike weighing seven pounds, in whose stomach was found another pike weighing over a pound, and in the mouth of the youthful fish was yet discovered a respectable perch. Even men, while wading in a pond, have been attacked by this fresh water wolf. He is so much of an exterminator, that when placed in a small lake with other fish, it is not long before he becomes "master of all he surveys," having depopulated his watery world of every species but his own. The following story, illustrating the savage propensity of this fish, is related by J. V. C. Smith. A gentleman was angling for pike, and having captured one, subsequently met a shepherd and his dog, and presented the former with his prize. While engaged in clearing his tackle, the dog seated himself unsuspectingly in the immediate vicinity of the pike, and as fate would have it, his tail was ferociously snapped at by the gasping fish. The dog was of course much terrified, ran in every direction to free himself, and at last plunged into the stream. The hair had become so entangled in the fish's teeth, however, that it could not release its hold. The dog again sought the land, and made for his master's cottage, where he was finally freed from his unwilling persecutor; but notwithstanding the unnatural adventure of the fish, he actually sunk his teeth into the stick which was used to force open his jaws.

The pike of this country does not differ essentially from the pike of Europe. His food usually consists of fish and frogs, though he is far from being particular in this matter. He loves a still, shady water, in river or pond, and usually lies in the vicinity of flags, bulrushes and water-lilies, though he often shoots out into the clear stream, and on such occasions frequently affords the rifleman a deal of sport. In summer he is taken at the top and in the middle, but in winter at the bottom. His time for spawning is March, and he is in season about eight months in the year. In speaking of the size of this fish, the anglers of Europe have recorded some marvelous stories, of which we know nothing, and care less. In this country they vary from two to four feet in length, and in weight from two to forty pounds; when weighing less than two pounds, he is called a jack. As an article of food he seems to be in good repute; but since we once found a large water-snake in the stomach of a monster fish, we have never touched him when upon the table. He suits not our palate, but as an object of sport we esteem him highly, and can never mention his name without a thrill of pleasure.

In this place we desire to record our opinion against the idea that the pike and maskalunge are one and the same fish. For many years we entertained the opinion that there was no difference between them, only that the latter was merely an overgrown pike. We have more recently had many opportunities of comparing the two species together, and we know that to the careful and scientific observer, there is a marked difference. The head of a maskalunge is the smallest; he is the stoutest fish, is more silvery in color, grows to a much larger size, and is with difficulty tempted to heed the lures of the angler. They are so precisely similar in their general habits, however, that they must be considered as belonging to the pike family. They are possibly the independent, eccentric and self satisfied nabobs of the race to which they belong; always managing to keep the world ignorant of their true character, until after their days are numbered.

We will now mention one or two additional traits, which we had nearly forgotten. The first is, that the pike is as distinguished for his abstinence as for his voracity. During the summer months, his digestive organs seem to be somewhat torpid, and this is the time that he is out of season. During this period he is particularly listless in his movements, spending nearly all the sunny hours basking near the surface of the water; and as this is the period when the smaller fry are usually commencing their active existence, we cannot but distinguish in this arrangement of nature the wisdom of Providence. Another habit peculiar to this fish, is as follows:—During the autumn, he spends the day-time in deep water, and the nights in the shallowest water he can find along the shores of river or lake. We have frequently seen them so very near the dry land as to display their fins. What their object can be in thus spending the dark hours, it is hard to determine : is it to enjoy the warmer temperature of the shallow water, or for the purpose of watching and capturing any small land animals that may come to the water to satisfy their thirst? We have heard it alleged that they seek the shore for the purpose of spawning, but it is an established fact that they cast their spawn in the spring; and, besides, the months during which they seek the shore as above stated, are the very ones in which they are in the best condition, and afford the angler the finest sport. Autumn is the time, too, when they are more frequently and more easily taken with the spear, than during any other season. And as to this spearing business, generally speaking, we consider it an abominable practice, but in the case of the savage and obstinate pike, it ought to be countenanced even by the legitimate angler.

We have angled for pike in nearly all the waters of this country where they abound. The immense quantity of book lore that we have read respecting the character of pike tackle, has always seemed to us an intelligent species of nonsense—a kind of literature originally invented by tackle manufacturers. Our own equipment for pike fishing we consider first-rate, and yet it consists only of a heavy rod and reel, a stout linen line, a brass snell, a sharp Kirby hook, and a landing net. For bait we prefer a live minnow, though a small shiner, or the belly of a yellow perch, is nearly as sure to attract notice. We have taken a pike with a gaudy fly, and also with an artificial minnow, but you cannot depend upon these allurements. Sinkers we seldom use, and the fashionable thing called a float we utterly abominate. We have fished for pike in almost every manner, but our favorite method has ever been from an anchored boat, when our only companion was a personal friend, and a lover of the written and unwritten poetry of nature. This is the most quiet and contemplative method, and unquestionably one of the most successful ones; for though the pike is not easily frightened, it takes but a single splash of an oar when trolling, to set him a-thinking, which is quite as unfortunate for the angler's success as if he were actually alarmed. Another advantage is, that while swinging to an anchor you may fish at the bottom, if you please, or try the stationary trolling fashion. To make our meaning understood, we would add, that an expert angler can throw his hook in any direction from his boat, to the distance of at least a hundred feet, and in pulling it in, he secures all the advantages that result from the common mode of trolling. The pike is a fish which calls forth a deal of patience, and must be humored; for he will sometimes scorn the handsomest bait, apparently out of mere spite; but the surest time to take him is when there is a cloudy sky and a southerly breeze. Live fish are the best bait, as we have before remarked, though the leg of a frog is good, and in winter a piece of pork, but nothing can be better than a shiner or a little perch; and it might here be remarked, that as the pike is an epicure in the manner of his eating, it is invariably a good plan to let him have his own time, after he has seized the bait. As to torchlight fishing for pike, though unquestionably out of the pale of the regular angler's sporting, it is attended with much that we must deem poetical and interesting. Who can doubt this proposition, when we consider the picturesque effect of a boat and lighted torch, gliding along the wild shores of a lake, on a still, dark night, with one figure noiselessly plying an oar, and the animated attitude of another relieved against the fire-light, and looking into the water like Orpheus into hell. And remember, too, the thousand inhabitants of the liquid element that we see, and almost fancy to be endowed with human sympathies? What a pleasure to behold the various finny tribes amid their own chosen haunts, leading, as Leigh Hunt has exquisitely written,

> "A cold, sweet, silver life, wrapped in round waves,
> Quickened with touches of transporting fear!"

In some of the Northern States fishing for pike with set lines through the ice, is practiced to a great extent. The lines are commonly attached to a figure four, by which the fisherman is informed that he has a bite, and if he has many lines out and the fish are in a humor to be captured, this mode of fishing is really very exciting. Especially so, if the ice is smooth and the fisherman can attend to his hooks with a pair of sharp skates attached to his feet.

Another mode for catching pike in the winter, and which we have seen practiced in the lakes and rivers of Michigan, is as follows. You cut a large hole in the ice, over which you erect a tent or small portable house; and after taking a seat therein, you let down a bait for the purpose of alluring the fish, and as they follow the hook, even to your feet, you pick them out with a sharp spear.

But it is time that we should change the tone of our discourse and mention the favorite waters of the American pike. The largest we have ever seen were taken in the Upper Mississippi, and on the St. Joseph and Raisin rivers of Michigan, where they are very abundant. They are also found in nearly all the streams emptying into Lakes Michigan, Erie, and Ontario;—also, in the Ohio and its tributaries. We have heard of them in the Upper St. Lawrence, and know them to abound in Lake Champlain, and in a large proportion of the lakes and rivers of New England. A very pretty lady once told us that she had seen a pike taken from Lake Champlain, which was as long as the sofa upon which we were seated together, and conversing upon the gentle art of fishing, and the tender one of love. Pike fishing with the hook we have not practiced to a very great extent. Our angling experience has been chiefly confined to the smaller lakes of Connecticut, particularly those in the vicinity of Norwich. Our favorite resort has been Gardner's Lake, whose shores are surrounded with pleasant wood-crowned hills, teeming with partridge and wood-cock, and the Sabbath stillness which usually reigns about it is seldom broken, save by the dipping oar or the laugh of the light-hearted fisherman. Dearly indeed do we cherish the memory of the pleasant days spent upon this picturesque lake; and we hope it may never be used for any other purpose than to mirror the glories of heaven, and never be visited by any but genuine sportsmen and true-hearted lovers of nature. Preston Lake is another beautiful sheet of water near Norwich, which reminds us of a night adventure. A couple of us had visited it for the purpose of taking pike by torch-light, having brought our spears and dry-pine all the way from Norwich in a one-horse wagon. It was a cold but still autumnal night, and as we tied our horse to a tree in an open field, we had every reason to anticipate a "glorious time." So far as the fish were concerned we enjoyed fine sport, for we caught about a dozen pike, varying from one to four pounds in weight; but the miseries we subsequently endured were positively intolerable.

Not only did we work an everlasting while to make our boat sea-worthy, but in our impatience to reach the fishing grounds, we misplaced our brandy bottle in the tall grass, and were therefore deprived of its warming companionship. About midnight a heavy fog began to arise, which not only prevented us from distinguishing a pike from a log of wood, but caused us to become frequently entangled in the top of a dry tree, lying on the water. Our next step, therefore, was to go home, but then came the trouble of finding our "desired haven." This we did happen to find, for a wonder, and having gathered up our plunder started on our course over the frosty grass after our vehicle and horse. We found them, but it was in a most melancholy plight indeed. Like a couple of large fools, we had omitted to release the horse from the wagon as we should have done, and the consequence was that he had released himself by breaking the fills and tearing off the harness, and we discovered him quietly feeding a few paces from the tree to which we had fastened him. What next to do, we could not in our utter despair possibly determine; but after a long consultation we both concluded to mount the miserable horse, and with our fish in hand we actually started upon our miserable journey home. Our fish were so heavy that we were compelled at the end of the first mile to throw them away, and as the day was breaking we entered the silent streets of Norwich, pondering upon the pleasures of pike fishing by torch-light, and solemnly counting the cost of our nocturnal expedition.

But the most successful pike fishing we ever enjoyed was at Crow Wing, on the Upper Mississippi. We were spending a few days with an isolated Indian trader of the wilderness, around whose cabin were encamped about three hundred Chippewa Indians. Seldom was it that we allowed a night to pass away, without trying our luck with the spear, and as a dozen canoes were often engaged in the same sport, the bosom of the river often presented a most romantic and beautiful appearance. Each canoe usually contained two or three individuals, and our torches, which were made of dried birch bark, threw such a flood of light upon the translucent water, that we could see every object in the bed of the river with the utmost distinctness. Beautiful indeed were those fishing scenes, and when the canoes had floated down the river for a mile or two, the homeward bound races that followed between the shouting Indians were exciting in the extreme. And what added to *our* enjoyment of this sporting was the idea that to grasp the hand of a white man (besides that of our host), we should have to travel one hundred miles through a pathless wilderness. We seldom took any note of time, and sometimes were throwing the spear even when the day was breaking. The largest fish that we saw taken at Crow Wing weighed upwards of forty pounds; and we have known five spearmen to take seventy pike and maskalunge in a single night.

But we must curtail our pike stories, for we purpose to append to our remarks a few interesting observations upon that and a kindred fish which have been kindly furnished to us by an accomplished scholar, a genuine angler and a valued friend, John R. Bartlett, Esq.

The pike bears the same relation to the finny tribes that the hyena and jackall do to animals, the vulture to birds, or the spider to insects —one of the most voracious of fishes. He feeds alike on the living or dead; and even those of his own brethren which are protected by nature against the attacks of other fish, find no protection against him. It is remarkable in the economy of animals, that while nature provides her weaker and smaller creatures with the means of defence against the stronger ones, she has, at the same time, furnished some of the latter with weapons, apparently for the very purpose of overcoming the feeble, however well they may be guarded. Thus, the pike, with its immense jaws, armed with innumerable teeth, is able to seize and crush every kind of fish. Its own kind do not escape, for instances are frequent when a pike of three or four pounds is found in the stomach of one of twelve or fifteen pounds weight.

It is interesting to notice the habits of the pike, which an angler may easily do in still, clear water. They have been characterized as a solitary, melancholy, and bold fish. Never are they found in schools, or even in pairs, as most other fish are, nor are they often seen in open water, where other fish would discover them and avoid their grasp. When in open water they lie very near the bottom, quite motionless, appearing like a sunken stick. Their usual and favorite place of resort is among the tall weeds where they cannot be seen. Here they lie, as it were, in ambush, waiting the approach of some innocent, unsuspecting fish, when they dart forth with a swiftness which none of the finny tribe can attain, seize their harmless victim, and slowly bear it away to some secluded spot. Here they crush their prey with their immense jaws, and leisurely force it into their capacious stomachs. Often, when angling for the pike with a live perch, from a wharf so far raised above the water that I could see every object for twenty feet on either side, a pike has so suddenly darted from a cluster of weeds, beyond the range of my vision, that the first intimation I had of his presence was, that he had seized my bait.

On one occasion, when angling in the St. Lawrence, where pike are very abundant, I put a minnow on my hook, and threw my line towards a mass of weeds, in the hope of tempting a perch to take it. Not many minutes had elapsed before my silvery minnow had tempted the appetite of one, which soon conveyed him to his maw. Knowing that my game was sure, I let him play about, first allowing him to run to the extent of my line and then drawing him towards me, when on a sudden a pike shot from his hiding place and seized my perch. I was obliged to let the fellow have his own way, and give him all the time he wanted to swallow the perch, when with a good deal of difficulty, I succeeded in disabling him and towed him in triumph to the shore. The perch weighed a pound and a half; the pike ten pounds.

The long and slender form of the pike, tapering towards the head and tail, enables him to move with great rapidity through the water, while his smooth and finless back facilitates his movements through the weeds or marine plants. Thus has nature provided this fish with a form adapted to its habits, and with large and well-armed jaws, to give it a pre-eminence among the finny tribes which inhabit the same waters. I have often thought why so great an enemy, so great a devourer of his race, should be placed among them, favored by so many advantages. May it not, nay, must it not be for some wise purpose? It is known how very prolific fishes are, and unless some way was provided to lessen the number, our inland waters could not contain the vast numbers which a few years would produce. Most fish live on each other, others on decomposing substances floating about. It is not always the largest that prey on each other, for the sturgeon is one of the largest fresh water fish, and he subsists on decomposing matter, or minute fish. A few pike placed in a lake, would very effectually prevent an over-population. May it not, then, be so ordered that the inhabitants of the seas, which are not so favored as those who dwell on the earth's surface, and who have a great variety of food to supply their wants, may have the means of providing their own sustenance by an immense increase of their own species?

Blaine observes that "the abstinence of the pike and jack is no less singular than their voracity; during the summer months their digestive faculties are somewhat torpid, which appears a remarkable peculiarity in pike economy, seeing it must be in inverse ratio to the wants of the fish, for they must be at this time in a state of emaciation from the effects of spawning. During the summer they are listless, and affect the surface of the water, where in warm sunny weather they seem to bask in a sleepy state for hours together. It is not a little remarkable, that smaller fish appear to be aware when this abstinent state of their foe is upon him; for they who at other times are evidently impressed with an instinctive dread of his presence, are now swimming around him with total unconcern. At these periods, no baits, however tempting, can allure him; but on the contrary, he retreats from everything of the kind. Windy weather is alone capable of exciting his dormant powers. This inaptitude to receive food with the usual keenness, continues from the time they spawn, until the time of their recovery from the effects of it."

The peculiarity above noticed does not entirely apply to the pike of the Northern States, and particularly of the great lakes and rivers, whose waters are not so sensibly affected by the heat of summer as shallow water is. In the smaller streams he lies in the listless state described by Mr. Blaine, but when he can reach the deep water he always does so.

Pike are found in all the lakes and inland waters of the Northern and Middle States of the Union. In the great lakes they grow to an enormous size. No fish is better known throughout Europe and the northern parts of Asia. In colder climes he attains the largest size, and is said by Walkenburg to disappear in geographical distribution with the fir. In our waters they are taken of all sizes, from four or five pounds to fifty or sixty. Their haunts are generally among the weeds or marine plants near the shore, or in deep bays where the water is not made rough by winds, and in all parts of rivers. They are rarely found on rocky bottoms or bars. A high wind and rough sea often drives them from their weedy haunts into deeper water. I have noticed this particularly on Lake Ontario. From wharves where basse are only taken on ordinary occasions, pike will bite with avidity when a severe gale is blowing and the water is in a disturbed state.

This fish, according to Donovan, attains a larger size in a shorter time, in proportion to most others. In the course of the first year it grows eight or ten inches; the second, twelve or fourteen; the third, eighteen or twenty inches. Some pike were turned into a pond in England, the largest of which weighed two and a half pounds. Four years after, the water was let off, when one pike of nineteen pounds, and others of from eleven to fifteen, were found. Mr. Jesse, in his Gleanings of Natural History, relates certain experiments by which he shows that the growth of pike is about four pounds a year, which corresponds with the growth of those before stated.

The various books on sporting give numerous instances of pike weighing from thirty to forty pounds, taken in England, though an instance is mentioned in Dodsley's Register for 1765, of an enormous pike weighing 170 pounds, which was taken from a pool near Newport, England, which had not been fished in for ages. In Ireland and Scotland, they are found larger than in England. In the Shannon and Lough Corrib, they have been found from seventy to ninety-two pounds in weight. At Broadford, near Limerick, one was taken weighing ninety-six pounds. Another was caught by trolling in Loch Pentluliche, of fifty pounds; and another in Loch Spey, that weighed 146 pounds. But these are small in comparison with a pike, which is stated by Gesner (and from him quoted by most writers on fish) to have been taken in a pool near the capital of Sweden, in the year 1497, which was fifteen feet in length, and weighed 350 pounds. Under the skin of this enormous fish was discovered a ring of cypress brass, having a Greek inscription round the rim, which was interpreted by Dalburgus, Bishop of Worms, to signify: "I am the fish first of all placed in this pond, by the hands of Frederic the Second, on the 5th of October, in the year of grace 1230;" which would make its age 267 years. The ring about his neck was made with springs, so as to enlarge as the fish grew. His skeleton was for a long time preserved at Manheim.

During the past summer, which I spent on the banks of the St. Lawrence, I had frequently tried the spool trolling, and always with success. Sometimes I would use two lines, one 70, the other 120 feet in length. On the larger one I had the best success, and my bait would be seized three times, when on the shorter one it would be but once; it being farther from the boat, the movements of which through the water, and the noise of the oars, drove the fish off. From experience I am satisfied that long trolling lines are the best. Basse will seize a fly or spoon at a few feet distance, but a pike will not. I have tried the experiment, when trolling for pike, to attach to one hook a bait of pork and red flannel, a very common bait, and to the other a brass spoon. The latter was invariably seized first, for the only reason, I suppose, that it made more show in the water. Neither resembled a fish, fly, or any living creature, but curiosity or hunger attracted the fish to the strange bait gliding through the water, which they seized, paying with their lives the penalty for so doing.

There is a large fish of the pike species commonly called the Maskinonge or Maskalunge before spoken of, of what specific character is not well understood by naturalists. Their habits and their haunts are the same as those of the pike, and they attain a larger size than any fish of our inland waters. I have seen them carried by two men of ordinary height, with a pole running through the gills and supported on the shoulders of the men. In this position the tail of the fish dragged on the ground. Forty or fifty pounds is not an unusual weight for them, and instances are known when much larger ones have been caught. Maskinonge are generally taken in seines, seldom with the hook. Their size is so large that the ordinary baits of anglers would be no temptation for them. In the several opportunities which I have had to examine the stomachs of these fish I have invariably found within them, fish of very large size, such as no angler would ever think of putting on his line. The largest perch I ever saw, about fifteen inches in length, was taken from the paunch of a Maskinonge, and I have often seen catfish, perch, and other fish, weighing from one to two pounds, taken from them; but in no instance small fish; and hence anglers have not taken them, as few would angle with live bait of that size, where there are no fish but these which would take it.

The most exciting sport I ever had on the St. Lawrence, or anywhere else, was in taking a maskinonge. It was a regular battle, such only as the salmon anglers enjoy when they hook a twenty pounder. As the method was quite different, I will send you all the particulars.

A friend and myself took a small skiff, with one trolling line, intending to take turns at the oars, and proceeded at once to a favorite spot among the "Thousand Islands."

I held the trolling line with a spoon hook attached, while my companion pulled the oars. We sailed among the secluded places, wherever weeds were seen below the surface of the water, and were rewarded with good sport by taking several fine pike, weighing from six to fifteen pounds, which we managed to secure with ease, save the largest, which gave us some trouble. We then thought we would try deeper water, in the hope of tempting larger fish. A few windings among the clusters of small islands brought us to the channel of the river, when I directed my companion to increase the speed of our skiff, determined that the curiosity of no fish should be satisfied, without first tasting my gilded spoon. We pulled for half a mile, when the river wound suddenly round an island, which presented a bold shore, from the rushing of the river's current. The tall forest trees extended to the very brink of the river, over which they hung, throwing a deep shadow on the water. This quiet spot looked as though it might be an attractive one for some solitary fish, and we accordingly took a sweep around the foot of the island.—Scarcely had we entered the deep shade spoken of, when I felt a tug at my line, which was so strong that I supposed my hook had come in contact with a floating log or fallen tree. My companion backed water with his oars to relieve my hook, when another violent pull at my line convinced me that it was no log, but some living creature of great weight. My line was already out its full length of 150 feet; no alternative was therefore left but to give my fish more line by rowing after him.

This we did for a few minutes, when I began to pull in the slack of my line, some fifty feet or more, when I felt my fish. The check was no sooner felt by him than he started forward with a velocity scarcely conceivable in the water, bringing my line taut, and the next moment our skiff was moving off stern foremost towards the river's channel. We soon perceived that our fish had turned his head up stream, and as the water was deep, there was no danger of his coming in contact with weeds or protruding rocks. We therefore allowed him to tow us for about five minutes, when he stopped. Then quickly backing water with our oars, and taking in our line, we carefully laid it over the skiff's side, until we had approached within twenty feet of our fish. I then gave him another check, which probably turned his head, for he again darted off in a contrary direction down stream. We pulled our skiff in the same direction as fast as possible to give the fish a good run before checking him again, but he soon had the line out its full length, and was again towing our skiff after him with more rapidity than before. This did not last long, however, for I then took the line and hauled towards him to lessen our distance. He made another slap, when I managed to keep my line taut, and with our oars moved towards him. Our victim now lay on the surface of the water with his belly upward, apparently exhausted, when we found him to be a maskinonge, between five and eight feet in length. We had no sooner got him alongside than he gave a slap with his tail and again darted off the whole length of the line, taking us once more in tow. His run was now short, and it was evident he was getting tired of the business. Again the line slacked and we drew the skiff up to the spot where he lay turned up on his back.

He now seemed so far gone that I thought we might draw him into our skiff, so I reached out my gaff and hooked him under the jaw, while my companion passed his oar under him. In this way we contrived to raise him over the gunwale of the skiff, when he slid to its bottom. I then placed my foot back of his head to hold him down, in order to disengage my hook, which passed through his upper jaw. No sooner had I attempted this than he began to flap about, compelling us to give him room to avoid his immense jaws. Every moment seemed to increase his strength, when my companion seized an oar in order to dispatch him, while I took out my knife for the same purpose. The first blow with the oar had only the effect to awaken our fish, which taking another and more powerful somerset, threw himself over the gunwale of our skiff, which was but a few inches above the water, and with a plunge disappeared in the deep water at our side. We had scarcely recovered from our surprise, when I found my line drawn out again to its full length, save a few tangles and twists, which had got into it in the struggle between us and our fish. We determined to trifle no longer with the fellow, with our small skiff, but to make for the shore and there land him. A small island, a short distance from us, seemed to present a convenient place, and here without further ceremony we pulled, towing our fish after us. I leaped into the water about ten feet from the shore, and tugged away at my victim, who floated like a log upon the water, while my companion stood by with an oar to make the capture more sure this time. In this way we landed him in safety just one hour and a quarter after he was first hooked. This maskinonge weighed 49 pounds, and had within him a pike of three pounds weight, a chub, partially decomposed, of four pounds, and a perch of one and a half pounds, which appeared to have been but recently swallowed; yet this fish's appetite was not satisfied, and he lost his life in grasping at a glittering bauble. Any person who has ever killed a pike of ten pounds or upwards, can readily imagine the strength of one five times its weight.

The great strength of these fish was shown in a sporting adventure which happened to a friend of mine when out a few evenings since, spearing by torch light. The person alluded to had never before tried his hand with the spear, although he was a skillful angler. On this occasion he had killed several fish, which he secured without trouble. He was then in about six or eight feet of water, when he discovered a large fish, either a very large pike or maskinonge. He planted himself with one foot below the flaming torch, the other a little behind, when he plunged his spear into the huge fish that lay so quietly before him; but whether he was so deceived in the depth of the water, or whether he had not braced himself properly in the boat is not known, at any rate he struck the fish, which darted off like lightning, taking the spear with him, as well as him who threw it. For the gentleman, probably deceived by the depth of the water, had reached forward too far and thereby lost his balance. So over he went head foremost, holding on to the spear. But he was satisfied without following the fish further, which escaped with the long spear, neither of which could be again seen. The gentleman made the best of his way into the skiff. Two days after a large maskinonge floated ashore several miles below the spot where the event took place, with the spear still clinging to him, just before the dorsal fin.

PLANTATION CUSTOMS.

WE profess to be neither a defender nor an advocate of slavery, but circumstances having brought us into frequent communication with the colored population of the Southern States, we have the satisfaction of knowing that our opinions, concerning their condition, whether correct or not, are the result of personal observation. We do indeed consider the institution as an evil, but we consider the fanaticism of the North to be a much greater evil. By birth and education are we a Northern man, and we willingly acknowledge that we started upon our first journey through the Southern States, harboring in our breast an unreasonable number of prejudices against the institution already mentioned. The tables, however, are now completely turned. Aside from the abstract idea which has ever and will ever trouble us, we have seen but little to mourn over and regret, but rather observed much, as touching the happiness of the negro and especially his customs, which we cannot but commend and admire. Instead of commenting upon these customs in a general manner, we propose to give an idea of them by describing two specimens—the negro manner of spending the Christmas Holidays, and the prominent features of one of their Corn Huskings.

The scene of our first description is a plantation in the interior of South Carolina. Within hailing distance of the planter's mansion is a collection of picturesque cabins, where are domiciled his negroes, numbering in all about one hundred souls. It is early morning and the day before Christmas. The slaves have obtained their accustomed furlough, which is to last until the close of the year, and they are now on the point of carrying to the market of some neighboring town the products they may have obtained from their allotted plots of ground during the bygone season. All the means of conveyance belonging to the plantation have been placed at their disposal, and the day has arrived when they are to receive in hard money, or merchandise, the fruit of their own industry, irrespective of their obligations to their masters. As a matter of course, the excitement among them is unusual, and is participated in by all—men, women, and children. All things being ready, the sable fraternity are upon the move, and as they enter upon a road winding through a succession of picturesque woods, we will glance at some of the characters belonging to the cavalcade. The leader thereof is probably the most industrious and frugal of the whole brotherhood, and he is taking to market, in a double wagon drawn by two horses, some two or three bales of cotton, which he will dispose of for one hundred and fifty dollars. The next vehicle is also a wagon, and in it are two or three old women, who have under their especial protection an assortment of poultry which it is their intention to exchange with the village merchant for any little conveniences that they may need, or any fancy articles that they may desire. Directly behind these we have a noisy party of girls and boys, who are footing their way to market more for the frolic or freedom of the thing than any desire to obtain money, albeit we doubt not but some of the boys may have stowed away in one of the wagons an occasional fox or coon skin which have accidentally come into their possession by means of their cunningly devised traps. In another wagon, drawn by a pair of mules, we notice a load of miscellaneous articles, including a supply of rudely wrought agricultural implements, a few bags of corn and other grain, and a neatly dressed hog, with his hoofs pointing to the sky. We now have a venerable negro, mounted upon an equally venerable horse, his only saddle consisting of a large bag of choice seeds, which he has been permitted to glean from his master's fields at the end of the harvest. And coming up in the rear, is the excessively miscellaneous portion of the procession, who ramble along, so far as their appearance is concerned, somewhat after the manner of a party of bedlamites, but as joyous and light-hearted as if they were the lords instead of the serfs of creation. And so much for the appearance of our friends on their way to market.

The thousand and one incidents which occur at the town, interesting and unique as they are, we will leave to the imagination of our readers. Towards the close of the day the party return to their cabins upon the plantation, and albeit some of the more indiscreet may have imbibed an undue quantity of the intoxicating beverage, the majority of them are as circumspect in their deportment as could be expected. And then, on their arrival home, commences the long-anticipated frolic of Christmas Eve. The banjos and fiddles are brought forth, and devoting themselves most heartily to the pleasures of dancing, singing, and comparing notes as to the acquisitions made during the day, the hours of night are soon numbered, and the revelry is only concluded by the approach of day.

Two hours after sunrise on Christmas morning the sable fraternity are all out of their beds and moving about with considerable activity, considering their loss of sleep, and a new order of things is about to occur. The house servants, and such of the field hands as think their services may be needed, place themselves in the way of the master and mistress of the plantation, and cheerfully perform any necessary work which may be allotted to them. This done, they return to their cabins, and plan the various means of enjoying themselves. Those old women, and others who are religiously disposed, jump into a wagon and drive to some neighboring church to hear the story of the Saviour. Others, who have relatives belonging to another plantation, start off upon a friendly visitation. Some, who have a passion for shooting, and have either borrowed or purchased the necessary fusees, depart upon a vagabondizing excursion into the woods; while others, who are particularly covetous, and have already experienced the satisfaction of owning a little property, remain about the premises for the purpose of accomplishing some newly-conceived scheme, which will most likely result at no distant day in his purchasing his freedom. As Christmas is passed, so are the remaining days of the week, an arrangement having been made among the negroes, that a portion of them should take turns with another portion, so that the necessary labor of the plantation might not be neglected. At the commencement of the year, the regular order of business is resumed upon the plantation, and so continues with occasional interruption until another Christmas arrives, to the entire satisfaction, both of master and slave.

The rural custom denominated *corn husking* or *corn shucking* is peculiar to the Southern States. It occurs at night, in the autumn of the year, is participated in by negroes alone, and has for its main object the husking and the gathering into barns of the yellow maize or corn. And the locality of our present description is a plantation in the State of Georgia.

Intelligence having previously been circulated throughout the district, that a husking is to occur on a certain night, at a certain plantation, the first step, as a matter of course, is to prepare for the contemplated meeting. The corn yielded by the present harvest is hauled in from the surrounding fields, and deposited in huge heaps, immedidiately around the crib or barn into which it is eventually to be deposited. The roof of the crib having been built so as to be easily removed, and for the purpose of allowing the corn to be thrown into the building from a considerable distance, it is accordingly transferred to some out-of-the-way place, there to remain until reappropriated to its legitimate use after the husking is ended. The next step is to bring together at convenient points around the barn and the stacks of corn, huge quantities of light wood, which is to be employed for the several purposes of tempering the night air, affording necessary light, and rendering the approaching scene as cheerful as possible. And while all these preparations are being made by the men, others of quite as much importance are occupying the attention of all the women belonging to the plantation, whose business it is to prepare the feast which necessarily follows the actual business of husking; while the children are probably spending their time in clearing away the rubbish from a level spot of ground in the vicinity of the bonfires, where it is more than probable we may yet have the pleasure of witnessing a negro dance.

Night has settled upon the world, and the whole space enclosed by the planter's mansion and his almost innumerable outhouses, is filled with a hum of talking and laughing voices—the loud talking and the hoarse laughing of perhaps two hundred negroes, exclusive of woman and children. The torch is now applied to the piles of dry wood, and by the brilliant light of the several fires the *huskers* move to their allotted places around the corn house and seat themselves upon the ground. They are divided into what might be termed four divisions (occupying or flanking the several sides of the house), each one of which is "*headed*" by one of the smartest men in the company, whose province it is not only to superintend his division, and with the assistance of several boys to throw the corn, as it is husked, into the crib, but to take the lead in the singing which, among the blacks, invariably, and we believe necessarily, accompanies the business of husking corn. All things being ready, a signal is given, and the whole party fall to work as if their very lives depended upon their handling a specified quantity of the white and yellow grain. At the same instant commences a mingled sound of shouting and singing voices, which presently swell into a loud and truly harmonious chorus, and the husking scene is in its prime. The very fires seem elated with the singular but interesting prospect which they illumine, and shoot their broad sheets of flame high into the air. Song follows song, in quick succession, and in every direction piles of beautiful corn seem to spring out of the earth as if by magic, and with the quickness of magic are transferred into the great receptacle, which is itself rapidly becoming filled. Rude indeed are the songs they sing, but harmonious and plaintive. The words are improvised and the ideas are simple, but there is invariably a pathos and harmony in the chorus which fails not to delight the ear. Amusing stories are occasionally told, and then resoundeth far over the quiet fields sleeping in moonlight, even as did the songs, boisterous peals of laughter. One, two, three, and perhaps four hours have elapsed, and it is now midnight, when the announcement is made by some patriarch of the company that the corn is all husked, and the crib is nearly full. One more song is called for, during the singing of which the roof is replaced upon the corn house, and after congregating around the fires, partly with a view of comparing notes as to the amount of labor performed, but more especially for the purpose of drying the sweat from their sable faces, the entire party of huskers move to the spacious kitchen attached to the planter's mansion.

And here an entirely new scene presents itself to our view. Board tables have been spread in every available corner, and even in the more sheltered portions of the adjoining yard, and everywhere is displayed a most sumptuous entertainment, consisting not only of the substantials of life, strangely served up in the form of a thick soup, but abounding even in luxuries. Good whisky and perhaps peach brandy is supplied in reasonable quantities, and the women, having finished their allotted duties, now mingle with the men, and the feasting company presents as merry and happy a picture of rural life as can well be imagined. Each negro devotes himself to his particular mess, and somewhat after the manner of the aborigines. Jokes of questionable elegance and delicacy are uttered to a considerable extent, and many compliments paid to the *"lib'ral and magnan'mous massa ob dis plantation."* On such occasions, as might not be supposed, acts of decided impropriety but seldom occur, and it is not often that a sufficient quantity of spirit is imbibed, either materially to injure the health or produce intoxication. In this particular, even the *"down-trodden"* slaves, as they are called, may often set a worthy example for the imitation of those who occupy a more elevated rank in society.

We now come to describe the concluding scene of the corn-husking entertainment, which consists of a dance upon the spot cleared away by the boys in the vicinity of the late fires, which are replenished for further use. The scraping of fiddles and the thumping of banjos having been heard above the clatter of *spoons*, *soup-plates*, and *gourds*, at the various supper tables, a new *stampede* takes place, and the musicians are hurried off to the dancing ground, as if to trip the light fantastic toe were deemed the climax of earthly happiness. "On with the dance, let joy be unconfined." But there seemeth no need of the poet's advice on the present occasion, for the sable congregation now assembled, seem animated with an almost frantic excitement. The dance, as a matter of course, is the famous *"Virginia Reel,"* and at least a hundred individuals have formed themselves in their proper places. No sooner do the instruments attain the necessary pitch, than the head couples dash into the arena, now slowly and disdainfully, now swiftly and ferociously, and now performing the *double shuffle* or the *pigeon-wing*. Anon they come to a stand, while others follow, and go through the same fantastic performances, with the addition perhaps of an occasional leap or whirl. The excitement is becoming more intense than ever, and it is evident that those whose business it is to stand still, are actually dancing in their shoes. Louder than ever wails the music—order is followed by confusion—and in the madness of the dance there is no method. The brilliant watch-fires cast a ruddy glow upon the faces of the dancers, and when, as it sometimes happens, an individual chances to wander without the circle, his leaping and uncouth figure pictured against the sky, resembles more the form of a lost spirit than a human being. Music, dancing, shouting, leaping, and laughing, with other indescribable matters, are mingled together in a most unique manner, constituting a spectacle only equaled by the midnight dances of painted savages. For hours does this frolic continue, and perhaps is only brought to an end by the crowing of a cock, or the first glimpse over the eastern hills, of the coming day. And then comes the breaking up of the assembly, so that by the usual breakfast hour, the negroes have reached the several plantations to which they belong, and after spending rather an idle day, are ready for any other *husking* to which they may be invited, and which their masters will permit them to attend.

FISHING IN GENERAL.

"We have, indeed, often thought that angling alone offers to man the degree of half-business, half-idleness, which the fair sex find in their needle-work or knitting, which, employing the hands, leaves the mind at liberty, and occupying the attention, so far as is necessary to remove the painful sense of a vacuity, yet yields room for contemplation, whether upon things heavenly or earthly, cheerful or melancholy." SIR WALTER SCOTT.

IN the preceding articles we have given the public the substance of our experience in regard to our five favorite fish, the salmon, trout, pike, rock, and black basse. On the present occasion we purpose to embody within the limits of a single article, our stock of information upon the remaining fish of the United States, which properly come under the jurisdiction of the angler. We shall proceed in our remarks after the manner of the dictionary-makers, and shall take up each variety without any regard to their order, but as they may happen to come into our mind.

The Perch.—With two members of this family alone are we personally acquainted, viz. the yellow perch and the white perch. The first is a beautiful fish, and found in nearly all the waters of the Northern and Middle States, and probably as well known throughout the world as any of the finny tribes. Its predominating color is yellow; it has an elegant form, is a bold biter, varies in weight from four ounces to a pound (although occasionally found in New England weighing two pounds); has a dry and sweet flesh, but ill adapted to satisfy the cravings of a hungry man on account of its bones, which are particularly numerous, hard, and pointed. They generally swim about in *schools*, and yet at the same time are not at all distinguished for their intelligence, being invariably allured to destruction by the most bungling anglers, and the more common kinds of bait. They spawn in the autumn, and recover, so as to be in fine condition, early in the spring. They delight in clear rivers or lakes, with pebbly bottoms, though sometimes found on sandy or clayey soils. They love a moderately deep water, and frequent holes at the mouth of small streams or the hollows under the banks. With regard to the white perch we have only to say that it is well described by its name, is a migratory fish, found in nearly all the rivers of the Atlantic coast, from Boston to Norfolk; and they weigh from six ounces to one pound, are in season during the spring and summer, are capital as an article of food, and afford the entire brotherhood of anglers an abundance of sport. As touching the name of the fish now before us, we desire to chronicle our opinion respecting an important instance in which it has been misapplied. Many years ago, while reading the remarkable and intensely interesting work of Audubon on the birds of America, we chanced upon the description of a fish, found in the Ohio, to which he gave the name of white perch. Subsequently to that period, while sojourning in the city of Cincinnati, we happened to remember Mr. Audubon's description, and one morning visited the market for the purpose of examining the fish. We found them very abundant, and were informed that they commanded a high price. On examining the fish, however, in view of certain doubts that we had previously entertained (for we knew that the white perch of the book was a native of salt water), we found it to be not a legitimate white perch, but simply the fish known on Lake Erie as the fresh water sheeps-head. But this misapplication of the term perch is not peculiar to the residents on the Ohio, for we know that, throughout the Southern States where the black basse is found, it is universally called the black perch; and that in the vicinity of Boston and Nahant the miserable little fish called the conner is there designated as a black perch. That there are several varieties of the real perch besides those which we have mentioned we do not deny, but we feel confident that the above correction cannot be refuted.

The Maskalunge and Pickerel.—Both of these fish are peculiar to the United States, and especially to the Great Lakes, and the waters of the St. Lawrence and Mississippi. The former belongs unquestionably to the pike family, although commonly weighing from twenty to forty pounds, while many people affirm that it is only an overgrown pike. They are valued as an article of food, and by those who are fond of killing the most savage of game at the expense of much labor, they are highly appreciated. The best and about the only valuable account of this fish that we have ever seen, was written by George W. Clinton, Esq., and published in the Buffalo Commercial Advertiser. As to the fish which we call the pickerel, we have to say that it occupies a position somewhere between the trout and perch; that it is a favorite with the anglers of Lake Champlain, Lake Erie, and Lake Michigan, and with those also who practice the gentle art along the borders of the Ohio and the Tennessee. It is an active fish, of a roundish form, with large mouth and sharp teeth, and covered with small scales, the predominating colors being a dark green and yellowish white. The name which it bears is the one so generally applied, but erroneously, to the legitimate pike. It is also the same fish known in the Southwest as the salmon, but as unlike the peerless creature of the far North as a gray wolf is unlike a deer. As is the case with the maskalunge, the pickerel is among the first of the finny tribes that run up our Western rivers early in the spring; and in the waters of Lake Champlain and the St. Lawrence they are found herding with the yellow perch, and we believe that in some districts they are considered as belonging to the perch family.

The Catfish.—This fish is distinguished for its many deformities, and is a great favorite with all persons who have a fancy for muddy waters. In the Mississippi they are frequently taken weighing upwards of one hundred pounds; and while they are taken in all the tributaries of that river, it has been ascertained that they decrease in size as you ascend towards the north. They are also found in the tributaries of Lake Erie. They are taken with any kind of bait; and as they are very strong the best of tackle is invariably necessary. This fish is also found in many of the lakes of New England, where they seldom weigh more than two pounds, being there known as the horn or bull pout, owing to a peculiar pictorial thorn with which they are adorned. Their flesh, though not particularly sweet, is said to be easily digested, and they are often sought for by people with weak stomachs. But it has always seemed to us that it required a very *powerful* stomach to eat a piece from one of the mammoths of the Western waters.

As to the remaining fresh-water fish of the country, we will content ourself by merely mentioning the names of those which are known to our anglers, to wit: the chub, dace, white basse, sunfish, roach, bream, and rock basse. The fish called in Virginia and Maryland the fall fish is identical with the dace. In the waters of the West the mullet, fresh water sheepshead, and sucker, are found in immense numbers, but they are all exceedingly poor eating, and as sporting fish are of no account. The sturgeon, we believe, is found almost everywhere, and known to almost everybody.

There is a fish found in Florida which we have never seen, but which, from all the descriptions that we have heard, belongs either to the trout or basse families. It abounds in all the rivers, lakes and springs of this State, is a bold biter, reaches the weight of fifteen pounds, has a white and sweet flesh, and is taken in very much the manner employed by northern anglers in capturing the pike, and with similar artificial baits.

We now come to our favorites of the ocean and tide-water rivers; and the first fish that we mention is the *black fish*, or *tautog*, as it was called by the Mohegan Indians. It is a stationary inhabitant of the salt water, and usually found upon reefs and along rocky shores. It is taken all along the Atlantic coast between New York and Boston, but it has been known north of Cape Cod only within a few years; its legitimate home is Long Island Sound. It is an active, bold, strong, and tough fish, highly esteemed as an article of food, and, like the cod, is brought to the principal markets in floating cars, in which confinement they are said to fatten. They are by no means a handsome fish, and their scales are so adhesive as to be taken off only with the skin. They are a summer fish, being taken as early as April, and no later than October. A three-pounder is considered a good fish, but we have often taken them weighing ten pounds, and have seen them weighing fifteen pounds. They are generally taken with the hand line, and no better bait can be employed than the lobster or soft-crab.

The Sheepshead.—This is a thick set but rather handsome fish, and, for the sweetness of its flesh, highly esteemed. They are seldom seen in the New York market, but very common in the Charleston and Mobile markets, from which we infer that they are partial to southern waters. They vary in weight from three pounds to fourteen; live exclusively upon shell fish, and invariably command a high price. They are popular with the anglers, for they swim in shoals and are captured with but little trouble.

The Blue Fish.—The name of this glorious fish reminds us of the ground swell, and sends through our whole frame a thrill of pleasure. They are a species of mackerel, attaining in certain places the weight of a dozen pounds. They swim in shoals, and are taken with a trolling line and an ivory squid. Our favorite mode for taking them has ever been from a small boat with a hand line, though many people prefer taking them from a sailboat when running before a breeze. They are quite as active a fish as we have ever seen, and the strength of their jaws is so great that we have known them to bite off a man's finger. When fresh and fat we consider them quite as delicate as the real mackerel, and much better than the black fish. They are found on the sea coast as far south as Norfolk (where they are called tailors), but they are particularly abundant along the shores of Connecticut and Rhode Island. In some places we have often found them so numerous that we have seen a dozen of them darting after our squid at the same instant. They are in season during the whole of summer and autumn.

Another capital fish that we have caught "all along shore" between New York and Cape Cod, is the *weak fish*, or *squeteague.* It never comes into the fresh water rivers, and usually makes its appearance about harvest time. Its habits are similar to those of the striped basse, and in appearance it closely resembles the *ciscovet*, of Lake Superior. They commonly weigh from three to five pounds, though they have been taken weighing nearly ten. They are bold biters, and highly esteemed for their sweetness.

With regard to the remaining fish found on our seaboard we are disposed to be quite brief. The *mackerel* we esteem, and have had rare sport in taking them, but we look upon them as the exclusive property of our merchants. The *halibut* we admire, but fear, for he reminds us of one of the most fatiguing piscatorial adventures we ever experienced, when we hooked a thirty pounder in the Atlantic, one hundred miles off Nantucket. As to the *cod*, we have only to say that we have caught them off Nahant by the hundred, and never wish to catch any more; like the *mackerel*, we consider them the exclusive property of the mercantile fraternity. With the *king fish* and *drum* we are wholly unacquainted. The *tom cod* and *conner* or *blue perch* we despise, and our antipathy to snakes has always caused us to avoid the eel. Of the *sea basse* and *paugee*, if we knew what to say, we would indite a long paragraph, for we esteem them both. As to the *shad* and *sea sturgeon*, we shall dismiss them with an angler's scorn, for they know not what it is to take the hook. And now that we have reached the bottom of our last page (devoted to the finny tribes), we are reminded of the very peculiar but sweet and valuable fish, which are ever found only at the bottom of the sea—the *flounder and flat-fish*. Many a time and oft have we taken them both with the hook and spear, and we can pay them no higher compliment than by mentioning the fact that they are particular favorites with the distinguished painter, *William S. Mount, Esq.*, of Long Island.

OUR MASTER IN LANDSCAPE.

"His departure has left a vacuity which amazes and alarms us. It is as if the voyager on the Hudson were to look to the great range of the Catskills, at the foot of which Cole, with a reverential fondness, had fixed his abode, and were to see that the grandest of its summits had disappeared, had sunk into the plain from our sight. I might use a bolder similitude; it is as if we were to look over the heavens on a starlight evening and find that one of the greater planets, Hesperus or Jupiter, had been blotted from the sky."

FUNERAL ORATION BY WILLIAM CULLEN BRYANT.

UPON the romantic life of the greatest of American landscape painters it is not our province to discourse, for that task has been assigned to a gifted poet and friend of the departed—the Reverend Louis L. Noble;—nor do we purpose to expatiate upon his beautiful character as a man, and his genius as an artist; for that labor of love has already been accomplished by the eminent poet from whom we have borrowed our motto. The only idea that we have in view, is simply to describe the truly Epic productions of the late Thomas Cole (in whose studio, which looked out upon the Catskill Mountains, we have spent many pleasant hours), for the edification of those of our readers who have never had an opportunity of examining them.

In the first place, then, we will turn our attention to the series of five pictures, entitled "*The Course of Empire.*" This work is an epitome of the life of man, and is conceived and executed in a manner which must convince the beholder that the artist possessed many of the attributes of the philosopher, the poet, and the Christian.

In the first picture we have a perfectly wild scene of rocks, mountains, woods, and a bay of the ocean, reposing in the luxuriance of a ripe spring. The clouds of night are being dissipated by the beams of the rising sun. On the opposite side of the bay rises a lofty promontory, crowned by a singular, isolated rock, which would ever be a conspicuous landmark to the mariner. As the same locality is preserved in each picture of the series, this rock identifies it, although the position of the spectator changes in the several pictures. The chase being the most characteristic occupation of savage life, in the foreground we see an Indian clothed in skins, pursuing a wounded deer, which is bounding down a narrow ravine. On a rock, in the middle ground, are other Indians, with their dogs surrounding another deer. On the bosom of a little river below are a number of canoes passing down the stream, while many more are drawn up on the shore. On an elevation beyond these is a cluster of wigwams, and a number of Indians dancing round a fire. In this picture we have the first rudiments of society. Men are already banded together for mutual aid in the chase. In the canoes, huts, and weapons, we perceive that the useful arts have commenced, and in the singing, which usually accompanies the dance of savages, we behold the germs of music and poetry. The Empire is asserted, to a limited degree, over sea, land, and the animal kingdom.

Ages have passed away, and in the second picture we have the Simple or Arcadian State of Society. The time of day is a little before noon, and the season early summer. The "untracked and rude" has been tamed and softened. Shepherds are tending their flocks; a solitary ploughman, with his oxen, is turning up the soil; and in the rude vessels passing into the haven of a growing village, and in the skeleton of a barque building on the shore, we perceive the commencement of Commerce. From a rude temple on a hill the smoke of sacrifice is ascending to the sky, symbolizing the spirit of Religion. In the foreground, on the left hand, is seated an old man, who, by describing strange figures in the sand, seems to have made some geometrical discovery, demonstrating the infancy of Science. On the right hand is a woman with a distaff, about crossing a stone bridge; beside her, a boy is drawing on a stone the figure of a man with a sword; and beyond these, ascending the road, a soldier is partly seen. Under some noble trees, in the middle distance, are a number of peasants dancing to the music of pipe and timbrel. All these things show us that society is steadily progressing in its march of usefulness and power.

Ages have again passed away, and in the third picture we have a magnificent city. It is now mid-day, and early autumn. The bay is now surrounded by piles of architecture, temples, colonnades, and domes. It is a day of rejoicing. The spacious harbor is crowded with vessels, war-galleys, ships, and barques, their silken sails glistening in the sunshine. Moving over a massive stone bridge, in the foreground, is a triumphal procession. The conqueror, robed in purple, is mounted on a car drawn by an elephant, and surrounded by captives and a numerous train of guards and servants, many of them bearing pictures and golden treasures. As he is about to pass the triumphal arch, beautiful girls strew flowers in his path; gay festoons of drapery hang from the clustered columns; golden trophies glitter in the sun, and incense rises from silver censers. Before a Doric temple, on the left, a multitude of white-robed priests are standing on the marble steps, while near them a religious ceremony is being performed before a number of altars. The statue of Minerva, with a Victory in her hand, stands above the building of the Caryatides, on a columned pedestal, near which is a company of musicians, with cymbals, "trumpets also, and shawms." From the lofty portico of a palace, an imperial personage is watching the procession, surrounded by her children, attendants, and guards. Nations have been subjugated, man has reached the summit of human glory. Wealth, power, knowledge, and taste have worked together and accomplished the highest meed of human achievement and Empire.

Another change—and lo! in the fourth picture, the Vicious State, or State of Destruction. Behold the consequences of luxury, in the weakened and debased condition of mankind. A savage enemy has entered the once proud and happy city; a fierce tempest is raging; walls and colonnades are lying in the dust, and temples and palaces are being consumed by the torch of the incendiary. The fire of vengeance is swallowing up the devoted city. An arch of the bridge over which the triumphal procession had before passed, has been battered down, and broken pillars, ruins of war-engines, and the temporary bridge which had been thrown over, indicate that this has been the scene of direst contention. Now there is a terrible conflict on the bridge, whose insecurity accelerates the horror of the conflict. Horses, and men, and chariots, are precipitated into the raging waves. War-galleys are contending; others in flames; and others still, sinking beneath the prow of a superior foe. Smoke and flames are issuing from the falling and prostrate edifices; and along the battlements and in the blocked-up streets the conflict is dreadful indeed. The foreground is strewed with the bodies of the dead and dying. Some have fallen into the basin of a fountain, tinging the water with blood. One female is sitting in mute despair over the dead body of her son; another leaping over a battlement, to escape the grasp of a ruffian soldier; and other soldiers drag a woman by the hair down the steps, that form the pedestal of a mutilated colossal statue, whose shattered head lies on the pavement below. A barbarous enemy has conquered the city; Carnage and Destruction have asserted their frightful Empire.

The last and most impressive picture of this series is the scene of Desolation. The sun has just departed, and the moon is ascending the twilight sky over the ocean, near the place where the sun rose in the first picture. The shades of evening are gradually stealing over the shattered and ivy-grown ruins of that once great city. A lonely column rises in the foreground, on whose capital a solitary heron has built her nest, and at the foot of it her mate is standing in the water, both of them apparently conscious of being a living mockery. The Doric temple and triumphal bridge may still be identified among the ruins, which are laved by the waters of the tranquil sea. But though man and his works have perished, the steep promontory with its isolated rock, still rears itself against the sky, unmoved, unchanged. Time has consumed the works of man, and art is resolving into its elemental nature. The gorgeous pageant has passed, the roar of battle has ceased, the multitude has mingled with the dust, the Empire is extinct.

The first, second, and last of these paintings are the best of the series, not only in the poetry they portray, but in their execution. The style is more varied and natural, and has less the appearance of paint than many of the artist's later productions. As to the third and fourth paintings, the conception of both is exceedingly fine and poetical, but they are deficient in execution. The architecture is admirably done, but the numerous figures which it was necessary to introduce, are poorly drawn and arranged; and there is a feebleness in the effect.

It would be, perhaps, too much to ask that an artist should be a great painter of scenery, and also a master of the human figure. As a whole, however, the Course of Empire is a work of art worthy of any nation or any painter. These pictures were painted for the late Luman Reed, at a cost of eight thousand dollars, but are now the property of the New York Gallery, which institution owes its existence to Mr. Reed, whose collection of pictures formed the foundation thereof.

The next work to which we would call the attention of our readers is called "*The Voyage of Life.*" It is a series of four pictures, allegorically portraying the prominent features of man's life, viz: childhood, youth, manhood, and old age. The subject is one of such universal interest, that it were almost impossible to treat it in an entirely original manner, but no one can deny that the conception of the painter displays a high and rare order of poetic power.

In the first, we behold the dawn of a summer morning. A translucent stream is issuing from an unknown source, out of a deep cavern in the side of a mountain. Floating gently down the stream, is a golden boat, made of the sculptured figures of the Hours, while the prow is formed by the present hour holding forth an emblem of Time. It is filled with flowers, and on these a little child is seated, tossing them with his upraised hands, and smiling with new-born joy, as he looks upon the unnumbered beauties and glories of this bright world around him; while a guardian angel is at the helm, with his wings lovingly and protectingly extended over the child. Love, purity, and beauty emanate like incense from the sky, the earth, and water, so that the heart of the gazer seems to forget the world, and lose itself in a dream of heaven.

A few fleeting years are gone, and behold the change! The Stream of Life is widened, and its current strong and irresistible, but it flows through a country of surpassing loveliness. The voyager, who is now a youth, has taken the helm into his own hands, and the dismissed angel stands upon the shore looking at him with "a look made of all sweet accord," as if he said in his heart, "God be with thee, thoughtless mortal!" But the youth heeds not his angel, for his eyes are now riveted by an airy castle pictured against the sky, dome above dome, reaching to the very zenith. The phantom of worldly happiness and worldly ambition has absorbed the imagination and eager gaze of the wayward voyager, and as he urges his frail bark onward, he dreams not of the dangers which may await him in his way. To the boat, only a few flowers are now clinging, and on closer observation we perceive that the castle in the air, apparently so real, has only a white cloud for its foundation, and that ere long the stream makes a sudden turn, rushing with the fury of a maddened steed down a terrible ravine. The moral of the picture it is needless to elucidate.

Another change, and lo! the verge of a cataract and a fearful storm. The rudderless bark is just about to plunge into the abyss below, while the voyager (now in the prime of manhood) is imploring the only aid that can avail him in the trying hour, that of heaven. Demoniacal images are holding forth their temptations in the clouds around him, but he heeds them not. His confidence in God supports him, the previous agony of his soul is dispelled or subdued, by a reflection of immortal light stealing through the storm, and by the smiles of his guardian angel, visibly stationed in the far-off sky.

The Voyage of Life is ended, and our voyager, now white with hoary hairs, has reached that point where the waters of time and eternity mingle together—a bold conception, which is finely embodied by the daring genius of the painter. The hour-glass is gone, and the shattered bark is ready to dissolve into the fathomless waters beneath. The old man is on his knees, with clasped hands and his eyes turned heavenward, for the greenness of earth is forever departed, and a gloom is upon the ocean of eternity. But just above the form of our good voyager is hovering his angel, who is about to transport him to his home; and, as the eye wanders upward, an infinite host of heavenly ministers are seen ascending and descending the cloudy steps which lead to the bosom of God. Death is swallowed up in life, the glory of heaven has eclipsed that of the earth, and our voyager is safe in the haven of eternal rest. And thus endeth the allegory of Human Life.

With regard to the mechanical execution of these paintings, we consider them not equal to some of the earlier efforts of the same pencil. They are deficient in atmosphere, and have too much the appearance of paint. The water in the first, second, and third pictures is superior, but the perspective and atmosphere in the second are masterly. In all of them the figures are very fine, considering the difficulty of managing such peculiar characters. In the first we are pleased with the simplicity of the composition : in the second, with the variety, there being portrayed the elm of England, the plains of Tuscany, the palm of tropic climes, the mountains of Switzerland, and the oak of America; in the third, with the genius displayed in using the very storm to tell a story; and in the fourth, with the management of the shadows, and the apparent reality of the light from heaven. These pictures were painted for the late Samuel Ward of New York city, and the price received for them was six thousand dollars. During the last year, however, they were purchased by the American Art Union, and distributed among the prizes at their annual lottery in December.

Duplicates of the above paintings were executed by Cole, and sold to a gentleman in Cincinnati in the year 1846.

The last, and in many respects the most impressive, of Cole's more ambitious productions, is a series of five pictures entitled *The Cross and the World.* The designs or studies for these pictures were all executed, but owing to the untimely death of the artist, only two out of the five were ever finished on a large scale. This series of pictures constitutes a Christian poem of a high order, and in describing them, we shall employ the language of the artist's friend Noble, who has probably studied the entire work more thoroughly than any other man. The idea is that two youths enter upon a pilgrimage—one to the cross and the other to the world.

In the first picture the eye of the beholder first strikes the bold termination of a chain of mountains, with craggy peaks lost in the clouds.

The same lofty range is seen through the entire series.

To the left, a straight and narrow path takes its way up a rugged gorge, down which there beams a silvery light from a bright cross in the sky. The path at first leads off through fields of real flowers, betokening the early part of the Christian life, neither difficult nor uninviting. In the distance a dark mist, hovering over the track, conceals from the advancing wayfarer the real difficulties of his journey, and betokens the sorrows which of necessity befall him. To the right, a gracefully winding way leads down into a gently undulating and pleasant vale. Stretching forward through delightful landscapes, it finally fades away, and leaves the eye to wander on to the dim pinnacles and domes of a great city. A golden light falls through an atmosphere of repose, and lends warmth, softness, and beauty, as well to crag and precipice as to the rich valley. By-paths, serpent-like, steal up upon the sunny slopes of the mountain, inviting the traveler to the enjoyment of the prospect and the coolness of the waterfall.

Vegetation of unnatural growth, and gorgeous and unreal flowers skirt the borders of the way.

At the foot of the mountain stands Evangelist with the open Gospel. A little in advance are the waters, symbolical of Baptism.

Two youths, companions in the travel of life, having come to the parting of their road, are affectionately and earnestly directed to the shining cross. While one, through the power of truth, enters with timid steps upon his holy pilgrimage, the other, caught by the enchantment of the earthly prospect, turns his back upon Evangelist and the Cross, and speeds forward upon the pathway of the world.

In the second picture we have a wild mountain region now opening upon the beholder. It is an hour of tempest. Black clouds envelop the surrounding summits. A swollen torrent rushes by, and plunges into the abyss. The storm, sweeping down through terrific chasms, flings aside the angry cataract, and deepens the horror of the scene below. The pilgrim, now in the vigor of manhood, pursues his way on the edge of a frightful precipice. It is a moment of imminent danger. But gleams of light from the shining cross break through the storm, and shed fresh brightness along his perilous and narrow path. With steadfast look, and renewed courage, the lone traveler holds on his heavenly pilgrimage.

The whole symbolizes the trials of faith.

In the third picture the beholder looks off upon an expanse of tranquil water. On the right are the gardens of pleasure, where the devotees of sensual delights revel in all that satiates and amuses. Near a fountain, whose falling waters lull with perpetual murmurs, stands a statue of the goddess of Love. An interminable arcade, with odorous airs and delicious shade, invites to the quiet depths of a wilderness of greenery and flowers. A gay throng dances upon the yielding turf, around a tree, to the sound of lively music. Near an image of Bacchus, a company enjoys a luxurious banquet.

On the left is the Temple of Mammon, a superb and costly structure, surmounted by the wheel of Fortune. Beneath its dome, a curiously-wrought fountain throws out showers of gold, which is eagerly caught up by the votaries below.

From the great censers, rising here and there above the heads of the multitude, clouds of incense roll up and wreath the columns of the temple—a grateful odor to the God. The trees and shrubbery of the adjacent grounds are laden with golden fruit.

Far distant, in the middle of the picture, a vision of earthly power and glory rises upon the view. Splendid trophies of conquest adorn the imposing gateway; suits of armor, gorgeous banners, and the victor's wreath. Colonnades and piles of architecture stretch away in the vast perspective. At the summit of a lofty flight of steps stand conspicuous the throne and the sceptre. Suspended in the air, at the highest point of human reach, is that glittering symbol of royalty, the crown. Between the beholder and this grand spectacle are the armies in conflict, and a city in flames, indicating that the path to glory lies through ruin and the battle-field. To the contemplation of this alluring scene the Pilgrim of the World, now in the morning of manhood, is introduced. Which of the fascinating objects before him is the one of his choice, is left to the imagination of the spectator. The picture symbolizes the pleasure, the fortune, and the glory of the world.

In the fourth picture, the pilgrim, now an old man on the verge of existence, catches a first view of the boundless and eternal. The tempests of life are behind him; the world is beneath his feet. Its rocky pinnacles, just rising through the gloom, reach not up into his brightness; its sudden mists, pausing in the dark obscurity, ascend no more into his serene atmosphere. He looks out upon the infinite. Clouds—embodiments of glory, threading immensity in countless lines, rolling up from everlasting depths—carry the vision forward toward the unapproachable light. The Cross, now fully revealed, pours its effulgence over the illimitable scene. Angels from the presence, with palm and crown of immortality, appear in the distance, and advance to meet him. Lost in rapture at the sight, the pilgrim drops his staff, and with uplifted hands, sinks upon his knees.

In the last picture, desolate and broken, the pilgrim, descending a gloomy vale, pauses at last on the horrid brink that overhangs the outer darkness. Columns of the Temple of Mammon crumble; trees of the gardens of pleasure moulder on his path. Gold is as valueless as the dust with which it mingles. The phantom of glory—a baseless, hollow fabric—flits under the wing of death to vanish in a dark eternity. Demon forms are gathering around him. Horror-struck, the pilgrim lets fall his staff, and turns in despair to the long-neglected and forgotten Cross. Veiled in melancholy night, behind a peak of the mountain, it is lost to his view forever.

The above pictures are in the possession of the artist's family. We did think of describing at length *all* the imaginative productions of our great master in landscape, but upon further reflection we have concluded merely to record their titles, by way of giving our readers an idea of the versatility of Cole's genius. They are as follows:—*The Departure and Return*, which is a poetical representation of the Feudal Times, *The Cross in the Wilderness*, *Il Penseroso*, *L'Allegro*, *The Past and Present*, *The Architect's Dream*, *Dream of Arcadia*, *The Expulsion of Adam and Eve*, and *Prometheus Bound*. As the last mentioned picture is owned in England, and is unquestionably one of the wildest and most splendid efforts of the painter's pencil, we cannot refrain from a brief description. The scene represented is among the snow-covered peaks of a savage mountain land, and to the loftiest peak of all, is chained the being who gives the picture a name. Immediately in the foreground, is a pile of rocks and broken trees, which give a fine effect to the distant landscape, while, just above this foreground, is a solitary vulture slowly ascending to the upper air, to feast upon its victim. The idea of leaving the devouring scene to the imagination, could only have been conceived by the mind of the most accomplished artist. The time represented is early morning—and the cold blue ocean of the sky is studded with one brilliant star, which represents Jupiter, by whose order Prometheus was chained to the everlasting rock.

This is one of the most truly sublime pictures we have ever seen, and possesses all the qualities which constitute an epic production. The unity of the design is admirable—one figure, one prominent mountain, a cloudless sky, one lonely star, one representative of the feathery tribes, and one cluster of rocks for the foreground—and it is also completely covered with an atmosphere which gives every object before us a dreamy appearance. In point of execution we cannot possibly find a fault with this glorious picture, and we do not believe that the idea of the poet was ever better illustrated by any landscape painter.

With regard to the actual views and other less ambitious productions of Cole, we can only say that the entire number might be estimated at about one hundred. The majority of them are illustrative of European scenery, but of those which are truly American, it may be said that they give a more correct and comprehensive idea of our glorious scenery, than do the productions of any other American artist. In looking upon his better pictures of American scenery we forget the pent-up city, and our hearts flutter with a joy allied to that which we may suppose animates the woodland bird, when listening in its solitude to the hum of the wilderness. Perpetual freedom, perpetual and unalloyed happiness, seem to breathe from every object which he portrays, and as the eye wanders along the mountain declivities, or mounts still farther up on the chariot-looking clouds, as we peer into the translucent waters of his lakes and streams, or witness the solemn grandeur and gloom of his forests, we cannot but wonder at the marvelous power of genius. The style of our artist is bold and masterly. While he did not condescend to delineate every leaf and sprig which may be found in nature, yet he gave you the spirit of the scene. To do this is the province of genius, and an attainment beyond the reach of mere talent. The productions of Cole appeal to the intellect more than to the heart, and we should imagine that Milton was his favorite poet. He loved the uncommon efforts in nature, and was constantly giving birth to new ideas. He had a passion for the wild and tempestuous, and possessed an imagination of the highest order. He was also a lover of the beautiful, and occasionally executed a picture full of quiet summer-like sentiment: but his joy was to depict the scenery of our mountain land, when clothed in the rich garniture of autumn. He was the originator of a new style, and is now a most worthy member of that famous brotherhood of immortals whom we remember by the names of Lorraine, Poussin, Rosa, Wilson, and Gainsborough.

The name of Cole is one which his countrymen should not willingly let die. A man of fine, exalted genius, by his pencil he has accomplished much good, not only to his chosen art, by becoming one of its masters, but eminently so in a moral point of view. And this reminds us of the influences which may be exerted by the landscape painter. That these are of importance no one can deny. Is not painting as well the expression of thought as writing? With his pencil, if he is a wise and good man, the artist may portray, to every eye that rests upon his canvass, the loveliness of virtue and religion, or the deformity and wretchedness of a vicious life. He may warn the worldling of his folly and impending doom, and encourage the Christian in his pilgrimage to heaven. He may delineate the marvelous beauty of nature, so as to lead the mind upward to its Creator, or proclaim the ravages of time, that we may take heed to our ways and prepare ourselves for a safe departure from this world, into that beyond the Valley of the Shadow of Death. A goodly portion of all these things have been accomplished by Thomas Cole. As yet, he is the only landscape painter in this country who has attempted imaginative painting, and the success which has followed him in his career, even in a pecuniary point of view, affords great encouragement to our younger painters in this department of the art. He has set a noble example, which ought to be extensively followed. Observe, we do not mean by this that his subjects ought to be imitated. Far from it; because they are not stamped with as decided a national character, as the proproductions of all painters should be. Excepting his actual views of American scenery, the paintings of Cole might have been produced had he never set foot upon our soil. Let our young artists aspire to something above a mere copy of nature, or even a picture of the fancy; let them paint the visions of their imagination. No other country ever offered such advantages as our own. Let our young painters use their pencils to illustrate the thousand scenes, strange, wild, and beautiful, of our early history. Let them aim high, and their achievements will be distinguished. Let them remember that theirs is a noble destiny. What though ancient wisdom and modern poetry have told us that "art is long and time is fleeting!"—let them toil and persevere with nature as their guide, and they will assuredly have their reward.

POVERTY.*

And wherefore do the poor complain?
The rich man asked of me:
Come walk abroad with me, I said,
And I will answer thee.

SOUTHEY.

ATTENDED by police officers, we once paid a visit to a building called the Old Brewery, which infests the city of New York as does a cancer the bosom of a splendid woman. At the time in question, it was a very large and rickety affair, and the *home* of about *eighty pauper families;* and we verily believe contained more unalloyed suffering than could have been found in any other building in the United States. It belonged to the city, and was rented by a woman, who, in her turn, rented it out by piecemeal to the paupers. For many years it was a dram shop or a college for the education of drunkards, and it is now the comfortless hospital or dying-place of those drunkards and their descendants. We visited this spot at midnight, and were lighted on our way by torches which we carried in our hands.

Having passed through a place called Murderer's Alley (on account of the many murders committed there), our leading officer bolted into a room, where was presented the following spectacle. The room itself was more filthy than a sty. In the fireplace were a few burning embers, above which hung a kettle, tended by a woman and her daughter. It contained a single cabbage, and was all they had to eat, and the woman told us she had not tasted food for twenty-four hours. The wretched being, it appears, had been engaged in a fight with some brute of a man, who had so severely bruised her face that one whole

* The unvarnished facts contained in this article were picked up by the writer in the autumn and winter of 1847, while he had charge of the city department of the New York Daily Express.

side was literally black and blue. We asked her some questions and alluded to her young daughter. She replied to our inquiries, and then burst into tears, and wept as if her heart was broken. The only comment which the daughter made was, "Mother, what are you crying about? Don't make a fool of yourself. Tears will not wipe away God's curse." The couch to which this pair of women were to retire after their midnight meal, was a pallet of straw, wet with liquid mud that came oozing through the stone walls of the subterranean room. This woman told us that her husband was in the State prison, and that she was the mother of seven daughters, all of whom but the one present had died in girlhood, utterly abandoned to every vice. "Yes," added the woman, "and I hope that me and my Mary will soon join them; there can be no worse hell than the one we are enduring." She mourned over her unhappy fate, and looked upon vice as a matter of necessity—for they could not starve.

In the next room that we entered, on a litter of straw, and with hardly any covering upon them, lay a man and his wife, the former suffering with asthma and the latter in the last stages of consumption. Covered as they were with the most filthy rags, they looked more like reptiles than human beings. In another corner of the same room, upon a wooden box, sat a young woman with a child on her lap; the former possessing a pale and intellectual countenance, while the latter was a mere skeleton. The woman uttered not a word while we were present, but seemed to be musing in silent despair. Her history and very name were unknown, but her silence and the vacant stare of her passionless eyes spoke of unutterable sorrow. She was the "queen of a fantastic realm."

Another room that we entered contained no less than five families, and in one corner was a woman in the agonies of death, while at her side sat a miserable dog, howling a requiem over the dying wretch. In another corner lay the helpless form of a boy, about ten years of age, who was afflicted with the small-pox, and had been abandoned to his miserable fate. He had rolled off the straw, and his cheek rested upon the wet floor, which was black with filth. All the rooms we visited were pretty much alike, crowded with human beings, but there were particular ones which attracted our attention. The faded beauty and yet brilliant eye of one woman attracted our notice, and we were informed that it was only about two years ago that she was performing Juliet at one of the principal theatres to the delight of thousands. She is now an outcast, and her only possession is a ragged calico gown. In another room we noticed the living remains of a German philosopher, who was once a preacher, then a professor in the Berlin and Halle Universities, an author, a rationalist, a doctor of philosophy, and now a—pauper. He came to this country about three years ago, supposing that his learning would here find a ready market. This man is master of the Hebrew, Greek, Latin, French, and German languages, and yet a bitter reviler of the Christian religion ! He was brought to his present state by the united influences of his infidel principles and the wine cup.

In one room we saw a husband and his wife with three children, sound asleep on a bed of shavings, and the furniture thereof consisted of only a pine box, a wooden bowl (partly filled with meal), and a teacup, while on the hearth of the empty fireplace were scattered a few meatless bones. In another we saw a woman in a state of gross intoxication, whose child, wrapped in rags, was lying on a bed of *warm ashes* in one corner of the fireplace. In one room a lot of half-clothed negroes were fighting like hyenas; and in another a forlorn old man was suffering with delirium tremens. In another, still, the fireplace was destitute of fire and the hearth of wood. On the floor were three litters of straw ; on one lay the corpse of a woman and a dead infant, and another child about three years of age, which had no covering upon its shivering body except the fragments of an old cloak. On one pile of straw lay a middle-aged man apparently breathing his last; and in the opposite corner was seated a drunken woman, a stranger to the dead and dying, who was calling down curses upon the head of her husband, who had abandoned her to her misery. As we rambled about the old building, peering into the dark rooms of poverty and infamy, we were forcibly reminded of Dante's description of hell. The majority of women that we saw were widows, and we were informed that the rent they paid varied from two to six shillings per week. Our guide, before leaving, directed our attention to the back yard, where, within the last two years, twenty people had been found dead. Their histories yet remain in mystery, and we were told of the singular fact that a funeral had not been known to occur at the Old Brewery for many years, as it has ever been a market-place for anatomists and their menials.

On giving the readers of the Express some of the above facts, a number of benevolent individuals remitted to us quite a large amount of money for the inmates of the Brewery. One lady (God bless the Christian!) sent us no less than ten dollars. In fulfilling our obligations to these charitable friends, we purchased clothing, bread, pork, fish, and vegetables, and, assisted by a couple of servants, took another walk over the mansion of suffering. As we went in the day time, we expected to see less misery than we did on our former visits, but were sadly disappointed. We entered several new rooms and saw new pictures of distress. In one was a very old negro, sitting in his desolate chimney corner, with no clothing on his person but a pair of pantaloons; he was afflicted with the asthma and shivering with cold, while his poor wife was weeping over their wretched condition. When we supplied the latter with food, we thought the overjoyed being would actually clasp me in her arms. On entering another room, we discovered a mass of rags in one corner, where lay an elderly woman who had lost the use of her limbs, and had not been able to move from her couch of shavings for upwards of two months. She was evidently the victim of consumption, and not far from the gateway to the grave. Her only attendant was a kindly-disposed woman who had the dropsy. When we gave her some food, she actually wept tears of gratitude, and begged me to *accept a rug,* which she had made of rags, probably picked up in the street. In another room, before an expiring fire, sat a sickly-looking girl, about ten years of age, holding in her arms a little babe, and the countenances of both were deeply furrowed by premature suffering. Her story was that her mother had been dead about a month, and she knew not the fate of her father, who had been arrested for stealing some two weeks before. She obtained her living by begging, and when too feeble to carry her infant sister in the street, was in the habit of leaving it in her room under the protection of a miserable dog, to which she directed my attention. We gave this sadly unfortunate girl a large supply of food, and was sorely grieved that it was not in our power to take her from her cheerless dwelling place to some other home, where she might be fed, clothed, and instructed. The act of adopting such a child would cover a multitude of sins. The condition of Mr. Dickens's fancy child "Little Nell" was real happiness compared to the condition of this living and yet dying orphan. God have mercy upon the *innocent* poor!

Another room into which we entered was completely crowded with human beings. On one bed of rags and straw lay a woman who was so very ill that she could not speak, and her only covering, strange as it may seem, was a tattered *American flag*. She was a stranger to all her companions, but supposed to be the wife of a sailor, who had died some months before. Immediately in front of the fireplace, lying on her side, was a colored woman moaning with the rheumatism, and in her immediate vicinity was her husband, suffering intensely with a cold. Here sat an Irish woman on a chest, holding an infant in her arms; she was *singing* a lullaby, and yet she told me that she had not eaten a hearty meal for many weeks. There, lying in his corner, was a middle aged man, confined to the floor by an ulcerated knee, and he had in charge a feeble babe, which had never been blessed with even a calico dress—it was not only naked, but a cripple from its birth. The wife of this man was dead, and those were her dying groans which chilled my blood with horror when we made a nocturnal visit to this miserable abode. His only helper in his hour of great need was a puny boy, about seven years old, who seemed to be an idiot. The appearance of this child we cannot possibly describe. The *happiest* individual in this room was a colored man, who appeared to be in good health, but he crawled about on crutches, for he had lost both his legs. He seemed to be an exceedingly worthy and amiable man, and we were lavish in our gifts to him and those in whom he was interested.

But enough, enough. There can be no use in continuing this painful record. We would assure our readers, however, that we have only sketched a small portion of the unimagined misery which lately existed and still exists in the Old Brewery. The spectacles we have witnessed there excel the most extravagant flights of fancy; we have never read the book which contained pictures of such complete and hopeless misery. We have told a simple tale of truth, contributed our pittance, and it now remains for the opulent of the great metropolis and the rulers thereof to do their duty. Is it right that such a building as the Old Brewery should be suffered to exist within a stone's throw of the City Hall? Is it right that the "hell hounds" (we now allude to a fact) should be permitted by the authorities to sell their poisons *under the same roof* where hundreds of people are dying from starvation, brought upon them by their own folly and those very dram shops? We would not make an issue upon the license question; but, we ask, is it right, is it humane, to allow this state of things? If the aged in iniquity cannot be reclaimed, ought not something to be done to save the children of the Old Brewery—the innocent, laughter-loving children, from spending their days in misery? If nothing else can be done, it would be a mercy to fire that abode of suffering, even though every soul within its walls should perish in the flames; the wail of agony would indeed be dreadful, but it would be of short duration. Why will not the superb city of New York wipe from her bosom this lump of leprosy, which is now preying upon her vitals? Can the rich now understand why it is that the poor complain?

An Irishman, his wife, and two children were brought to the almshouse in a complete state of starvation. They landed in the city from an emigrant ship, and had not tasted food for several days. The mother was wellnigh a perfect skeleton, and the sunken cheeks and eyes of the whole family told the melancholy truth that they were the victims of the most intense suffering. One of the children was so near dead that it could not walk, whilst it was with the utmost difficulty that even the father could totter over the floor. They were as nearly dead as it is possible for the living to be, and want of food was the principal cause which had brought them to this miserable state. In answer to all questions asked them, their replies were, "We want some bread; do give us some bread; we will die if you do not give us some bread." As a matter of course their wants were immediately supplied, but the utmost caution was necessary in administering food. When they were seated at the table, the first thing the mother did was to feed her youngest child. In doing this she took not the least notice of herself, but uttered a strange wild laugh; and, when the child was made quite sick by even a spoonful of rice, the mother wept most bitterly, and said: "Oh, my child is going to die!—what shall I do to save its darling life?" Four days afterwards every member of this exiled family had passed into the unknown future.

On another occasion an intemperate woman was taken to the almshouse, ragged and reeling at the time, and bearing a little child, supposed to be about sixteen months old. It was literally a skeleton, entirely destitute of flesh, a mere fragment of humanity. The smaller portions of its arms and legs were not more than half an inch in thickness, while the corners of its mouth were drawn down, and its eyes so deeply sunken that it had the appearance of an old and decrepit woman. Its face was white as snow, its body almost as cold, and wrinkles upon its cheek and brow were distinctly marked; and what made the picture still more wretched was the fact that the poor child had the *whooping cough* and was *totally blind.* The opinion of the attending physician was that the child had been famished. On questioning the mother about her offspring it was ascertained that the child had never taken any food but what came from her breast; its condition was partly attributed to this fact, and it was evident that all its sufferings were inherited from its mother; that *it had been a drunkard even from the hour of its birth.* It was found necessary to take the child away from its mother; but, as she would not give it up, she was taken to the Tombs, and at midnight, when the parent was in a deep sleep, the child was taken from her filthy and inflamed bosom, and placed in the hands of a careful nurse. The weeping and wailing of that forsaken mother, on the following morning, were terrible in the extreme. Her brain was on fire, and at the setting of the sun she was numbered with the dead. In less than a week thereafter the pauper child had followed its mother to Potter's Field.

It was recorded in the newspapers that the dead body of an aged man had been found, tied up in a coffee bag, and floating in the East river. His throat was cut from ear to ear, and it was supposed he had been murdered, but later developments explained the mystery.

The name of the deceased was subsequently ascertained; he belonged to one of the oldest and most respectable families of Connecticut, and was related to one of its former governors. The individual in question spent the morning and noon of his life in the lap of luxury; in old age, however, his wealth, wife, children, and nearly all his kindred, were taken away from him, and he became a man acquainted with many sorrows. Some months previous to the time when his body was found, and while actually suffering from hunger, it so happened that he entered a certain dwelling for the purpose of asking alms. The principal inmate of that dwelling was a widow who had once been on the most intimate terms with the family of the beggar, having been born in the same town. The friends of other days recognized each other, a long conversation ensued, which recalled a thousand recollections of childhood, and they were very happy. The only thought which oppressed the spirit of the mendicant was, that his bones, when he came to die, would be deposited in the soil of strangers, and his only prayer was that he might be buried among his kindred. His kind friend assured him that, if her own life was spared, the desire of his heart should be fully gratified.

Weeks passed on, and, contrary to the wishes of his friend, the old man became an inmate of the almshouse. In process of time the silver cord of the pilgrim's life was broken, and he was buried in the public graveyard. Subsequently to this his body was disinterred, used for purposes of dissection, and rudely thrown into the river. In the meanwhile the widow had sent to the coroner to inquire how she might obtain the pauper's body, as she wished to bury him elsewhere than in Potter's Field, but she could meet with no encouragement. A number of days was the man's body tossed to and fro in the East River, but by the hand of Providence it was washed ashore and given in charge to the coroner. This gentleman suspected that the deceased was the friend of the widow who had consulted him some days before, and it so happened that his suspicions were well founded, for the body in due time was recognized. It was given into the custody of the good woman, who had it placed in a decent coffin, and the aged pauper was buried in the vault of the W———, in Connecticut, by the side of his wife and children. It is indeed a fact that fiction is often not one-half so strange as truth; and it is also certain that human life is but a dream, and the ways of God unsearchable.

Beautiful were the orphan minstrels of whom we are now to speak; beautiful in mind and heart. The party was composed of three individuals, two sisters and a little brother, the eldest of whom had not yet seen her thirteenth summer. Remarkable singers they were not, but yet there was something wild and plaintive in their voices which cannot easily be forgotten. The instruments they used, however—the harp, the tamborin, and flute—were uncommonly musical, and played upon with facility and taste.

We became acquainted with these minstrels in this wise. They had stopped for a few moments, about nine o'clock in the evening, in the hall of Rathbun's hotel. After delighting a crowd of listeners, and receiving a few pennies, they courtesied and bowed, and then continued on their way. We had an hour's leisure at the time, and resolved as a matter of curiosity, that we would follow the children. We did so; and saw them enter two or three hotels, where they performed a number of pieces. The night was now far advanced, and they turned Barclay Street on their way home. Onward did they trip, with gladness in their hearts, talking together in the French tongue; and, in a few moments after, we saw them turn down Washington street into an emigrant boarding house. We were now in a predicament, and afraid to lose our game. But resolving to defend our conduct by inquiring after some imaginary person, we bolted into the house and followed the children up two flights of stairs. They entered a room where were seated a very old man and an equally old woman. The meeting between this aged pair and the little children was quite touching, for, when the money was counted and laid away, the latter were rewarded by a loving embrace. Soon as this scene was ended we made our appearance, and introduced ourselves by asking the intended question. This having been promptly and politely answered, we proceeded a little further in our queries, and obtained the following information: The senior members of this family were the grandparents of the children, and their only relatives in the world. The old man said they were all natives of France; that they had been in this country four months; and that their only support was derived from the *unwearied labors of the minstrel children.* As the old man told his story his eyes were filled with tears; he was mourning over his own helplessness, and yet rejoicing over the *living blessings* of his old age. Having apologized for my rudeness, and uttered what I thought would be a word of comfort, we bade each member of the family a kind good night, and left them to obtain the repose they needed, and to dream perchance of church bells ringing in one of the beautiful valleys of their native land.

We happened to be out at an unusually late hour on a certain night, and while on our way home witnessed the following picture. In passing one of the more splendid mansions in the upper part of Broadway our attention was attracted by a singular looking object, which we thought was attempting to effect an entrance into the house. Curiosity led us to draw near, when we beheld a group of three little girls nestled in the corner of the marble doorway. One of them appeared to be about twelve years of age, and the other two had perhaps seen seven and nine years. The former was seated in the Turkish fashion on the coarse matting, apparently half asleep, whilst the heads of the other two were pillowed on her lap, and both evidently enjoying a dream of peace and comfort. As we remembered the sumptuous and fashionable entertainment in which we had just participated, and reflected upon the picture before us, we were almost disposed to doubt the evidence of our senses. It was already past midnight, and the sleet which beat upon our head assured us that we ought to make an effort to relieve the vagrant children from their miserable condition, for they were almost naked and barefooted.

After some difficulty we found a watchman, when we awoke the children and asked them about their home. They reluctantly told us where their parents resided, and it was with the utmost difficulty that we could induce them to accompany us. We succeeded, however, in taking them *home,* which was a comfortless dwelling with one room, where we witnessed the following spectacle. On a bed of straw lay the father of these children in a state of senseless intoxication, and on the bare floor in another corner of the room was the mother, moaning with pain, and bleeding from wounds which had been inflicted by her cruel husband. One of the little girls told us they had not eaten as much food as they wanted for ten days, that they had been forced into the street for the purpose of begging, and that the scene before us was an old story to them. My opulent and happy readers, it is probable, can scarcely believe that such things actually exist in the Christian city of New York; but what we assert is as true as the fact, that the scourge intemperance is annually destroying some thirty thousand souls in our land alone.

This allusion to intemperance reminds me of another melancholy picture, which we once witnessed in the great emporium. We had been enjoying a walk among the shipping in South street, when we discovered, partly hidden from view by a pile of casks and boxes, a man and two guardian angels. It was the insensible form of a poor drunkard, lying on the ground, and at his side two little girls, one of whom looked upon me with a most wo-begone expression of countenance, while the pale temples of the other were resting on the bloated bosom of the man. He was their father, and they were motherless.

We once visited the Children's Hospital connected with the Almshouse of New York, and the spectacles we there witnessed were even more touching than those connected with the Old Brewery. The entire building (which is on Blackwell's Island) contained over one hundred children, about one-half of whom were so ill as to be confined to their beds, and it is the room where these were harbored to which we now allude. The beds were arranged along the walls, about three feet apart, and each end of every bed or cot was occupied by a sick child. The majority of them were motherless and fatherless, and entirely dependent upon strangers for those kind and delicate attentions which commonly smooth the pathway to the grave. Some of them were the offspring of intemperate parents, now confined in the State Prison; while many of them had not even inherited a name. Not one of the whole number but presented a feeble and haggard appearance, and the pains of many were intense, for their mingled moans actually fills the room with a heart-sickening chorus. One poor little thing, about three years of age, was sitting in its bed, eating a dry crust of bread, to satisfy a morbid appetite, and the disease which preyed upon the vitals of this child was consumption in its most ghastly form. Hollow and wrinkled were its cheeks, eyes large and deeply sunken, and, while looked upon, hot tears trickled upon its pillow. In the same bed was another of these unhappy children, dying from the terrible malady of scrofula. It had been a cripple from its birth, and could hardly be recognized as a human being. We caught a glimpse of the creature's countenance as it slumbered, and was positively startled by its surpassing beauty. It was as bright and spiritual as the light of a star. It was certain, however, that death had marked it for the grave, and we remembered the poet's words:—

> "The good die first,
> And they, whose hearts are dry as summer dust,
> Burn to the socket."—WORDSWORTH.

This deformed but yet lovely fragment of humanity had been picked up as a foundling, and was without a name. Another child which attracted my attention, though only about twelve years of age, had the appearance of being thirty. She had been brought from an emigrant ship, suffering with fever associated with bronchitis. She had a finely developed head, a beautiful and highly intellectual face, but it was deeply marked with the lines of suffering, and her cheeks were flushed with the hue of approaching death. She was also troubled with a hollow cough, and her body was a mere skeleton. The attending physician patted her upon the head and asked her how she felt to-day; when she looked up with a smile, "made of all sweet accord," and answered: "I am going to die, doctor. Tell them to have my coffin ready; and, dear doctor, will they not bury me by the side of my mother and little sister, in that place you call Potter's Field?" Who now can ask the question: "And wherefore do the poor complain?"

Four Irishmen, all afflicted with the ship fever, had landed from an emigrant ship in the city of New York. The party consisted of a father and three sons. They were friendless and without money. In the company of three hundred beings, as miserable as themselves, had they landed in the city, and, in the confusion attendant upon the discharge of the ship, it so happened that they were separated, and the father knew not the fate of the sons, nor the sons the fate of the father.

A number of weeks elapsed, when the elder brother of this family called upon the commissioner of the almshouse, praying for assistance that he might find his relatives, if yet in the land of the living. The story that he told of his own sufferings since his arrival was most melancholy; for he had been living the life of a sick vagrant, in and about the Tombs. The commissioner took pity upon him and gave him all the assistance he desired, and the pauper, with a guide, started upon the hunting expedition. The first place they visited was the New York Hospital, where it was ascertained the second brother had died of the loathsome ship fever, and whence his remains had been taken to Potter's Field. They next went to the Bellevue Hospital, and heard precisely the same story with regard to the third brother. They also visited the Lunatic Asylum, where it was ascertained that the father had been confined as a raving maniac, but had paid the debt of nature, and was now a resider in the city of the dead. As to the feelings of the forlorn man, who had thus been stripped of every tie which bound him to the earth, I cannot attempt to describe them. His only prayer was that one little spot of earth might be granted to him, where he might rebury his dead relatives, provided their bodies could be recognized, and where his own ashes might be deposited after his race was run. The commissioner promised to do all in his power to bring out this result, and in less than one week *the pauper's prayer was answered!*

It was an emigrant ship, and when boarded by a New York pilot he was informed that she had left England with two hundred poverty-stricken passengers, some twenty-five of whom had died on the passage, and been buried in the deep. Among the departed were a father and mother, who had left behind them a little girl nine years old. Desolate indeed was her lot before she became an orphan; but when the "silver cord" which bound her to her parents was broken, her condition became more deplorable than ever; and, as the ship glided into the noble bay of New York, the child was also numbered with the dead—none knowing whence she came, none knowing even her baptismal name.

In due time the ship was safely moored, and, while the usual discharging bustle was going on, an almshouse coffin was sent for, into which the pauper child was placed (with her ragged clothes carefully tucked round her body), and then given into the charge of the almshouse sextons. Not one tear was shed as they mounted the hearse, and not one word of regret or sorrow was uttered by the multitude around as the sextons started for Potter's Field.

Long was the way to the crowded city of the dead. The sextons were in a merry mood, and, as their carriage rattled over the stony streets, they cracked their jokes and laughed as if going to a wedding instead of the tomb. But how could these men be blamed? They were following their vocation and receiving liberal pay. Once in a while, however, a troublesome thought seemed to pass their minds, but it was only when fearful that they might lose their dinner on account of the great number of paupers who were to be buried before the coming on of night. They hurried by a school-house, before which a flock of little girls were playing and laughing in their glee, but these happy children thought not upon the sister spirit whose remains were going to the grave. Onward rattled the hearse, and after turning the corner of a street it came to a halt, and the senior sexton stepped into his house for a drink of water. A number of laughing children met him at the door, and after he had satisfied his thirst he gave each one of them a kiss, and again, in a jovial mood, started for the public grave-yard. Another mile and the hearse reached the margin of the East River, where the Potter's Field boat was in waiting, managed by the keeper of the field. Carelessly was the coffin transferred from the hearse to the boat, and the journey of the dead was continued. The boat was now moored at the landing place on Randall's Island, where the coffin was taken away on a man's shoulder, and deposited in a deep trench covered with a few shovels full of sand, and lying in the midst of a multitude of unknown dead from every nation on the globe. And thus endeth the story of the pauper child, who crossed the ocean only to find a grave *in a land she never saw, and where the very name she bore is utterly unknown.*

It was the twilight hour, and we saw an old and deformed woman standing in front of St. Paul's, asking alms. We happened to be in the mood just then, and tarried for a few moments to watch the charity of the world. Many, in the passing tide of human life, were to us unknown, but of the few that we recognized the following attracted our particular attention :

First came a gentleman whom we knew to be a merchant of great wealth ; and, as he approached the beggar, we surely thought that he would listen to her petition. But no—he was thinking of his last importation, or the sum total of his rents, and he passed on with these words as a donation : "You must go to the poor-house, my good woman." We thought upon the days of darkness.

Then came a scholar-like looking young man, whom we knew to be a struggler with poverty; but he approached the beggar with a smile upon his countenance, dropped a shilling into her withered hand, called for God's blessing to rest upon her head, and resumed his way. My fancy now wandered to that blessed region where ever floweth the river of life.

Next came an intemperate and selfish man. When the imploring look of the cripple met his own, he coolly frowned upon her, uttered a wicked curse, and reeled onward to a hall of sinful revelry. And now we pondered on the worm that never dieth.

Finally came a little flock of boys and girls, returning from school. The woman smiled upon them, but spoke not a single word. The children knew her to be a beggar, and paused to talk with her a moment. She told them briefly the story of her life, and they were melted to tears. All the pennies that the children could raise were given to the woman; and each child, with an immortal jewel in its heart, passed on its way to receive a shower of kisses from its fond parents. And now our mind reveled in a dream of heaven-born loveliness.

And now, by way of giving our readers an idea of *self-inflicted* poverty, we will furnish them with a brief sketch of an old miser residing in the Empire city:

He is an old man—a very old man; he is also a strange man—a very strange man; whose history and name are alike unknown. His business is that of a paper scavenger, and the spoil which he collects in his journeying about the city he disposes of at the rate of one cent per pound. Many pounds does he often gather in a single day; but, as it only costs him four shillings per week to live, it is certain he lays up a few shillings at the close of every day. He commences his daily business in the down-town streets even when the day is breaking, and continues at his monotonous employment until the dark hours. He never goes home to dinner, but, when hungry, generally purchases a dry crust of bread, and eats it sitting upon the lower steps of the Custom-house or the City Hall. Never does he utter a word to a living soul; and when the stranger looks upon him he feels disposed to exclaim, "what a poor miserable being!" He is, indeed, a pitiable object to look upon, for his leather clothes are glossy and hard with the accumulated filth of many years, and his countenance is furrowed all over with deep wrinkles which no one could believe were ever moistened with a tear. He is a hard-visaged man, repulsive and even terrible to look upon. For fifteen years have we known this singular being, and "even then he was so old he seems not older now." There are people in this great city who have been familiar with his form for upwards of twenty years, and they affirm that he has been a paper scavenger during all that time. At all times, when the winds of winter howl through the streets, and also when the dog-star reigns, does he pursue his laborious and degrading employment.

And now, that I have introduced my hero to the reader, it is meet that we should mention what we know of his actual condition. He is a miser—a narrow-minded and mean miser, who can count his dollars by tens of thousands. If the reader doubts my word, let him, when next he meets the miserable man in the public highway, ask him the time of day, and he will be promptly answered, on the authority of a superb gold watch, hidden in his filthy vestments. A dry crust of bread, and a cast-off bone constitute his daily food, and yet this man carries the deeds in his pocket which prove him to be the proprietor of at least five handsome dwelling houses, located in a fashionable part of the city; certificates of bank stock and other valuable papers are also hidden in his pockets. He is a widower, but the father of an only daughter, whom he has established over a superbly furnished house as the sole mistress and only tenant. She has all she needs in the way of household things, and every luxury of the season, and, though her servants may prepare a sumptuous feast, none participate with her in its enjoyment. Though it would add to her happiness on such occasion to call in a neighboring friend, yet the privilege of giving an invitation is denied by her father in the most positive and imperative manner. In the rear of this daughter's dwelling is located a rickety shell of a cabin, resembling more the appearance of a sty than a human habitation, and this is the only dwelling-place of our miser; and here he spends the precious hours of his leisure life, counting his gold and examining the signatures of his deeds by the light which rests upon his oaken table, and seldom is it extinguished until after the hour of midnight; and when exhausted with his strange vigils, carefully does he fasten, with heavy iron bolts, the door of his den, and sink to sleep upon his bed of rags.

THE FATAL VALENTINE.

Mary Marlowe was a beautiful girl, and the only child of devoted parents. Her father was a merchant in moderate circumstances, and resided in one of the more secluded streets of the great emporium of our land. The society to which they belonged was of the highest respectability, but the life led by each member of this family was distinguished for its peacefulness.

All the young men who were acquainted with the only daughter, were charmed by her accomplished mind, personal beauty, and the sweetness of her voice. But among those who aspired to win her hand and heart, was one who had been received as an accepted lover. The parties were worthy of each other, and the love which was daily uniting them almost into one being, was eminently refined and pure. Charming beyond compare were the scenes which the lover was constantly picturing to his mind, but the smiles of his lady constituted the sunlight of every scene; and she, too, cherished many a vision of unalloyed happiness, and the thought never entered her mind that the world contained a single cloud that could possibly cast a shadow over her heart. Like a young and vigorous tree of the forest, the young man stood among his fellows; and like a flower in a remote dell dwelt the heroine of our story, in her quiet home.

It was the evening of St. Valentine's Day, and Mary Marlowe was seated before a comfortable fire; now thoughtfully peering into the glowing grate, and anon enjoying some of the fine passages of her favorite authors. Her father was absent from home on some charitable errand, while her mother and a country cousin, who was making her a winter visit, were spending the evening with a neighboring family. And it so happened, too, that Mary's lover was absent from the city, so the beautiful damsel was entirely alone. Yes, she was indeed alone, but far from being in a lonely mood, for her thoughts were with her lover, and she amused herself by dwelling upon the treasures of her newly-discovered ideal world.

But now the damsel is startled by the sudden ringing of the street door bell, and the servant presently makes his appearance in the parlor with a note addressed to Mary Marlowe. She recognizes the handwriting—it is from her lover, and quickly does she fix herself comfortably in the old arm-chair to enjoy the anticipated luxury. She opens the letter, and reads as follows:—

"MY DEAR MARY—You are indeed dear to me, but at the same time I think you are a cold-hearted girl, and I fear that you possess a timid and bashful disposition, which would never be reconciled to my sterner nature. In view of this deeply-rooted belief, I have conceived the idea of bringing our intimacy of half a year to an immediate close. And what more appropriate season could be selected for our separation than the present, when, as I doubt not, you are well-nigh overwhelmed with the missives of St. Valentine, and can, in a moment, select a worthy lover from the many who have sought your hand? And now that I may be in the fashion, I subscribe myself,

YOUR FRIEND AND VALENTINE."

The cruel arrow has pierced the maiden's heart, and by the calm despair now resting on her brow, we tremble for her fate. Tears come not to her relief—the crimson current in her veins has ceased to flow, and she falls into the hollow of her chair in a deep swoon. And now she is visited by a dream, and if we are to believe the story of her countenance, strange and fearful must be the character of that dream.

* * * * * * *

It is now ten o'clock; the family have all returned, and our Mary has recovered from her swoon. Laughingly does her mother talk to her about her housekeeping duties, for her drooping eyelids intimate the idea that she has enjoyed a comfortable nap. To this a pleasant reply is returned, accompanied with a kiss for all present, but none, save our poor Mary, can see the heavy cloud brooding upon the household. A few moments more, and the family have all retired to their several apartments, and the house is shrouded in silence.

As usual, Mary and her cousin are to occupy the same bed, and the latter, being uncommonly drowsy, is soon lost in a sweet slumber. And now let us watch with care the movements of her companion, who, when last noticed by the sleeper, was poring over the pages of her Bible. Noiselessly do her footsteps fall upon the carpet, as she goes to a closet for a small vial, which she examines, and then places upon her dressing-case. Drawer after drawer is opened, and on one or two chairs are displayed the various articles which compose the dress of a bride. And now the lady retires to her bath, and then comes forth with a ruddy glow upon her cheek; her flowing hair is bound into its beautiful folds, and in a short time she stands before her mirror decked in spotless white, as if for a virgin festival. What does all this mean? Alas! our Mary is "the queen of a fantastic realm."

But, lo! another change. The lamp has been extinguished, and our Mary is upon her knees at prayer, with her hands closely clasped, and her full liquid eyes turned heavenward. The mellow moonlight steals sweetly through the open curtains, adding an unwonted brightness, as it were, to the figure of the praying girl. Not a sound is there to break the holy silence of the place—no sound save the almost inaudible words of this strange prayer:—

"Father in heaven, I cannot understand the decree of thy Providence, but I submit to thy dispensation without a murmur. I knew that in my womanly idolatry I was forgetting thee, and I now beseech thee, in thine infinite love, to have mercy upon me, and wash my soul from every transgression. Have mercy also, O God, upon him who has broken my heart; comfort my parents in their declining years, and answer my prayer through the merits of thy Son, the Redeemer of the world. I come to dwell with Thee, if thou wilt receive me to thy bosom. Amen and Amen."

* * * * * * *

Morning dawned, and the pleasant sunshine was flooding the world with beauty. Our Mary's cousin was the first to awaken from slumber, when she encircled her bedfellow with her arms, and imprinted an affectionate kiss upon her lips; one moment more, and she was petrified with horror—for Mary Marlowe was numbered with the dead.

On the third day after that of St. Valentine, the lover of the unhappy suicide returned to the city. He found not his beloved in the pleasant parlor of her father, but a sleeper in the voiceless and desolate tomb. The fatal valentine was found and submitted to his inspection. He avowed his utter ignorance of it, and having fallen into a settled melancholy, is now a raving maniac. As to the thoughtless and wicked man who wrote the foolish valentine, his name and purpose are alike unknown.

NOTE.—The prominent features of this incident actually occurred in the city of New York in February, 1847.

INDIAN LEGENDS.

NOTE PRELIMINARY.

THE following romantic but authentic legends have been collected by the writer from a variety of sources, and are now presented to the public as an addition to the aboriginal lore, already published in his several books of travel.

INDIAN LEGENDS.

THE SHOOTING METEORS.

Among the Indians who live upon the north-eastern shore of Lake Huron, a remnant of the Iroquois, it is believed that the heavens contain only four meteors which have the power of shooting through the sky. It is thought they severally occupy the four quarters of the compass, and that they never perform their arrowy journey excepting for the purpose of warning the Huron Indians of approaching war. The meteors in question, or Pun gung-nung, are recognized by their peculiar brilliancy, and universally considered the Manitoes or guardian spirits of the entire Indian race. They came into existence at the same period of time which witnessed the creation of Lake Huron itself, and the legend which accounts for their origin is distinguished for the wild and romantic fancies of the aborigines. I obtained it from a chief named *On qwa-sug*, or Floating Wood.

It was the winter time, and an Indian with his wife and two children, a daughter and a son, were living in a wigwam on a bleak peninsula of the Great Lake. The game of that section of country had nearly all disappeared, and the fish were spending the season in such deep water, that it was quite impossible to secure any of them for food. Everything seemed to go wrong with the poverty-stricken Indian, and he was constantly troubled with the fear that the Master of Life intended to annihilate his family and himself by starvation. He expressed his anxiety to his wife, and was surprised to hear her answer him with a song.

Nearly half a moon had passed away, and the sufferings of this unfortunate family were melancholy in the extreme. Whole days did the father spend roaming through the forests, with his bow and arrows, and on four several evenings had he returned without even a pair of tiny snow-birds for a supper. The ill-luck which attended him in his expeditions made him very miserable, but he was frequently astonished and alarmed, on such occasions, by the conduct of his wife and children. When he gave them an account of his ill-luck in obtaining game, instead of manifesting any anxiety, they usually ran about the wigwam with their fingers on their mouths, and uttering a singular moan. He noticed with fear that they were becoming greatly emaciated for the want of food. So deeply grieved was the poor man, that he almost resolved to bury himself in the snow and die. He made a better resolution and again went out to hunt.

On one occasion he had wandered into the woods to an unusual distance, and, as fortune would have it, was successful in finding and shooting a single rabbit. With the speed of a deer did he return to his cabin (with his braided shoes over the crusted snow), but he now met with a new disappointment. On entering his lodge he found the fire entirely out, and the simple utensils for cooking all scattered about in great confusion; but what was far more melancholy, his wife and children were gone, and he knew not where to find them. The more he thought upon what had happened for many days past, the more bewildered did he become. He threw down his game almost in despair, and hurried out of his cabin in search of his missing family. He looked in every direction, but could see no signs of their appearing, and the only noise that he could possibly hear was a singular and most doleful moan, resembling the wail of a loon, which seemed to come from the upper air. By a natural instinct he raised his eyes towards the heavens, and beheld perched upon the dry limb of a tall tree which stood a short distance off, all the members of his family. He shouted with delight at the unexpected spectacle, and, rushing towards the tree, told his wife and children that they must come down, for he had killed a rabbit and they would now have a good feast. But again was he astonished to find his words unheeded. Again did he beseech them to come down, but they replied not a single word, and looked upon him with eyes that seemed made of fire. And what was still more wonderful it was evident that they had thrown aside their beaver and deerskin dresses, and were now decked out in newly fashioned robes made of the fur of the white fisher and the white fox. All this was utterly inexplicable, and the poor husband re-entered his lodge, bewildered and perplexed to a marvelous degree.

Then it was that the idea entered his head that he would try an experiment, by appealing to the hunger of his obstinate wife and children. He therefore cleaned the rabbit and boiled a sweet soup which he carried out, and with which he endeavored to allure his friends to the earth. But this attempt was all in vain. The mother and her children expressed no desire for the food, and still remained upon the tree, swaying to and fro like a flock of large birds. Again in his wretchedness was he about to destroy himself, but he took the precaution to appropriate the soup to its legitimate purpose. Soon as this business was accomplished, he relapsed into his former state of melancholy, from which he was suddenly aroused by the moans of his wife, which he was sure had an articulate tone. Again was he riveted to his standing place under the magic tree, and from the moaning of his wife he gathered the following intelligence. She told him that the Master of Life had fallen in love with her and her two children, and had therefore transformed them all into spirits, with a view of preparing them for a home in the sky. She also told him that they would not depart for their future home until the coming spring, but would in the meantime roam in distant countries till the time of his own transportation should arrive. Having finished her communication, she and her children immediately commenced a song, which resembled the distant winds, when they all rose gracefully from the tree, and leaning forward upon the air, darted away across the lake toward the remote South.

A cheerless and forlorn moon did the poor Indian spend in his lonely lodge on the margin of the Great Lake. Spring came, and just as the last vestige of snow had melted from the woods, and at the quiet evening hour, his spirit-wife again made her appearance, accompanied by her two children. She told her husband that he might become a spirit by eating a certain berry. He was delighted with the idea, and, complying with her advice, he suddenly became transformed into a spirit, and having flown to the side of his wife and children, the party gradually began to ascend into the air, when the Master of Life thought proper to change them into a family of Shooting Stars. He allotted to each a particular division of the heavens, and commanded them to remain there forever, as the guardians of the great nation of Lake Huron.

THE MAIDEN OF THE MOON.

The following legend was obtained from the lips of a Chippeway woman named Penaqua, or the Female Pheasant, and I hardly know which to admire most, the simple beauty of the plot, or the graphic and unique manner of the narrative, of which, I regret to say, I can hardly give a faithful translation.

Among the rivers of the North, none can boast of more numerous charms than the St. Louis, and the fairest spot of the earth which it waters is that where now stands the trading post of Fond du lac. Upon this spot, many summers ago, there lived a Chippeway chief and his wife, who were the parents of an only daughter. Her name was Weesh—Ko-da-e-mire, or the Sweet Strawberry, and she was acknowledged to be the most beautiful maiden of her nation. Her voice was like that of the turtle-dove, and the red deer was not more graceful and sprightly in its form. Her eyes were brilliant as the star of the northern sky, which guides the hunter through the wilderness, and her dark hair clustered around her neck like grape vines around the trunk of the tree they loved. The young men of every nation had striven to win her heart, but she smiled upon none. Curious presents were sent to her from the four quarters of the world, but she received them not. Seldom did she deign to reply to the many warriors who entered her father's lodge, and when she did, it was only to assure them that while upon earth she would never change her condition. Her strange conduct astonished them, but did not subdue their affection. Many and noble were the deeds they performed, not only in winning the white plumes of the eagle, but in hunting the elk and the black bear. But all their exploits availed them nothing, for the heart of the beautiful girl was still untouched.

The snows of winter were all gone, and the pleasant winds of spring were blowing over the land. The time for making sugar had arrived, though the men had not yet returned from the remote hunting grounds, and in the maple forests bright fires were burning, and the fragrance of the sweet sap filled all the air. The ringing laugh of childhood and the mature song of women were heard in the valley, but in no part of the wilderness could be found more happiness than on the banks of the St. Louis. But the Sweet Strawberry mingled with the young men and maidens of her tribe in a thoughtful mood and with downcast eyes. She was evidently bowed down by some mysterious grief, but she neglected not her duties; and though she spent much of her time alone, her buchère-bucket was as frequently filled with the sugar juice as any of her companions.

Such was the condition of affairs when a party of young warriors from the far North came upon a frolic to the St. Louis River. Having seen the many handsome maidens of this region, the strangers became enamored of their charms, and each one succeeded in obtaining the love of a maiden, who was to become his bride during the marrying season of summer.

The warriors had heard of the Sweet Strawberry, but, neglected by all of them, she was still doomed to remain alone. She witnessed the happiness of her old playmates, and, wondering at her own strange fate, spent much of her time in solitude. She even became so unhappy and bewildered that she heeded not the tender words of her mother, and from that time the music of her voice was never heard.

The sugar making season was now rapidly passing away, but the brow of the Sweet Strawberry was still overshadowed with grief. Everything was done to restore her to her wonted cheerfulness, but she remained unchanged. Wild ducks in innumerable numbers arrived with every southern wind, and settled upon the surrounding waters, and proceeded to build their nests in pairs, and the Indian maiden sighed over her mysterious doom. On one occasion she espied a cluster of early spring flowers peering above the dry leaves of the forest, and, strange to say, even these were separated into pairs, and seemed to be wooing each other in love. All things whispered to her of love, the happiness of her companions, the birds of the air, and the flowers. She looked into her heart, and, inwardly praying for a companion whom she might love, the Master of Life took pity upon her lot and answered her prayer.

17

It was now the twilight hour, and in the maple woods the Indian boys were watching their fires, and the women were bringing in the sap from the surrounding trees. The time for making sugar was almost gone, and the well-filled mokucks, which might be seen in all the wigwams, testified that the yield had been abundant. The hearts of the old women beat in thankfulness, and the young men and maidens were already beginning to anticipate the pleasures of wedded life and those associated with the sweet summer time. But the brow of the Sweet Strawberry continued to droop, and her friends looked upon her as the victim of a settled melancholy. Her duties, however, were performed without a murmur, and so continued to be performed until the trees refused to fill her buchère-bucket with sap, when she stole away from the sugar camp and wandered to a retired place to muse upon her sorrows. Her unaccountable grief was very bitter, but did not long endure; for, as she stood gazing upon the sky, the moon ascended above the hills and filled her soul with a joy she had never felt before. The longer she looked upon the brilliant object, the more deeply in love did she become with its celestial charms, and she burst forth into a song—a loud, wild, and joyous song. Her musical voice echoed through the woods, and her friends hastened to ascertain the cause. They gathered around her in crowds, but she heeded them not. They wondered at the wildness of her words, and the airy-like appearance of her form. They were spell-bound by the scene before them, but their astonishment knew no limits when they saw her gradually ascend from the earth into the air, where she disappeared, as if borne upward by the evening wind. And then it was that they discovered her clasped in the embraces of the moon, for they knew that the spots which they saw within the circle of that planet were those of her robe, which she had made from the skins of the spotted fawn.

Many summers have passed away since the Sweet Strawberry became the Maiden of the Moon, yet among all the people of her nation is she ever remembered for her beauty and the mystery of her being.

THE GHOSTLY MAN-EATER.

THERE is an idea existing among the Chippeway Indians, which corroborates a statement made by the early travelers on this continent relative to the belief that there once existed among the aboriginal tribes, a species of vampire, or ghostly man-eater. The Chippeways do not assert that there ever lived more than one of these unearthly beings; but they pretend that such an one did, and does exist, and that he has his residence upon an island in the centre of Lake Superior —which island can never be seen by mortal man, excepting when darkness has settled upon the world. The stories they relate of his appearance and deeds, are horrible in the extreme, and resemble much the creations of a mind suffering under the influence of the nightmare. For example, they describe this monster as possessing the material appearance of the human form—but of such a nature as not to be susceptible to the touch. He is said to have the body of a serpent, with human legs and arms—all supplied with immense nails, which he employs for the double purpose of digging up the earth, and dissecting the bodies upon which he feeds; his head is like that of the wolf, and his teeth of a peculiar sharpness.

The deeds which he performs are worthy of his personal appearance —and some of them are as follows: When the Indian mother, during a long journey, has lost her infant child, and placed it on the rude scaffold, that she may return to it at some future day, the Ghostly Man-Eater only waits until she is fairly out of his sight, and then proceeds to the sacred place, and feasts himself upon the tender flesh and blood of his victim. And therefore it is, that the traveler sometimes sees, in the remote wilderness, fragments of human bones scattered on the ground, as if a wolf had been suddenly interrupted, while devouring his prey. But the Man-Eater sometimes enters the house, or half-buried receptacle of the dead; and, after digging his way to the decaying body, coils himself up, as if in delight, and gluts his appetite with the unholy food. How it is that he travels, with lightning speed, from one distant place to another, has never been ascertained; but the strange sounds which the Indian occasionally hears, high in the air above his wigwam, is thought to be the song of the Man-Eater, as he hurries upon the wings of the wind, from a recent banquet, to his mysterious island on the lake.

But I once heard a legend in the Chippeway country, which accounted for the origin of the man-eating monster—and I now record it in the English tongue, for the benefit of those who feel an interest in the mythology of the Indian, and the peculiarities of his mind. The individual from whom I obtained this story was named Ka-yon-kee-me, or the Swift Arrow; and his words, as near as we can remember them, were as follows:—

I ask the white man to listen. At an early period in the history of the world, an old Indian hunter and a little boy who was his grandson, lived in an isolated cabin on the north shore of Lake Superior. They were the only remnants of a once powerful tribe of Indians, whose name is not now remembered. It was the middle of a long and dreary winter, and the entire country was covered with snow, to the height of the tallest wigwam. The section of country where resided the hunter and child was particularly desolate, and destitute of almost every species of game; and whilst the former was too feeble to wander far, after the necessary food, the latter was too young and inexperienced. The very wood which the unequal pair collected to keep them warm, was brought to their cabin with the greatest difficulty; and the thought occasionally entered the old man's mind, that the Great Spirit was about to give him up to the pains of starvation. He uttered not a murmur, however; but, as he reflected upon his impending fate, he bit his lips with a scornful smile.

One, two, and three days had passed away and the old man, as well as the child, had not tasted a particle of food. But, on the evening of the fourth day, the boy came tottering into the comfortless lodge and threw at the feet of his grandfather the lifeless body of a white-partridge, which he had fortunately killed with his own arrow. Immediately was the bird divested of its feathers—and, while yet its very blood was warm, it was devoured by the starving man and child.—Sweet was the slumber of the noble boy on that night—but, as the story goes, that aged man was visited by a dreadful dream at the same time, which made him a maniac.

Another day was nearly gone, and the unhappy pair were standing in front of their wigwam watching the western sky, as the sun enlivened it with his parting beams. The old man pointed to the bright picture, and told the boy that there was the gateway to the Spirit Land, where perpetual summer reigned, and game was found in great abundance. He spoke too of the child's father and mother, and of his little brother, whom he described as decked out in the most beautiful of robes, as they wandered through the forests of that distant, shadowy land. The boy, though suffering with the pangs of hunger, clapped his little hands in glee, and told his grandfather that it would make him very happy if he could go to the land of perpetual summer. And then it was that the old man patted the boy upon his head, and told him that his desires should be realized before the sun again made its appearance above the snow-covered mountains and plains of the east.

It was now the hour of midnight. Intensely cold was the wind which swept over the wilderness, but the sky was very blue, and studded with many stars. No sound broke upon the air, save the occasional groan of the ice along the lake shore, and the hissing whisper of the frost. Within the Indian lodge, which was the very home of desolation, the child was sweetly sleeping, enveloped in his robes, while the old man bent over the burning embers as if in despair. Some inhuman thought had crazed his brain, and he was nerving himself for an unheard of crime. One moment more, and in the dim light of that lonely lodge, gleamed the polished blade of a flinty weapon—a sudden groan was heard—and the Indian maniac was feeding upon the body of his child.

I have given the white man a sorrowful history, but it is one which the Chippeway nation believe. On the morning which followed the event I have now narrated, a party of Indian hunters came to the cabin of the unknown man, and they found him lying dead upon the ground, with the mangled remains of the boy at his side. This was the most terrible deed which ever happened in the Chippeway country

—and the one which so greatly offended the Great Spirit, that he pronounced a curse upon the man who had destroyed his child for food—and he, therefore, doomed him to live upon the earth forever, tormented with an appetite which nothing can ever appease, but the decaying flesh of the human race.

THE FIRE-WATER SACRIFICE.

THE historical tradition which I am now to narrate, is said to have occurred at an early day on the extreme western point of what is now called Drummond's Island, in the northern waters of Lake Huron. I obtained it from the lips of Kah-ge-ga-gah-bowh, or *Upright Standing*, a young chief of the Chippeway nation, who assured me that it commemorated the first introduction of the baneful Fire-water into the Indian country.

It was the afternoon of a pleasant day in the autumn-time, when a trading canoe landed on Drummond's Island, in the immediate vicinity of a Chippeway village. It belonged to a French trader, and was laden with a barrel of whisky, which he had brought from the lower country. Soon as he had deposited his barrel upon the beach, he called together the men of the village, and told them that he had it in his power to supply them with a beverage which would make them exceedingly happy, and that he was willing to supply them with what they wanted, provided they would give into his hands all the furs they had in their possession. A bargain was consequently made, and while the entire population of the village were quaffing the baneful fire-water, the trader packed away his treasures in the canoe, and under cover of the night, started upon his return to Detroit.

The moon and stars came forth in the northern sky, and the only sound which broke the solitude of the wilderness issued from the Indian village, where the medicine man and the chief, the Indian mother and her infant, were shouting and dancing and fighting in a delirium of madness. The carousal did not end until the break of day, and soon as the sun was fairly risen above the horizon, it was rumored in every wigwam that a young hunter named Ne-mo-a-Kim, or *Purple Shell*, had taken the life of a brother hunter, who happened to be his dearest friend. An apparent gloom rested upon every countenance, and as the more aged Indians reflected upon the sudden disappearance of the trader, and upon the headache which many of them endured, they became greatly enraged, and attributed the calamity which had befallen them to the burning water. But the trader who had brought it to them was beyond their reach; so they buried the murdered man with appropriate honors, and then announced that a council should be immediately held to decide upon the fate of the murderer. Blood for blood was demanded by the relatives of the deceased; the time-honored law of the Chippeways could not be evaded, and a delegation was appointed to prepare Ne-mo-a-Kim for the sacrifice. His lodge was entered by the ministers of death, but Ne-mo-a-Kim was not there. They hunted for him in all the wigwams of the village, but nowhere could he be found. The old men who had suffered with him in the remote wilderness, and had never known him to be guilty of a cowardly deed, now shook their heads in sorrow and disappointment. Another council was held, another ancient law remembered, and it was again decided that the only relative and brother of Ne-mo-a-Kim should suffer in his stead. The name of that brother was Ma-Ko-nah, or *The Unbending Pine*, and when they informed him of his fate, he uttered not a murmur, but demanded that his execution should take place on the following night at the rising of the moon.

And now for another scene in our strange story. The sun has long been absent from the western sky, and once more has the solemn midnight settled upon the world. The inhabitants of the Indian village have assembled upon a level green. Firmly in the earth have they planted a stake, on either side of which are burning a couple of huge fires, while at the distance of about one hundred feet may be discerned a crowd of eight or ten young men, who are bending their bows and straightening their arrows for the cruel deed. A small white cloud makes its appearance above the horizon, and a murmur of excitement issues from the crowd of human beings. The proud form of an Indian is now seen marching across the green, when the name of Ma-Ko-nah is whispered from ear to ear, and an unearthly shout ascends into the upper air. The heroic man stands before the stake, and looks with scorn upon the withes lying at his feet. The people have confided in his bravery, and they will not humble his proud spirit by resorting to the disgraceful implements of security. Upon his naked breast has the Indian hero painted the uncouth figure of a swan, as a certain mark for the arrows which are to deprive him of life. Around his waist has he carefully adjusted his richest robe, and by a motion of his hand, has signified his intention of delivering a speech; an intense silence reigns throughout the surrounding multitude, and Ma-Ko-nah thus addresses his cowardly brother, whose spirit he imagines to be hovering near.

"Willingly do I die for you, my brother, but you have disgraced your nation. Your name will hereafter be hissed at by the little boys, when they pick up the purple shells on the lake shore. I am going to the Spirit Land, and while I shall be happy in the possession of every good, you will be despised by all who learn your history. Your food will be bitter, and the ground upon which you will have to sleep will always be uneven, and covered with thorns and stones. You are a coward, my brother; but Ma-Ko-nah is a brave man, and not afraid to die."

Loud and long was the shout which replied to this proud speech. All things were now ready, and the fatal moment, when the rim of the moon should appear above the distant waters, was nigh at hand. Another snowy cloud floated into view, and just as the signal to fire was about to be given by the great medicine man, Ne-mo-a-Kim suddenly burst through the crowd, and threw himself upon the ground before his brother Ma-Ko-nah. To describe the confusion which followed were quite impossible. It were sufficient to know that Ma-Ko-nah was released from his obligation, and while he was to continue in the land of the living, his repentant brother was to perish. But though he now yielded himself as a willing sacrifice, his integrity had been doubted, and the lately untouched thongs were used to bind him to the stake. All things were again ready, the signal was given, the loud twang of the bow-strings pulled at the same instant was heard, and the Chippeway murderer was weltering in his own blood.

The night was far spent, the silence of the grave rested upon the wilderness village, and all the Indians, save one, were asleep in their wigwams. But Ma-Ko-nah was filled with grief, and the remaining hours of that night did he spend in his lodge, mourning over the body of his unfortunate and only brother. His father and mother were both dead, and so also was his wife, and the heart of Ma-Ko-nah was very desolate. So endeth the story of The Fire-Water Sacrifice.

ORIGIN OF THE CATAWBA INDIANS.

THERE was a time when the world was an unbroken waste of rocks, hills, and mountains, save only one small valley, which was distinguished for its luxuriance, and where reigned a perpetual summer. At that time, too, the only human being who inhabited the earth was a woman, whose knowledge was confined to this valley, and who is remembered among the Catawbas as the mother of mankind. She lived in a cavern, and her food consisted of the honey of flowers, and the sweet berries and other fruits of the wilderness. Birds without number, and the wild streams which found a resting place in the valley, made the only music which she ever heard. Among the wild animals, which were very numerous about her home, she wandered without any danger; but the beaver and the doe were her favorite companions. In personal appearance she was eminently beautiful, and the lapse of years only had a tendency to increase the brightness of her eyes and the grace of her movements. The dress she wore was made of those bright green leaves which enfold the water lilies, and her hair was as long as the grass which fringed the waters of her native vale. She was the ruling spirit of a perennial world, for even the very flowers which bloomed about her sylvan home were never known to wither or die. In spite of her lonely condition, she knew not what it was to be lonely; but ever and anon a strange desire found its way to her heart, which impelled her to explore the wild country which surrounded her home. For many days had she resisted the temptation to become a wanderer from her charming valley, until it so happened, on a certain morning, that a scarlet butterfly made its appearance before the door of her cave, and by the hum of its wings invited her away. She obeyed the summons, and followed the butterfly far up a rocky ravine, until she came to the foot of a huge waterfall, when she was deserted by her mysterious pilot, and first became acquainted with the emotion of fear. Her passage of the ravine had been comparatively smooth; but when she endeavored, in her consternation, to retrace her steps, she found her efforts unavailing, and fell to the ground in despair. A deep sleep then overcame her senses, from which she was not awakened until the night was far spent; and then the dampness of the dew had fallen upon her soft limbs, and for the first time in her life did she feel the pang of a bodily pain. Forlorn and desolate indeed was her condition, and she felt that some great event was about to happen, when, as she uncovered her face and turned it to the sky, she beheld, bending over her prostrate form, and clothed in a cloud-like robe, the image of a being somewhat resembling herself, only that he was more stoutly made, and of a much fiercer aspect. Her first emotion at this strange discovery was that of terror; but as the mysterious being looked upon her in kindness, and raised her lovingly from the ground, she confided in his protection, and listened to his words until the break of day.

He told her that he was a native of the far off sky, and that he had discovered her in her forlorn condition while traveling from the evening to the morning star. He told her also that he had never before seen a being so soft and beautifully formed as she. In coming to her rescue he had broken a command of the Great Spirit, or the Master of Life, and, as he was afraid to return to the sky, he desired to spend his days in her society upon earth. With joy did she accept this proposal; and, as the sun rose above the distant mountains, the twain returned in safety to the luxuriant vale, where, as man and woman, for many moons, they lived and loved in perfect tranquillity and joy.

In process of time the woman became a mother; from which time the happiness of the twain became more intense, but they at the same time endured more troubles than they had ever known before. The man was unhappy because he had offended the Master of Life, and the mother was anxious about the comfort and happiness of her newly-born child. Many and devout were the prayers they offered to the Great Spirit for his guidance and protection, for they felt that from them were to be descended a race of beings more numerous than the stars of heaven. The Great Spirit had compassion on these lone inhabitants of the earth; and, in answer to their prayers, he caused a mighty wind to pass over the world, making the mountains crowd closely together, and rendering the world more useful and beautiful by the prairies and valleys and rivers which now cover it, from the rising to the setting sun. The Master of Life also told his children that he would give them the earth and all that it contained as their inheritance; but that they should never enjoy their food without labor, should be annually exposed to a season of bitter cold, and that their existence should be limited by that period of time when their heads should become as white as the plumage of the swan. And so endeth the words of the Catawba.

THE LONG CHASE.

It was a summer day, and my birchen canoe, paddled by a party of Chippeway Indians, was gliding along the southern shore of Lake Superior. We had left the Apostle Islands, and were wending our way towards the mouth of the Ontonagon, where we intended to spend the night. Behind us reposed in beauty the Emerald Islands, in our front appeared the Porcupine Mountains, the sky above was without a cloud, and the waste of sleeping waters was only broken by the presence of a lonely swan, which seemed to be following in our wake, apparently for the sake of our companionship. I was delighted with the scene which surrounded me, and having requested my comrades to refill their pipes from my tobacco-pouch, I inquired for an adventure or a story connected with this portion of the lake. I waited but for a moment, when the chief of the party, *O-gee-maw-ge-zhick*, or Chief of the Sky, signified his intention by a sudden exclamation, and proceeded with the following historical tradition :

The Indian warrior of other days seldom thought that distance ought to be considered when he went forth to battle against his enemies, provided he was certain of winning the applause of his fellow men. Fatigue and hunger were alike looked upon as unimportant considerations, and both endured without a murmur.

The white man had not yet become the owner of this wilderness, and our nation was at war with the Iroquois, who had invaded our territory. At this time it was that a party of six Iroquois runners had been sent by their leading chiefs from Ke-wa-we-non, on the southern shore of Lake Superior, to examine the position of the Chippeways, who were supposed to be on an island called Moo-ne-quah-na-kon-ing. The spies having arrived opposite to the island where their enemies were encamped (which island was about three miles from the main shore), they built a war-canoe out of the bark of an elm-tree, launched it at the hour of midnight, and, having implored the god of war to smile upon them and keep the lake in peace, they landed on the island, and were soon prowling through the village of the unconscious Chippeways.

They were so cautious in all their movements, that their footsteps did not even awaken the sleeping dogs. It so happened, however, that they were discovered, and that, too, by a young woman, who, according to ancient custom, was leading a solitary life previous to becoming a mother. In her wakefulness she saw them pass near her lodge and heard them speak, but could not understand their words, though she thought them to be of the Na-do-was tribe. When they had passed, she stole out of her own wigwam to that of her aged grandmother, whom she informed of what she had seen and heard. The aged woman only reprimanded her daughter for her imprudence, and did not heed her words. "But, mother," replied the girl, "I speak the truth; the dreaded Na-do-was are in our village; and if the warriors of the Buffalo Race do not heed the story of a foolish girl, their women and their children must perish." The words of the girl were finally believed, and the warriors of the Crane and Buffalo tribes prepared themselves for the capture. The war-whoop echoed to the sky; and the rattling of bows and arrows was heard in every part of the island. In about an hour, the main shore was lined with about eight hundred canoes, whose occupants were anxiously waiting for the appearance of the spies. These desperate men, however, had made up their minds to try the mettle of their oars to the utmost, and, as the day was breaking, they launched their canoe from a woody cove, shot round the island, and started in the direction of the Porcupine Mountains, which were about sixty miles distant. Soon as they came in sight of the Chippeways, the latter became quite frantic, and, giving their accustomed yell, the whole multitude started after them swift as the flight of gulls. The mighty lake was without a ripple; and the beautiful fish in its bosom wandered about their rocky haunts in perfect peace, unconscious of the dreadful strife which was going on above. The canoes of the pursued and the pursuers moved with magic speed. The Iroquois were some two miles ahead, and while they strained every nerve for life, one voice rose high into the air, with a song of invocation to the spirits of their race for protection; and, in answer to their petition, a thick fog fell upon the water, and caused great confusion. One of the Chippeway warriors laid down his paddle, seized his mysterious rattle (made of deer's hoof), and, in a strange, wild song, implored the spirits of his race to clear away the fog, that they might only see their enemies. The burthen of the song was :—

> "Mon-e-tou ne bah bah me tah wah
> Ke shig ne bah bah me tah goon
> Ah bee ne nah wah goom me goon
> Men ke che dah awas—awas."

Which may be translated as follows :—

> "Spirit! whom I have always obeyed,
> Here cause the skies now to obey,
> And place the waters in our power.
> We are warriors—away, away."

Just as the last strain died upon the air, the fog quickly rolled away, and the Iroquois spies were discovered hastening towards the shore, near Montreal river. Then came the fog again, and then departed, in answer to the conflicting prayers of the nations. Long and awfully exciting was the race. But the Great Spirit was the friend of the Chippeway, and just as the Iroquois were landing on the beach, four of them were pierced with arrows, and the remaining two taken prisoners. A council was then called, for the purpose of deciding what should be done with them; and it was determined that they should be tortured at the stake. They were fastened to a tree, and surrounded with wood, when, just as the torch was to be applied, an aged warrior stepped forth from the crowd of spectators, and thus addressed the assembly :—

"Why are you to destroy these men? They are brave warriors, but not more distinguished than we are. We can gain no benefit from their death. Why will you not let them live, that they may go and tell their people of our power, and that our warriors are numerous as the stars of the northern sky." The council pondered upon the old man's advice, and there was a struggle between their love of revenge and love of glory; but both became victorious. One of the spies was released, and, as he ascended a narrow valley, leading to the Porcupine Mountains, the fire was applied to the dry wood piled round the form of the other; and in the darkness of midnight, and amid the shouting of his cruel enemies, the body of the Iroquois prisoner was consumed to ashes. The spot where the sacrifice took place has been riven by many a thunderbolt since then, for the god of war was displeased with the faintheartedness of the Chippeway, in valuing a name more highly than the *privilege* of revenge; and the same summer, of the following year, which saw the humane Chippeway buried on the shore of Superior, also saw the remains of the pardoned spy consigned to the earth on the shore of Michigan.

Thus endeth the legend of Shah-gah-wah-mik, one of the Apostle Islands, which the French named La Pointe, and which was originally known as Moo-ne-quah-na-kon-ing. The village stood where the old trading establishment is now located; and among the greenest of the graves in the hamlet of La Pointe is that where lie the remains of the Indian girl who exposed herself to reproach for the purpose of saving her people.

THE LONE BUFFALO.

AMONG the legends which the traveler frequently hears, while crossing the prairies of the Far West, I remember one which accounts in a most romantic manner for the origin of thunder. A summer-storm was sweeping over the land, and I had sought a temporary shelter in the lodge of a Sioux, or Dahcotah Indian on the banks of the St. Peters. Vividly flashed the lightning, and an occasional peal of thunder echoed through the firmament. While the storm continued my host and his family paid but little attention to my comfort, for they were all evidently stricken with terror. I endeavored to quell their fears, and for that purpose asked them a variety of questions respecting their people, but they only replied by repeating, in a dismal tone, the name of the Lone Buffalo. My curiosity was of course excited, and it may be readily imagined that I did not resume my journey without obtaining an explanation of the mystic words; and from him who first uttered them in the Sioux lodge I subsequently obtained the following legend:—

There was a chief of the Sioux nation whose name was the Master Bear. He was famous as a prophet and hunter, and was a particular favorite with the Master of Life. In an evil hour he partook of the white man's fire-water, and in a fighting broil unfortunately took the life of a brother chief. According to ancient custom blood was demanded for blood, and when next the Master Bear went forth to hunt, he was waylaid, shot through the heart with an arrow, and his body deposited in front of his widow's lodge. Bitterly did the woman bewail her misfortune, now mutilating her body in the most heroic manner, and anon narrating to her only son, a mere infant, the prominent events of her husband's life. Night came, and with her child lashed upon her back, the woman erected a scaffold on the margin of a neighboring stream, and with none to lend her a helping hand, enveloped the corpse in her more valuable robes, and fastened it upon the scaffold. She completed her task just as the day was breaking, when she returned to her lodge, and shutting herself therein, spent the three following days without tasting food.

During her retirement the widow had a dream, in which she was visited by the Master of Life. He endeavored to console her in her sorrow, and for the reason that he had loved her husband, promised to make her son a more famous warrior and medicine man than his father had been. And what was more remarkable, this prophecy was to be realized within the period of a few weeks. She told her story in the village, and was laughed at for her credulity.

On the following day, when the village boys were throwing the ball upon the plain, a noble youth suddenly made his appearance among the players, and eclipsed them all in the bounds he made and the wildness of his shouts. He was a stranger to all, but when the widow's dream was remembered, he was recognized as her son, and treated with respect. But the youth was yet without a name, for his mother had told him that he should win one for himself by his individual prowess.

Only a few days had elapsed, when it was rumored that a party of Pawnees had overtaken and destroyed a Sioux hunter, when it was immediately determined in council that a party of one hundred warriors should start upon the war-path and revenge the injury. Another council was held for the purpose of appointing a leader, when a young man suddenly entered the ring and claimed the privilege of leading the way. His authority was angrily questioned, but the stranger only replied by pointing to the brilliant eagle's feathers on his head, and by shaking from his belt a large number of fresh Pawnee scalps. They remembered the stranger boy, and acknowledged the supremacy of the stranger man.

Night settled upon the prairie world, and the Sioux warriors started upon the war-path. Morning dawned, and a Pawnee village was in ashes, and the bodies of many hundred men, women, and children were left upon the ground as food for the wolf and vulture. The Sioux warriors returned to their own encampment, when it was ascertained that the nameless leader had taken more than twice as many scalps as his brother warriors. Then it was that a feeling of jealousy arose, which was soon quieted, however, by the news that the Crow Indians had stolen a number of horses and many valuable furs from a Sioux hunter as he was returning from the mountains. Another warlike expedition was planned, and as before, the nameless warrior took the lead.

The sun was near his setting, and as the Sioux party looked down upon a Crow village, which occupied the centre of a charming valley, the Sioux chief commanded the attention of his braves and addressed them in the following language:

"I am about to die, my brothers, and must speak my mind. To be fortunate in war is your chief ambition, and because I have been successful you are unhappy. Is this right? Have you acted like men? I despise you for your meanness, and I intend to prove to you this night that I am the bravest man in the nation. The task will cost me my life, but I am anxious that my nature should be changed and I shall be satisfied. I intend to enter the Crow village alone, but before departing, I have one favor to command. If I succeed in destroying that village, and lose my life, I want you, when I am dead, to cut off my head and protect it with care. You must then kill one of the largest buffaloes in the country and cut off his head. You must then bring his body and my head together, and breathe upon them, when I shall be free to roam in the Spirit-land at all times, and over our great prairie-land wherever I please. And when your hearts are troubled with wickedness remember the Lone Buffalo."

The attack upon the Crow village was successful, but according to his prophecy the Lone Buffalo received his death wound, and his brother warriors remembered his parting request. The fate of the hero's mother is unknown, but the Indians believe that it is she who annually sends from the Spirit land the warm winds of spring, which cover the prairies with grass for the sustenance of the Buffalo race. As to the Lone Buffalo, he is never seen even by the most cunning hunter, excepting when the moon is at its full. At such times he is invariably alone, cropping his food in some remote part of the prairies; and whenever the heavens resound with the moanings of the thunder, the red man banishes from his breast every feeling of jealousy, for he believes it to be the warning voice of the Lone Buffalo.

LEGENDS OF MACKINAW.

The original Indian name of this island was Mich-il-i-mack-i-nack, signifying the mammoth turtle. It is a beautiful spot of earth, and its origin is accounted for by the following Ottaway legend:—

When the world was in its infancy, and all the living creatures were wandering over its surface from their several birth-places, for a permanent home, it so happened that a multitude of turtles came to the southern shore of Lake Erie. They found the country generally level, and were delighted with the muddy waters of the lake, and also with the many stagnant rivers and ponds which they discovered in its vicinity. But while the race were generally satisfied with their discoveries, and willing to remain where they were, the mammoth leader of the multitude resolved upon extending his journey to the north. He was allured to this undertaking by a strange light of exceeding loveliness (supposed to be the Aurora Borealis), which he had frequently observed covering the horizon. He endeavored to obtain a few companions for his intended pilgrimage, but without success. This disappointment did not dishearten him, however, and as he remembered that the summer was only half gone, he determined to depart alone. Long and very circuitous was his journey, and many, beautiful and lonely, the bayous and swamps where he frequently tarried to rest himself and obtain refreshment. Summer, and nearly the whole of autumn were now passed, and the traveling turtle found himself on a point of land which partially divided the two lakes of Huron and Michigan. Already he had been numbed by chilly winds, but his ambition was so great that he still persisted in his foolish pilgrimage. The day on which he made his final launch upon the waters, was particularly cold and desolate, and it so happened that in the course of a few days his career was stopped by the formation of an icy barrier, which deprived him of life and left him, a little black spot, on the waste of frozen waters.

Spring returned once more, but while the ice gradually dissolved itself into beautiful blue waves, the shell of the turtle was fastened to a marine plant or tall reed, and in process of time became an island, which the Indians appropriately named Mich-il-i-mack-i-nack, or the Mammoth Turtle.

The individual from whom I obtained the above story was an Ottaway Indian; and he told it to me as we sat together on the brow of the arched rock which has, from time immemorial, been considered the principal natural curiosity of Mackinaw. The following legend I obtained from the same source, and, like the majority of Indian stories, it is uncouth and unnatural; but interesting for the reason that it bears a curious analogy to a certain passage in the Old Testament. But this remark is applicable, I believe, to the early traditions of nearly all the aboriginal nations of North America. But to the tradition:—

Very many winters ago, the sun was regularly in the habit of performing his daily circuit across the heavens, and when the stars made their appearance in the sky, he invariably descended into an immense hole supposed to be located in the remote west. But in process of time it so happened that a chief of the Ottaways committed an unheard of crime against the person of his only daughter, and the Master of Life became so offended, that he caused a mighty wind to come upon the earth, whereby the rocky hills were made to tremble, and the waters which surrounded them to roar with a dreadful noise. During this state of things, which lasted for one whole day, the sun shot through the heavens with an unsteady motion, and when it had reached the zenith suddenly became fixed, as if astonished at the red man's wickedness. All the people of the Ottaway nation were greatly alarmed at this phenomenon, and while they were gazing upon the luminary, it gradually changed into the color of blood, and with a dreadful noise, as if in a passion, it fell upon the earth. It struck the northern shore of Mackinaw, formed the cavity of the Arched Rock, and so entered the earth, from which it issued in the far east, at an early hour on the following morning, and then resumed its usual journey across the heavens.

Many, very many winters have passed away since the last mentioned incident occurred, and it is true that even the present race of Indians can seldom be persuaded to approach the brow of the Arched Rock. Never have I heard of one who was sufficiently bold to walk over the arch, though the feat might be easily accomplished by any man with a steady nerve. The shores of the island of Mackinaw are almost entirely abrupt—and their general altitude is about one hundred and fifty feet; but the summit of the Arched Rock has been estimated to be at least two hundred feet above the water. In connection with the above stories, I might introduce a description of the island they commemorate, but such a description has already been published in my "Summer in the Wilderness."

GREEN-CORN CEREMONIES OF THE CHEROKEES.

My main object in the present paper is to record a complete account of the ceremonies which were once practised by the Cherokee Indians, in connection with their principal agricultural pursuit of raising maize or Indian corn. For the great majority of my facts I am indebted to Mr. Preston Starritt, of Tennessee. While this is the case, however, I beg my readers to understand that I shall speak of the tribe in question as it existed in the times of old, when its members were the sole proprietors of the southern Alleghanies. Let us, then, banish from our minds the unhappy relations which brood over the Cherokees at the present time, and, by the aid of our fancy, mingle with the nation as it existed when in its pristine glory.

The snows of winter have melted from the mountain peaks, the rains are over and gone, the frosts are out of the ground, and the voice of the turtle is heard in the land. The beautiful valley to which we have journeyed is entirely surrounded with mountains, about five miles square, watered by a charming stream, and inhabited by two thousand aborigines, who are divided into seven clans, and located in seven villages. The ruling men of the tribe have signified to their people that the period for planting corn has arrived, and that they must gather themselves together for the purpose of submitting to the annual ceremonies of purification. For doing this they have a double object: they would, in the first place, expunge from their bodies every vestige of all the colds and diseases with which they may have been afflicted during the past winter; and, in the second place, they would propitiate the Great Spirit, so as to secure his blessing upon the crops which they are about to deposite in the ground. The moon being now at its full, and a fitting location having been selected, the chiefs and magicians congregate together, and the preliminary measures are thus managed. A magic circle is made to keep out all evil spirits and enemies, and the medicine men then proceed to walk in single file, and with measured steps, completely around the spot which they would render sacred, and which is generally half a mile in diameter, marking their route by plucking a single leaf from every tree or bush which they may happen to pass, all these leaves being carefully deposited in a pouch carried for the purpose. In the mean time, the brotherhood of chiefs have not been unemployed, for while the most aged individual of all has been making a collection of roots, the remainder have built a rude dam, and thereby formed a pond or pool of water on the creek which invariably waters the sacred enclosure. The entire population of the valley are now summoned to the outskirts of the sacred enclosure, and a general invitation extended to all to approach and join the chiefs and magicians in the rite they are about to perform; it being understood, however, that no man, under penalty of death, shall venture to participate who has left a single wrong unrevenged or committed any unmanly deed, and no woman who has given birth to a child since the preceding full moon. In the centre of the sacred ground, and in the vicinity of the pool, a large fire is now made, around which the multitude are congregated. The night is clear, and the moon and stars are flooding the earth with light. An earthen pot is now placed upon the fire, the roots gathered by the old chief, numbering seven varieties, are placed therein, also the leaves plucked by the magicians, when the pot is filled with water by seven virgins, who are promoted to this honor by the appointment of the senior chief. After the contents of the pot have been thoroughly boiled, and a most bitter but medicinal beverage been made, all the persons present are called upon to take seven sips of the bitter liquid, and then directed to bathe no less than seven times in the neighboring pool, the waters of which have been rendered sacred by the incantations of the priests. All these things being done, the multitude assemble around the fire once more, and, to the music of a strange wild singing, they dance until the break of day, and then disperse to their several homes. The friendship of the Great Spirit has now been secured, and therefore, as opportunity offers, the Indians proceed to loosen their ground, as best they may, and then plant their corn. This labor is performed chiefly by the women, and the planted fields are considered as under their especial charge. Though planted in the greatest disorder, they keep their cornfields entirely free of weeds, and the soil immediately around the corn in a loose condition. At every full moon they are commonly apprehensive that some calamity may befall their crop, and, by way of keeping the Great Spirit on their side, the women have a custom of disrobing themselves, at the dead hour of night, and of walking entirely around the field of corn.

And now that the sunshine and showers of summer are performing their ministry of good in bringing the corn to its wonted perfection, it may be well to make the reader acquainted with the following facts: As the Indians purify themselves and perform all their religious rites only when the moon is at its full, so do they refrain from plucking a single ear of corn until they have partaken of their annual harvest or green-corn feast. This feast occurs on that night of the full moon nearest to the period when the corn becomes ripe; and, by a time-honored law of the nation, no man, woman, or child is ever permitted, under penalty of death, to pluck a single roasting-ear. So rigidly enforced is this law that many Cherokees are known to have lost their lives for disobeying it, while many families have suffered the pangs of hunger for many days, even while their fields were filled with corn, merely because the harvest moon had not yet arrived, and they had not partaken of their annual feast. If a full moon should occur only one week after the corn has become suitable to pluck, the Indians will not touch a single ear until the next moon, even if it should then be so hard as to require pounding before becoming suitable for food. During the ripening period the cornfields are watched with jealous care, and the first stalk that throws out its silken plume is designated by a distinguishing mark. In assigning reasons for this peculiar care, the Indians allege that until the harvest feast has taken place the corn is exclusively the property of the Great Spirit, and that they are only its appointed guardians; and they also maintain that, when the corn is plucked before the appointed moon has arrived, the field which has thus been trespassed upon is sure to be prostrated by a storm or be afflicted with the rot; and wherefore it is that they are always greatly alarmed when they discover that a cornfield has been touched, as they say, by the Evil One.

But the harvest moon is now near at hand, and the chiefs and medicine men have summoned the people of the several villages to prepare themselves for the autumnal festival. Another spot of ground is selected, and the same sanctifying ceremony is performed that was performed in the previous spring. The most expert hunter in each village has been commissioned to obtain game, and while he is engaged in the hunt the people of his village are securing the blessing of the Great Spirit by drinking, with many mystic ceremonies, the liquid made from seven of the most bitter roots to be found among the mountains. Of all the game which may be obtained by the hunters, not a single animal is to be served up at the feast whose bones have been broken or mutilated; nor shall a rejected animal be brought within the magic circle, but shall be given to those of the tribe who, by some misdeed, have rendered themselves unworthy to partake of the feast. The hunters are always compelled to return from the chase at the sunset hour, and long before they come in sight of their villages they invariably give a shrill whistle, as a signal of good luck, whereupon the villagers make ready to receive them with a wild song of welcome and rejoicing.

The pall of night has once more settled upon the earth, the moon is in its glory, the watch-fire has been lighted within the magic circle, and the inhabitants of the valley are again assembled together in one great multitude. From all the cornfields in the valley the magicians have collected the marked ears of corn, and deposited them in the kettles with the various kinds of game which may have been slaughtered, from the bear, the deer, and the turkey, to the opossum, the squirrel, and the quail. The entire night is devoted to eating, and the feast comes not to an end until all the food has been dispatched, when, in answer to an appropriate signal from the medicine men, the bones which have been stripped of their flesh are collected together and pounded to a kind of powder, and scattered through the air. The seven days following this feast are devoted to dancing and carousing, and at the termination of this period the inhabitants of the valley retire to their various villages, and proceed to gather in their crops of the sweet maize or Indian corn.

THE OVERFLOWING WATERS.

A TRADITION OF THE CHOCTAWS.

The world was in its prime, and time rolled on with its accustomed regularity. The tiny streams among the hills and mountains shouted with joy, and the broad rivers wound their wonted course along the peaceful valleys. Many a tall oak had grown from the acorn, spread its rich foilage to the summer winds, decayed with age, and mingled with its mother earth. The moon and stars had long made the night-skies beautiful, and guided the Indian hunter through the wilderness. The sun, which the red man calls the glory of the summer time, had never failed to appear at his appointed periods. Many generations of men had lived and passed away.

In process of time the aspect of the world became changed. Brother quarreled with brother, and cruel wars frequently covered the earth with blood. The Great Spirit saw all these things and was displeased. A terrible wind swept over the wilderness, and the red men knew that they had done wrong, but they lived as if they did not care. Finally a stranger prophet made his appearance among them, and proclaimed in every village the news that the human race was to be destroyed. None believed his words, and the moons of summer again came and disappeared. It was now the autumn of the year. Many cloudy days had occurred, and then a total darkness came upon the earth, and the sun seemed to have departed forever. It was very dark and very cold. Men laid themselves down to sleep, but they were troubled with unhappy dreams. They arose when they thought it was time for the day to dawn, but only to see the sky covered with a darkness deeper than the heaviest cloud. The moon and stars had all disappeared, and there was constantly a dismal bellowing of thunder in the upper air. Men now believed that the sun would never return, and there was great consternation throughout the land. The great men of the Choctaw nation spoke despondingly to their fellows, and sung their death songs, but those songs were faintly heard in the gloom of the great night. It was a most unhappy time indeed, and darkness reigned for a great while. Men visited each other by torch-light. The grains and fruits of the land became mouldy, and the wild animals of the forest became tame and gathered around the watch-fires of the Indians, entering even into the villages.

A louder peal of thunder than was ever before heard now echoed through the firmament, and a light was seen in the North. It was not the light of the sun, but the gleam of distant waters. They made a mighty roar, and, in billows like the mountains, they rolled over the earth. They swallowed up the entire human race in their career, and destroyed everything which had made the earth beautiful. Only one human being was saved, and that was the mysterious prophet who had foretold the wonderful calamity. He had built him a raft of sassafras logs, and upon this did he float safely above the deep waters. A large black bird came and flew in circles above his head. He called upon it for aid, but it shrieked aloud, and flew away and returned to him no more. A smaller bird, of a bluish color, with scarlet eyes and beak, now came hovering over the prophet's head. He spoke to it, and asked if there was a spot of dry land in any part of the waste of waters. It fluttered its wings, uttered a sweet moan, and flew directly towards that part of the sky where the newly-born sun was just sinking in the waves. A strong wind now arose, and the raft of the prophet was rapidly borne in the same direction which the bird had pursued. The moon and stars again made their appearance, and the prophet landed upon a green island, where be encamped. Here he enjoyed a long and refreshing sleep, and when morning dawned he found that the island was covered with every variety of animals, excepting the great *Shakanli*, or mammoth, which had been destroyed. Birds, too, he also found here in great abundance. He recognized the identical black one which had abandoned him to his fate upon the waters, and, as it was a wicked bird and had sharp claws, he called it *Ful luh-chitto*, or bird of the Evil One. He also discovered, and with great joy, the bluish bird which had caused the wind to blow him upon the island, and because of its kindness to him and its beauty, he called it *Puch che-yon-sho-ba,* or the soft-voiced pigeon. The waters finally passed away, and in process of time that bird became a woman and the wife of the prophet, from whom the people now living upon the earth are all descended. And so endeth the story of The Overflowing Waters.

THE NAMELESS CHOCTAW.

THERE once lived in the royal Indian town of *E-ya-sho* (Ya-zoo) the only son of a war chief, who was eminently distinguished above all his fellows for his elegant form and noble bearing. The old men of the nation looked upon him with pride, and said that he was certainly born to occupy a high position as a warrior. He was also an eloquent orator, and none ever thought of doubting his courage. But, with all these qualities, he was not allowed a seat in the councils of his nation, because he had not distinguished himself in war. The renown of having slain an enemy he could not claim, nor had he ever been fortunate enough to take a single prisoner. He was universally beloved, and, as the name of his childhood had been abandoned according to an ancient custom, and he had not yet succeeded in winning a name worthy of his ability, he was known among his kindred as the Nameless Choctaw.

In the town of E-ya-sho there also once lived the most beautiful maiden of her tribe. She was the daughter of a hunter, and the betrothed of the Nameless Choctaw. They met often at the great dances, but, because she hoped to become his bride, she treated him as a stranger. Often, too, did they meet at the setting of the sun, but then they listened to the song of the whipporwill or watched the rising of the evening star, when each could hear the throbbing of the other's heart. They loved with a wild passion and were very happy. At such times one thought alone entered their minds to cast a shadow. It was this: They knew that the laws of their nation were unalterable, and that she could not become his bride until he had won a name. She knew that he could always place at the door of her lodge an abundance of game, and would deck her with the most beautiful of shells and wampum; but all this availed them nothing; that he must go upon the war-path was inevitable. She belonged to a proud family, and she never would consent to marry a man who had not a loud sounding name, and who could not sit in the councils of her people. She was willing to become his bride at any time, and therefore left him, by his prowess, to decide upon that time.

It was now midsummer and the evening hour. The Nameless Lover had met his promised bride upon the summit of a small hill, covered with pines. From the centre of a neighboring plain arose the smoke of a large watch-fire, around which were dancing a party of four hundred warriors. They had planned an expedition against the Osages, and the present was the fourth and last night of the preparation ceremonies. Up to that evening the Nameless Choctaw had been the leader in the dances, and even now his absence was only temporary, for he had stolen away to express his parting vows to his beloved. The last embrace was given, and then the maiden was alone upon the hill-top, looking down in sadness upon the dancing warriors, among whom she beheld none who commanded more attention than the being whom she loved.

Morning dawned, and the Choctaw warriors were upon the war-path leading to the country of their enemies, far up on the headwaters of the Arkansas. Upon that stream they found a cave, and in that cave, because they were on a prairie land, they secreted themselves. Two men were then selected to act as spies, one of whom (the Nameless Choctaw) was to reconnoitre in the west and the other in the east. Night came, and the party in the cave were discovered by an Osage hunter, who had traveled thither for the purpose of sheltering himself until morning from the heavy dews. By the light of the stars did he then travel to the nearest village, and having warned his people of the proximity of their enemies, they hurried in a large body to the cave. At its mouth they built a fire, and when the sun rose into the horizon the entire party of Choctaws had been smothered to death by the cunning of their enemies.

The Choctaw spy who had journeyed towards the east, had witnessed the surprise and unhappy fate of his brother warriors, and, returning to his own country, he called a council and revealed the sad intelligence. As to the fate of the Nameless Choctaw, who had journeyed to the westward, he knew that he too must have been overtaken and slain.

Upon the heart of one being this last intelligence fell with a most heavy weight, and the promised bride of the Nameless Lover pined in melancholy grief. From the night on which she was made wretched, she began to droop, and before the reigning moon had passed away she died, and was buried on the identical spot where she had parted with her lover.

But what became of the Nameless Choctaw? It was not true that he had been overtaken and slain. He was indeed discovered by the Osages, and far over the prairies and across the streams was he closely pursued. For many days and through the watches of many nights did the race continue, but the Choctaw warrior finally made his escape. His course had been exceedingly winding, and when he came to a pause he was astonished to find that the sun rose in the wrong quarter of the heavens. Everything appeared to him wrong and out of order, and the truth was he became a bewildered and forlorn man, and everywhere did he wander. He found himself at the foot of a mighty range of mountains, which were covered with grass and unlike any that he had ever before seen.

It so happened, however, at the close of a certain day, that he sauntered into a wooded valley, and having built him a rude bower and killed a rabbit, he lighted a fire, and prepared himself for one quiet meal and a night of repose. Morning dawned, and he was still in trouble. Many moons passed away and the Choctaw was still desolate and forlorn. It was now summer, and he called upon the Great Spirit to make his pathway plain; and having hunted the forests for a spotted deer, and slain her, on a day when there was no wind he offered a sacrifice, and that night supped upon a portion of the animal's sweet flesh. His fire burnt brightly, and though somewhat forlorn, he found that his heart was at peace. But now he hears a footstep! A moment more, and a snow-white wolf of immense size is crouching at his feet, and licking his torn moccasins. "How came you in this strange country?" inquired the wolf; and the poor Indian related the story of his unsuccessful exploit and subsequent escape. The wolf took pity upon the Choctaw and told him that he would conduct him in safety to the country of his kindred; and on the following morning did they take their departure. Long, very long was the journey, and many and very wild and turbulent the streams which they had to cross. The wolf helped the Choctaw to kill game for their mutual sustenance, and by the time that the moon for weeding the corn had arrived the nameless Choctaw had entered his native village again. This was on the anniversary of the day he had parted with his betrothed, and he was sorely grieved to find his people mourning her untimely death. Time and fatigue had so changed the returned Choctaw that his relatives and friends did not recognize him, and he chose not to reveal himself. From many a mouth, however, did did he learn the story of her death, and many a wild song, to the astonishment of all his friends, did he sing to the memory of the departed, whom he called by the beautiful name of IMMA, or the idol of warriors. And on a cloudless night did he wander to the grave of his beloved, and at a moment when the Great Spirit cast his shadow upon the moon (alluding to an eclipse) did he throw himself thereon and die. For three nights thereafter were the inhabitants of the Choctaw village alarmed by the continual howling of a wolf, and when it ceased, the pine forest, upon the hill where the lovers were resting in peace, took up the dismal howl or moan, and has continued it to the present time.

THE SPIRIT SACRIFICE.

It was midsummer, and there was a terrible plague in the wilderness. Many a Chippeway village on the borders of Lake Superior had been depopulated. The only band of the great northern nation which had thus far escaped, was the one whose hunting grounds lay on the northern shore of the St. Mary's River. Their principal village stood upon a gentle promontory overlooking the Great Lake, immediately at the head of the *Sault* or Falls, and at this village the chiefs and warriors of the tribe were assembled in council. Incantations of every possible description had for many days been performed, and yet nightly tidings were received, showing that the fatal disease was sweeping over the land, like the fires of autumn over the prairies. The signs in the sky, as well as these tidings, convinced the poor Indians that their days were numbered. It was now the last night of their council, and they were in despair. They knew that the plague had been sent upon the earth by the Great Spirit, as a punishment for some crime, and they also knew that there was but one thing that could possibly appease his anger. And what was this? The sacrifice of the most beautiful girl of her tribe. And such was the decree, that she should enter her canoe, and throwing away her paddle, cast herself upon the waters, just above the *Sault.*

Morning dawned, and loud and dismal beyond compare, was the wail of sorrow which broke upon the silent air. Another council was held, and the victim for the sacrifice was selected. She was an only child, and her mother was a widow, feeble and infirm. They told the maiden of her fate, and she uttered not a repining word. The girls and women of the village flocked around their long-loved companion, and decked her hair and her neck with all the brightest wampum, and the most beautiful feathers and shells that could be found in all the tribe. The time appointed for the sacrifice was the sunset hour; and as the day was rapidly waning, the gloom which pervaded the entire village gradually increased, and it even seemed as if a murmuring tone mingled with the roar of the mighty waterfall. The day had been one of uncommon splendor, and as the sun descended to the horizon a retinue of gorgeous clouds gathered around him, and the great lake, whose waters receded to the sky, was covered with a deeper blue than had ever before been seen.

All things were now ready, and the Indian maiden was ready for the sacrifice. In silence was she conducted to her canoe, and loud was the wail of lamentation. It died away; and now, to the astonishment of all the people, a strange echo came from over the waters. What could it mean? A breathless silence ensued, and even the old men listened with fear. And now a louder and a clearer continuation of the same echo breaks upon the air. A speck is seen upon the waters. The sun has disappeared, and a small canoe is seen rapidly approaching, as if from the very spot where the orb touched the waters. The song increases; and as the fairy-like canoe sweeps mysteriously over the watery waste, it is now seen to contain a beautiful being, resembling a girl, clothed in a snow-white robe. She is in a standing attitude, her arms are folded, and her eyes are fixed upon the heavens. Her soul is absorbed in a song, of which this is the burden:—

"I come from the Spirit land,
To appease the Great Spirit,
To stay the plague,
And to save the life of the beautiful Chippeway."

Onward she came, and her pathway lay directly towards the mighty rapids. With utter astonishment did the Indians look upon this unheard of spectacle, and while they looked they saw the canoe and its spirit voyager pass directly into the foam, where it was lost to them for ever.

And so did the poor Indians escape the plague. The St. Mary is a beautiful river; and during the summer time its shores are always lined with lilies, large, and of a marvelous whiteness; and it is a common belief among the Chippeways, that they owe their origin to the mysterious spirit, from whose mutilated body they sprang. And so endeth the Legend of the Spirit Sacrifice.

THE PEACE MAKER.

The following story was obtained by the writer, directly from the lips of a Seneca Indian, and the hero is said to have been the grandfather of the celebrated orator Red Jacket.

THERE was a time when all the Indian tribes in the world were at war with the great Seneca nation, whose hunting grounds were on the borders of Lake Ontario. So fearful had they become of their enemies, that the bravest hunters and warriors never left their wigwams without bending their bows, and little children were not permitted by their mothers to gather berries or hickory nuts in the neighboring woods. The head chief of the nation at that time, was *Sa-go-you-wat-ha*, or *Always Awake*. He was a good man, and being sorely grieved at the unhappiness of his people, he conceived the idea of securing a permanent peace. It was true, he said, that his father had been a cruel and unpopular chief, but he did not think it right that the generation which followed his father should be made miserable for crimes never committed by them. And therefore it was that he prayed to the *Great Ha-nee* to tell him, in a dream, what he must do to accomplish his end. Night came, and in spite of his name, *Always Awake* fell into a deep sleep and had a dream.

He was told that in the direction whence came the warm winds of summer, and distant from his village a journey of one moon, there was a very large mountain. On the summit of that mountain, as he was told, were living a few people from all the nations of the earth, excepting the Senecas. The place alluded to was called the *Mountain of Refuge*, and it was so sacred a place, that its soil had never been wet with human blood, and the people who lived there, were the peculiar favorites of the Great Ha-nee, and were the law makers of the world. The dream also told the Seneca chief, that he could secure a permanent peace only by visiting the sacred mountain; but as the intervening distance was so great, and his trail would be only among enemies, the dangers of the expedition would be very numerous. By traveling at night, however, and sleeping in the day time, the task might be accomplished, and he was at liberty to try *his* fortune.

Always Awake pondered a long time upon this strange vision, but finally determined to start upon the appointed expedition. Great was the fatigue that he endured, and oftentimes was he compelled to satisfy his hunger with the roots and berries of the forest. Many a narrow escape did he make from his enemies; but in due time he reached the Mountain of Refuge. He was warmly welcomed among the Indians of the mountain, and when he told his story and talked of peace, they honored him with many a loud shout of applause. A council was held, and a decree passed, to the effect that the important question at stake should be settled by another council composed of the head chiefs of all the Indian nations in the land. The fleetest runners were employed to disseminate the news, and at the appointed time the council of chiefs was held. They formed themselves into a confederacy, and with one exception, the nations of the wilderness became as one people, and so continued until the white man crossed the great waters and taught them the vices which have almost consumed them from the face of the earth. The only nation that would not join the confederation was the Osage nation, and because of their wickedness in so doing, they were cursed by the Great Ha-nee, and have ever since been a by-word and a reproach among their fellows.

And when the Seneca chief returned to his own country, he was very happy. His trail through the forests and over the mountains was lined with bonfires, and in every village that he tarried, he was feasted with the best of game. One moon after he returned to his people he died and was buried on the banks of the beautiful lake where he lived; and ever since that time the Great Ha-nee has permitted his people to live upon the land inherited from their fathers.

ORIGIN OF THE DEER.

A SHAWNEE LEGEND.

WA-PIT-PA-TASKA, or the Yellow Sky, was the daughter of a Shawnee or Snake hunter. His lodge was not one of the handsomest in the village where it stood, but the paths leading to it were more beaten than those leading to any other, for the daughter of the hunter was a great favorite among the young men of her tribe. The exploits of those who sought her hand had no charm for her ear, and her tastes were strangely different from those common among women. She knew that she had not many years to live upon the earth, and her dreams had told her she was created for an unheard-of mission. There was a mystery about her being, and none could comprehend the meaning of her evening songs. On one condition alone did she avow her willingness to become a wife, and this was, that he who became her husband should never, under any circumstances, mention her name. If he did so, a sad calamity would befall him, and he would forever thereafter regret his thoughtlessness. By this decree was the love of one of her admirers greatly enhanced, and before the summer was gone the twain were married and dwelt in the same lodge.

Time flew on and the Yellow Sky sickened and died, and her last words were that her husband should never forget her admonition about breathing her name. The widower was very unhappy, and for five summers did he avoid his fellow men, living in solitude, and wandering through the forests alone. The voices of autumn were now heard in the land, and the bereaved husband had, after his many journeyings, returned to the grave of his wife, which he found overgrown with briers and coarse weeds. For many moons had he neglected to protect the remains of his wife, and he now tried to atone for his wickedness by plucking up the briers and covering the grave with a soft sod. In doing this he was discovered by a stranger Indian, who asked him whose grave it was of which he was taking so much care? "It is the grave," said he, "of *Wa-pit-pa-taska*;" and hardly had the forbidden name (which he thoughtlessly uttered) passed from his lips, before he fell to the earth in a spasm of great pain. The sun was setting, and his bitter moans echoed far through the gloomy woods, even until the darkness settled upon the world.

Morning came, and near the grave of the Yellow Sky a large buck was quietly feeding. It was the unhappy husband, whom the Great Spirit had thus changed. The trotting of a wolf was heard in the brake, and the deer pricked up his ears. One moment more, and the wolf started after the deer. The race was very long and painful, but the deer finally escaped. And thus from a man came into existence the beautiful deer, or *mu-rat-si;* and because of the foolishness of this man, in not remembering his wife's words, the favorite animal of the Shawnee has ever been at the mercy of the wolf.

LEGEND OF THE WHITE OWL.

It was in the country of the Winnebagoes, or people of the turbid water, and there was a great scarcity of game. An Indian hunter, while returning from an unsuccessful expedition, at the sunset hour, chanced to discover in the top of a tree a large white owl. He knew that the flesh of this bird was not palatable to the taste, but as he thought of his wife and children, who had been without food for several days, he concluded to bend his bow and kill the bird. Hardly had he come to this determination, before he was astonished to hear the owl speaking to him in the following strain: "You are a very foolish hunter. You know it is against the laws of your nation to kill any of my tribe, and why should you do wrong because you happen to be a little hungry? I know that your wife and children are also hungry, but that is not a good reason for depriving me of life. I too have a wife and several children, and their home is in the hollow of an old tree. When I left them a little while ago, they were quite as hungry as you are, and I am now trying to obtain for their enjoyment a red squirrel or a young opossum. Unlike you, I have to hunt for my game only at night, and if you will go away and not injure me, I may have it in my power to do you a kindness at some future time."

The Indian hunter was convinced, and he unbent his bow. He returned to his wigwam, and after he had told his wife what had happened to him, she told him she was not sorry, for she had been particularly fortunate in gathering berries. And then the Indian and his family were contented, and game soon afterwards became abundant in the land.

Many seasons had passed away, and the powerful nation of the Iroquois were making war upon the Winnebagoes. The hunter already mentioned had become a successful warrior and a chief. He was a mark for his enemies, and the bravest among them started upon the war-path for the express purpose of effecting his destruction. They hunted him as they would the panther, but he always avoided their arrows. Many days of fatigue had he now endured, and, believing that his enemies had given up the chase, he stopped, on a certain evening, to rest himself and enjoy a repast of roots. After this comfortless supper was ended, he wrapped himself in his skins and thought that he would lie down and enjoy a little sleep. He did so, and the only sounds which broke the stillness of the air were caused by the falling of the dew from the leaves, and the whistling of the whippor-will. It was now past midnight, and the Winnebago was yet undisturbed. A whoop is heard in the forest, but so remote from his grassy couch as not to be heard by the unconscious sleeper. But what can this shouting mean? A party of the Iroquois warriors have fallen upon the trail of their enemy, and are in hot pursuit. But still the Winnebago warrior is in the midst of a pleasant dream. On come his enemies, and his death is inevitable. The shouting of the Iroquois is now distinct and clear, but in the twinkling of an eye it is swallowed up in a much louder and more dismal shriek, which startled the Winnebago to his feet. He is astonished, and wonders whence comes the noise. He looks upwards, and lo! perched upon one of the branches of the tree under which he had been resting, the form of a large white owl. It rolls its large yellow eyes upon him, and tells him that an enemy is on his trail, and that he must flee for his life. And this is the way in which the white owl manifested its gratitude to the Winnebago hunter for his kindness in sparing its own life many years before. And since that time the owl has ever been considered a very good and a wise bird, and when it perches above the wigwam of the red man it is always safe from harm.

DEATH OF THE GIANT CANNIBAL.

The following story was obtained from the lips of a Chippeway warrior named *Maw-gun-nub*, or Setting-ahead. He told it with as serious an air as if it had been a matter of actual and important history, and was evidently a firm believer in the wonders therein contained.

An Indian village stood upon the borders of the Lake of the Woods. It was a summer day, and a heavy rain storm had passed over the country, when a large Giant or Cannibal suddenly made his appearance in the village. He was as tall as the tallest hemlock, and carried a club in his hand which was longer than the longest canoe. He told the Indians that he had come from a far country in the North; that he was tired and hungry; and that all the wild rice and the game in the village must be immediately brought to his feet, that he might satisfy his appetite. His orders were obeyed, and when the food was brought, and the inhabitants of the village were collected together to see him enjoy his feast, the Giant told them he was not yet satisfied; whereupon, with one blow of his huge club, he destroyed, with one exception, all the people who had treated him so kindly. The only person who escaped the dreadful blow was a little boy, who happened to be sick in one of the wigwams.

After the Giant had committed his cruel deed, he devoured a number of the dead bodies, and during the night disappeared without discovering the boy. In a few days the boy was well enough to move about, and as he went from one wigwam to another, he thought of his friends who had been so suddenly killed, and was very unhappy. For many seasons did he live alone. While very young his food consisted of such birds as the partridge, but as he grew up to the estate of manhood, he became a successful hunter, and often feasted upon the deer and the buffalo. He became a strong man, but was very lonely, and every time he thought of the Giant who had destroyed his relatives and friends he thirsted for revenge.

Time passed on, and the Chippeway hunter became uneasy and discontented. He fasted for many days, and called upon the Great Spirit to give him power to discover and destroy the Giant who had done him so much harm. The Great Spirit took pity upon him, heard his prayer, and sent to his assistance a troop of a hundred men, from whose backs grew the most beautiful of wings. They told the hunter that they knew all about the Giant, and would help him to take his life. They said that the Giant was very fond of the meat of the white bear, and that if the hunter would give a bear feast they were certain that the Giant would make his appearance and ask for a portion of the choice food. The time for giving the feast was appointed, and it was to take place in a large natural wigwam, formed by the locked branches of many trees; whereupon the strange people disappeared and the hunter started towards the north after a bear.

The hunter was successful; the appointed time arrived, the feast was ready, and the strange people were on the ground. The dancing and the singing were all over, and the hot bear soup filled the wigwam with a pleasant odor. A heavy tramp was heard in the woods, and in a little time the Giant made his appearance, attracted to the place by the smell of the soup. He came rushing to the wigwam like one who knew not what it was to fear; but when he saw the array of people with wings he became very quiet, and asked the hunter if he might participate in the feast. The hunter told him that he might, on condition that he would go to the mouth of a certain stream that emptied into the lake, and bring therefrom to the wigwam a large rock which he would find there. The Giant was angry at this request, but as he was afraid of the people with wings he dared not disobey. He did as he was bidden, and the thong which he used to hold the rock on his back cut a deep gash in his forehead.

The hunter was not yet satisfied, and he told the Giant that before he could be admitted to the feast he must bring to the wigwam a gill-net that would reach across the widest stream. The Giant departed, and, having obtained a beautiful net from a *mammoth spider* that lived in a cave, he brought it to the hunter. The hunter was well pleased, but not yet fully satisfied. One more thing did he demand from the Giant before he could be admitted to the feast, which was this, that he must make his appearance at the feast wearing a robe made of weasel skins, with the teeth and claws all on. This robe was obtained, the Giant was admitted, and the feast proceeded.

It lasted for several days and nights, and the hunter, the strange people, and the Giant danced and caroused together as if they had been the best of friends. The Giant was delighted with the singing of his entertainers, and while he praised them to the skies he did not know that in his bowl of soup the Chippeway hunter, who had not forgotten the death of his friends, had placed a bitter root, which would deprive him of his strength. But such was, indeed, the case. On the last night of the feast the Giant became very tired and stupid, and asked permission to enjoy some sleep. Permission was granted, and in the centre of the great lodge was spread for his accommodation his weasel-skin robe. Upon the stone which he brought from the river did he rest his head, and over him was spread the net he had obtained from the mammoth spider. He then fell into a deep sleep, and the men with wings and the hunter continued the revelry. Each man supplied himself with a war club, and they performed the dance of revenge. They formed a ring around the sleeping Giant, and at a signal made by the hunter they all gave him a severe blow, when the spirit-men disappeared into the air, and the weasel-skin robe suddenly became alive. The little animals feasted upon the Giant with evident satisfaction, and by morning there was nothing left of him but his bones. These did the hunter gather into a heap, and having burnt them to ashes, he threw them into the air, and immediately there came into existence all the beautiful birds which now fill the world. And in this manner was the great Giant of the Chippeways destroyed, and instead of his living to feast upon the flesh of man, his own body, by the wisdom of the Great Spirit, was turned into the birds, which are the animal food of man.

THE CHIPEWAY MAGICIAN.

THIS legend, with at least a score of variations, was related to me by a Chippeway hunter named *Ka-zhe-osh*, or the *Fleet Flyer*. It is excessively romantic, but will most certainly enlist the sympathies of the ladies.

Near the head of the Mississippi is Sandy Lake. In the centre of this lake there is an island, and on this island, in the olden times, stood a Chippeway village. The chief of this village had a daughter, and that daughter had a lover, who was the greatest warrior of his tribe, and a magician. He had the power of turning himself into any kind of animal he pleased, and for this reason he was looked upon with suspicion by the females of his acquaintance. He lived in a secluded lodge on the outskirts of the village, and none ever disturbed him in his seclusion without express permission; and a greater number of scalps hung from the poles of his lodge than from those of any other in the tribe. The chief's daughter admired him for his noble bearing and his exploits, but she could not reconcile herself to become his wife. She was afraid of the strange power that he possessed, but she loved her father, and had promised him that she would never disobey his commands in regard to choosing her husband, though she trusted that the magician would never be mentioned in that connection.

In view of this state of things the magician made interest with the entire brotherhood of warriors and hunters, and proclaimed his intention of leading them upon the war-path to a distant country. He was unhappy, and hoped to find peace of mind by wandering into strange lands. At an appointed time the party assembled upon a neighboring plain, and they went through the ceremonies of the war-dance. They also shouted a loud war song, with the following burden:—

"We love the whoop of our enemies;
We are going to war,
We are going to war, on the other side of the world."

On witnessing these preparations, the chief of the village became troubled. He well knew that if the old men and the women and children under his charge should be abandoned by the fighting men and hunters of the tribe, they would be visited by much suffering, and he determined to avoid the calamity. But how could this be done? He thought of only one method, which was to give the magician his daughter. He told the daughter, and she promised to obey. He made the proposition to the magician, and it was accepted. It was on certain conditions, however, and these were as follows:—

The magician was first to capture the largest white-fish in the lake, then kill a white deer, and finally win a foot-race of fifteen miles against the swiftest runner in the tribe. All these things the magician promised to do, and he did them all. He turned himself into an otter, and by the assistance of the chief of the otters secured the largest fish that had ever been seen, and appearing in his own form again, deposited it in the lodge of the chief. He also turned himself into a black wolf, and having ranged the forest for a white deer he caught it, and again resuming his natural form carried it to the lodge where lived his betrothed. In running the race that had been proposed he had one hundred competitors, and at the end of the fifteen miles was stationed the chief's daughter, with a belt of wampum in her hand to crown the victor. The magician started upon the race in the form of a man, but before he had run a mile he turned himself into a hawk, and swooping to the side of the maiden, demanded that she should now become an inmate of his lodge. She consented, and the chief gave her to the magician. Before he took her away he called together the men of his tribe who had competed with him for the prize, and complimented them for their great activity in running the race, and condoled with them in their disappointment. He then told the chief that he did not thank him for what he had done, and turning to the daughter he said that as she had cost him so much trouble she must enter his camp and do all his work for him, even to the end of her days. And ever since that time has it been the lot of all Indian women to act as the servants of their husbands.

THE LOVER STAR.

I obtained the following legend from the lips of an Indian trader, whom I met at the island of La Pointe, in Lake Superior. He said it was related to him by a hunter of the Chippewyan nation, and that he had heard a similar story among the Chippeways.

There was once a quarrel among the stars, when one of them was driven away from its home in the heavens and descended to the earth. It wandered from one tribe of Indians to another, and had been seen hovering over the camp-fires of a thousand Indians, when they were preparing themselves to sleep. It always attracted attention and inspired wonder and admiration. It often lighted upon the heads of little children, as if for the purpose of playing with them, but they were invariably frightened and drove it away by their loud crying. Among all the people in the world, only one could be found who was not afraid of this beautiful star; and this was a little girl, the daughter of a Chippewyan warrior. She was not afraid of the star, but rather than this, she loved it with her whole heart, and was very happy in her love. That she was loved by the star in return there could be no doubt, for wherever she traveled with her father through the wilderness there, as the night came on did the star follow, but it was never seen in the day time. When the girl awoke at night, the star floated just above her head; and, when she was asleep, it was so constant in its watchfulness, that she never opened her eyes, even at midnight, without beholding its brilliant light. People wondered at this strange condition of things, but how much more did they wonder, when they found that the father of the girl never returned from the hunt without an abundance of game. They therefore concluded that the star must be the son of the Good Spirit, and they ever after spoke of it with veneration.

Time passed on, and it was midsummer. The Indian girl had gone into the woods for the purpose of gathering berries. Those of the wintergreen were nearly all eaten up by the pigeons and the deer, and, as the cranberries were beginning to ripen, she wandered into a large marsh with a view of filling her willow basket with them. She did so, and in the tangled thickets of the swamp she lost her way. She became frightened and cried aloud for her father to come to her assistance. The only creatures that answered her cries were the frogs and the lonely bittern. The night was rapidly coming, and the farther she wandered the more intricate became her path. At one time she was compelled to wade into the water even to her knees, and then again would she fall into a deep hole and almost become drowned among the poisonous slime and weeds. Night came, and the poor girl looked up at the sky, hoping that she might see the star that she loved. A storm had arisen, and the rain fell so rapidly that a star could not live in it, and therefore was there none to be seen. The storm continued, the waters of the country rose, and in rushing into the deeper lakes, they destroyed the Indian girl, and washed her body away so that it never could be found.

Many seasons passed away and the star continued to be seen above the watch-fires of the Chippewyans; but it would never remain long in one place, and its light appeared to have become dimmed. It ever seemed to be looking for something that it could not find, and people knew that it was unhappy on account of the untimely death of the girl it had loved. Additional years passed on, and with the leaves of autumn, it finally disappeared. A cold and long winter soon followed, and then the hottest summer that had ever been known. During this season it so happened that a hunter chanced at night to follow a bear into one of the largest swamps of the land, when to his astonishment he discovered a small light hanging over the water. It was so beautiful that he followed it for a long distance, but it led into such dangerous places that he gave up the pursuit, and returned to tell his people what he had seen. And then it was that the oldest men of the tribe told him that the light he had seen was the star that had been driven from heaven, and that it was now wandering over the earth for the purpose of finding the beautiful girl it had loved. And that same star is still upon the earth, and is often seen by the hunters as they journey at night through the wilderness.

ORIGIN OF THE POTTOWATOMIES.

According to the belief of the Pottowatomies, there once lived on the western shore of Lake Michigan two great spirits. Their names were *Kit-che-mo-ne-to*, or the Good Spirit, and *Mat-che-mo-me-to*, the Evil Spirit. They were equally powerful, but the creation of the world was attributed to the former. When he had piled up the mountains, and filled the valleys with running streams, he proceeded to people the world with living creatures, and allotted to each variety its peculiar sphere. He then endeavored to create a being that should resemble himself, but in this attempt he did not succeed. The animal that he made looked and acted more like a wolf than any other creature. Disappointed at this failure the Good Spirit became angry, and seizing the strange creature he had made he threw it into a great lake, and it was drowned. A storm arose, and the waters of the lake made a terrible noise as they beat upon its rocky shores. Among the shells and pebbles washed upon the sands were the bones of the strange animal that the Good Spirit had made, and when the storm had abated the bones were turned into a being who bore a strong likeness to the present race of Pottowatomies, and that being was the first woman. So well pleased with this creation was the Good Spirit that he made five other beings resembling her in form, but only more rugged, who were to help her in all her employments; and these were the first men. One of them was named *U-sa-me*, or Smoking-Weed; another *Wa-pa-ho*, or Pumpkin; another *Esh-kos-sim-in*, or the Melon; another *Ko-kees*, or the Bean; and the other *Mon-ta-min*, or Yellow Maize. The business of these several beings was to protect and gather the various productions of the earth after which they were named, and in doing this they continued to be employed from the time that the acorn fell to the ground until it became one of the largest trees of the forest.

The world had now become very beautiful, and the few men who had the care of it very proud. They became the friends of the Evil Spirit. They quarreled among themselves, and in process of time with the woman, whom they had for a long time obeyed. They looked upon her as the queen of the world, and coveted her power and happiness. They tried to take her life, but without success. She became acquainted with the wickedness of their hearts, and regretted that she had ever been created. So unhappy did she become that she prayed to the Good Spirit to take her to the sky; and when the following evening came she was transformed into a star, and ever since that time has been the first to take her station in the horizon after the sun has disappeared behind the distant hills. And it is thought that so long as this star remains unchanged no misfortune can happen to the world.

When the five young men found themselves alone they were sorry for the unkind feelings they had manifested towards the woman, and were constantly missing the brightness of her smiles and the music of her voice, which they now remembered with mingled feelings of pleasure and pain. They were in great tribulation, and expected to perish from the face of the earth for their wickedness. They called upon the Evil Spirit for comfort and power, but he heard them not; he had abandoned them to their fate. They then thought that they would implore the assistance of the Good Spirit. They did so, and told him that they only wanted each the companionship of a woman, like the one that had been taken away. Their prayer was answered, and thus did they become the husbands of affectionate wives, from whom are descended the nation of Pottowatomies, or *the people who make their own fires.*

ORIGIN OF THE CHOCTAWS.

The *sea* alluded to in this legend is supposed to be the *Gulf of Mexico*, and the *mighty river* the *Mississippi*. So said the educated Choctaw *Pitchlyn*, from whom it was obtained. The idea that the Choctaws were the original mound builders, will strike the reader as something new.

According to the traditions of the Choctaws, the first of their race came from the bosom of a magnificent sea. Even when they first made their appearance upon the earth they were so numerous as to cover the sloping and sandy shore of the ocean far as the eye could reach, and for a long time did they follow the margin of the sea before they could find a place suited to their wants. The name of their principal chief has long since been forgotten, but it is well remembered that he was a prophet of great age and wisdom. For many moons did they travel without fatigue, and all the time were their bodies strengthened by pleasant breezes, and their hearts, on the other hand, gladdened by the luxuriance of a perpetual summer. In process of time, however, the multitude was visited by sickness, and one after another were left upon the shore the dead bodies of old women and little children. The heart of the Prophet became troubled, and, planting a long staff that he carried in his hand, and which was endowed with the miraculous power of an oracle, he told his people that from the spot designated they must turn their faces towards the unknown wilderness. But before entering upon this portion of their journey he designated a certain day for starting, and told them that they were at liberty, in the meantime, to enjoy themselves by feasting and dancing, and performing their national rites.

It was now early morning, and the hour appointed for starting. Heavy clouds and flying mists rested upon the sea, but the beautiful waves melted upon the shore as joyfully as ever before. The staff which the Prophet had planted was found leaning towards the north, and in that direction did the multitude take up their line of march. Their journey lay across streams, over hills and mountains, through tangled forests, and over immense prairies. They were now in an entirely strange country, and as they trusted in their magic staff they planted it every night with the utmost care, and arose in the morning with great eagerness to ascertain the direction towards which it leaned. And thus had they traveled for many days when they found themselves upon the margin of an *O-kee-na-chitto*, or great highway of water. Here did they pitch their tents, and having planted the staff, retired to repose. When morning came the oracle told them that they must cross the mighty river before them. They built themselves a thousand rafts, and reached the opposite shore in safety. They now found themselves in a country of surpassing loveliness, where the trees were so high as almost to touch the clouds, and where game of every variety and the sweetest of fruits were found in the greatest abundance. The flowers of this land were more brilliant than any they had ever before seen, and so large as often to shield them from the sunlight of noon. With the climate of the land they were delighted, and the air they breathed seem to fill their bodies with a new vigor. So pleased were they with all that they saw that they built mounds in all the more beautiful valleys they passed through, so that the Master of Life might know that they were not an ungrateful people. In this new country did they conclude to remain, and here did they establish their national government with its benign laws.

Time passed on, and the Choctaw nation became so powerful that its hunting grounds extended even to the sky. Troubles now arose among the younger warriors and hunters of the nation, until it came to pass that they abandoned the cabins of their forefathers, and settled in distant regions of the earth. Thus from the very body of the Choctaw nation have sprung those other nations which are known as the Chickasaws, the Cherokees, the Creeks or Mukogees, the Shawnees and the Delawares. And in the process of time the Choctaws founded a great city, wherein their more aged men might spend their days in peace; and, because they loved those of their people who had long before departed into distant regions, they called this city *Yazoo*, the meaning of which is, *home of the people who are gone.*

THE DANCING GHOSTS.

THAT beautiful phenomenon known to the white man as the Aurora Borealis, or Northern Lights, is called by the Chippeway Indians *Je-bi-ne-me-id-de-wand*, or the Dancing Ghosts. The legends accounting for it are numerous, and the following, which was related to the translator by a Chippeway hunter, named *Keesh-Chock*, or Precipice Leaper, is quite as fantastic as the phenomenon itself. That it is a very ancient tradition is evident from the fact that the sacrifice to which it alludes has not been practiced by the Chippeways for at least a century.

There was a time when all the inhabitants of the far North were afflicted by a famine. It was in the depth of winter, and the weather had for a long time been so cold that even the white bear was afraid to leave his hiding place. The prairies were so deeply covered with snow that the deer and the buffalo were compelled to wander to a warmer climate, and the lakes and rivers were so closely packed with ice that it was only once in a while that even a fish could be obtained. Such sorrow as reigned throughout the land had never before been known. The magicians and wise men kept themselves hidden in their cabins. The warriors and hunters, instead of boasting of their exploits, crowded around their camp-fires, and in silence meditated upon their unhappy doom. Mothers abandoned their children to seek for berries in the desolate forests, and the fingers of the young women had become stiff from idleness, for they had not any skins out of which to make the comfortable moccasin. From one end of the Chippeway country to the other was heard the cry of hunger and distress. That the Great Spirit was angry with his people was universally believed, but for what reason none of the magicians could tell. The chief of the Chippeways was the oldest man in the nation, and he was consulted in regard to the impending calamity. He could give no reason for the famine, but stated that he had been informed in a dream that the anger of the Great Spirit could be appeased by a human sacrifice. How this should come to pass, however, he could not tell, and therefore concluded to summon to his lodge all the medicine-men who lived within a day's journey, for the purpose of consulting with them. He did so, and when the council was ended it was proclaimed that three Chippeways should be immediately bound to the stake and consumed. They were to be selected by lot from among the warriors of the tribe; and, when this sad intelligence was promulgated, a national assembly was ordered to convene.

The appointed time arrived, and, in the presence of a large multitude, the fatal lots were cast, and three of the bravest men of the tribe were thus appointed to the sacrifice. They submitted to their fate without a murmur. Whilst their friends gathered around them with wild lamentations, and decked them with the costliest robes and ornaments to be found in all the tribe, the youthful warriors uttered not a word about their untimely departure, but only spoke in the most poetical language of the happy hunting grounds upon which they were about to enter. The spot selected for the sacrifice was the summit of a neighboring hill which was covered with woods. Upon this spot had three stakes been closely erected, around which there had been collected a large pile of dry branches and other combustible materials. To the stakes, at the hour of midnight, and by the hands of the magicians, unattended by spectators, were the three warriors securely fastened. They performed their cruel duty in silence, and the only sounds that broke the stillness of that winter night were the songs and the shoutings of the multitude assembled in the neighboring village. The incantations of the priests being ended, they applied a torch to the fagots, and, returning to their village, spent the remainder of the night in performing a variety of strange and heart-sickening ceremonies.

Morning dawned, and upon the hill of sacrifice was to be seen only a pile of smouldering ashes. On that day the weather moderated, and an unusual number of hunters went forth in pursuit of game. They were all more successful than they had been for many seasons, and there was an abundance of sweet game, such as the buffalo, the bear, and the deer in every wigwam. A council was called, and the patriarch chief proclaimed the glad tidings that the Great Spirit had accepted their sacrifice, and that it was now the duty of his children to express their gratitude by a feast—the feast of *bitter roots.*

The appointed night arrived, and the bitterest roots which could be found in the lodges of the magicians were collected together and made into a soup. The company assembled to partake of this feast, was the largest that had ever been known, and, as they were to conclude their ceremony of thankfulness by dancing, they had cleared the snow from the centre of their village, and on this spot were they duly congregated. It was a cold and remarkably clear night, and their watch-fires burnt with uncommon brilliancy. It was now the hour of midnight, and the bitter soup was all gone. The flutes and the drums had just been brought out, and the dancers, decked in their most uncouth dresses, were about to enter the charmed ring, when a series of loud shoutings were heard, and the eyes of the entire multitude were intently fixed upon the northern sky, which was illuminated by a most brilliant and unearthly light. It was a light of many colors, and as changeable as the reflections upon a summer sea at the sunset hour. Across this light were constantly dancing three huge figures of a crimson hue, and these did the magicians proclaim to be the ghosts of the three warriors who had given up their bodies for the benefit of their people, and who had thus become great chiefs in the spirit-land. The fire by which their bodies had been consumed had also consumed every feeling of revenge; and ever since that remote period it has been their greatest pleasure to illume by their appearance on winter nights the pathway of the hunters over the snowy plains of the north.

THE STRANGE WOMAN.

It was in olden times, and two Choctaw hunters were spending the night by their watch-fire in a bend of the river Alabama. The game and the fish of their country were with every new moon becoming less abundant, and all that they had to satisfy their hunger on the night in question, was the tough flesh of a black hawk. They were very tired, and as they mused upon their unfortunate condition, and thought of their hungry children, they were very unhappy, and talked despondingly. But they roasted the bird before the fire, and proceeded to enjoy as comfortable a meal as they could. Hardly had they commenced eating, however, before they were startled by a singular noise, resembling the cooing of a dove. They jumped up and looked around them to ascertain the cause. In one direction they saw nothing but the moon just rising above the forest trees on the opposite side of the river. They looked up and down the river, but could see nothing but the sandy shores and the dark waters. They listened, and nothing could they hear but the murmur of the flowing stream. They turned their eyes in that direction opposite the moon, and to their astonishment, they discovered standing upon the summit of a grassy mound, the form of a beautiful woman. They hastened to her side, when she told them she was very hungry, whereupon they ran after their roasted hawk, and gave it all into the hands of the strange woman. She barely tasted of the proffered food, but told the hunters that their kindness had preserved her from death, and that she would not forget them, when she returned to the happy grounds of her father, who was the *Hosh-tah-li*, or Great Spirit of the Choctaws. She had one request to make, and this was, that when the next moon of midsummer should arrive, they should visit the spot where she then stood. A pleasant breeze swept among the forest leaves, and the strange woman suddenly disappeared.

The hunters were astonished, but they returned to their families, and kept all that they had seen and heard, hidden in their hearts. Summer came, and they once more visited the mound on the banks of the Alabama. They found it covered with a new plant, whose leaves were like the knives of the white man. It yielded a delicious food, which has since been known among the Choctaws as the sweet toncha or Indian maize.

THE VAGABOND BACHELOR.

In the great wilderness of the north, midway between Hudson's Bay and Lake Ontario, lies a beautiful sheet of water called Stone Lake. It is surrounded with hills, which are covered with a dense forest, and the length thereof is about twelve miles. On the shore of this lake there stood, in the olden time, an Ottawa village, and the most notorious vagabond in said village was an old bachelor. He was a kind-hearted rogue, and though he pretended to have a cabin of his own, he spent the most of his time lounging about the wigwams of his friends, where he was treated with the attention usually bestowed upon the oldest dog of an Indian village. The low cunning for which he was distinguished made him the laughing-stock of all who knew him, and his proverbial cowardice had won for him the contempt of all the hunters and warriors. Whenever a war party was convened for the purpose of pursuing an enemy, Wis-ka-go-twa, or the White Liver, always happened to be in the woods; but when they returned, singing their songs of victory, the vagabond bachelor generally mingled conspicuously with the victors.

But, in process of time, Wis-ka-go-twa took it into his head to get married, and from that moment began the troubles of his life. As soon as his resolution had become known among the young women of the village, they came together in secret council, and unanimously agreed that not one of them would ever listen to the expected proposals of the bachelor, for they thought him too great a coward to enjoy the pleasures of matrimony. Years elapsed, and the vagabond was still in the enjoyment of his bachelorhood.

In the meanwhile a beautiful maiden, named Muck-o-wiss, or the Whipporwill, had budded into the full maturity of life. She was the chief attraction of the village, and the heart of many a brave warrior and expert hunter had been humbled beneath her influence. Among those who had entered her lodge in the quiet night, and whispered the story of his love, was Wis-ka-go-twa. She deigned not to reply to his avowals, and he became unhappy. He asked the consent of her father to their union, and he said that he had no objections provided the daughter was willing. It so happened, however, that the maiden was not willing, for she was a member of that female confederacy which had doomed the vagabond lover to the miseries of single life. Time passed on, and he was the victim of a settled melancholy.

The sunny days of autumn were nearly numbered, and an occasional blast from the far north had brought a shudder to the breast of Wis-ka-go-twa, for they reminded him of the long winter which he was likely to spend in his wigwam alone. He pondered upon the gloomy prospect before him, and in his frenzy made the desperate resolution that he would, by any means in his power, obtain the love of his soft-eyed charmer. He consequently began to exert himself in his daily hunts, and whenever he obtained an uncommonly fat beaver, or large bear, he carefully deposited it before the lodge of Muck-o-wiss, and he now mingled, more frequently than ever before, in the various games of the village, and was not behind his more youthful rivals in jumping and playing ball. In a variety of ways did he obtain renown, but it was at the expense of efforts which nearly deprived him of life. Again did he sue for the smiles of Muck-o-wiss, but she told him he was an old man, and that he did not wear in his hair a single plume of the eagle, to show that he had ever taken a scalp.

The disappointed vagabond now turned his attention to war. It so happened, however, that a permanent peace had been established between the Ottawas and the neighboring tribes, so that our hero was baffled on this score also. But he had heard it reported in the village that a party of Iroquois warriors had been seen on that side of the Great Lake, and as they were heartily hated by his own tribe, he conceived the idea of absenting himself for a few days, for the purpose of playing a deceptive game upon the maiden of his love and the entire population of the village where he lived. Having formed his determination, he kept it entirely to himself, and on a certain morning he launched his canoe upon the lake and disappeared, as if going upon a hunting expedition.

Four or five days had elapsed, and the vagabond bachelor was not yet returned. On the afternoon of the sixth day, a couple of Indian boys, who had been frolicking away the morning in the woods, returned to the village in an uncommonly excited mood. They visited almost every wigwam, and related a grand discovery which they had made. While chasing a deer into a secluded bay, about ten miles down the lake, they announced that they had seen Wis-ka-go-twa engaged in a most singular employment. They were aware of his peculiar reputation, and when they saw him in this out-of-the-way place, they watched him in silence from behind a fallen tree. The first act which they saw him perform was, to shoot into the side of his little canoe some twenty of his flint-headed arrows, which mutilated the canoe in a most disgraceful manner. He next took some unknown instrument, and inflicted a number of severe wounds upon his arms and legs. But the deepest incision which he made was on his leg, just above the knee, into which they were astonished to see him place, with a small stick, a kind of white material, which resembled the dry shell of a turtle. All this being accomplished, they saw the vagabond embark in his leaky canoe, as if about to return to the village. They suspected the game that was being played, so they made the shortest cut home and related the foregoing particulars.

An hour or two passed on, and, as the sun was setting, the villagers were attracted by a canoe upon the lake. They watched it with peculiar interest, and found that it was steadily approaching. Presently it made its appearance within hailing distance, when it was discovered to be occupied by the vagabond bachelor. Every man, woman, and child immediately made their appearance on the shore, apparently for the purpose of welcoming the returning hunter, but in reality with a view of enjoying what they supposed would turn out a good joke. The hunter looked upon the crowd with evident satisfaction, but he manifested his feelings in a very novel manner, for he was momentarily uttering a long-drawn groan, as if suffering from a severe wound. As the canoe touched the sand it was found to be half full of bloody water, and one of the sides had evidently been fired into by the arrows of an enemy. A murmur ran through the crowd that Wis-ka-go-twa must have had a dreadful time, and he was called upon to give the particulars, when he did so in a few words. He had been overtaken, he said, by a party of Iroquois, consisting of some twenty men, who attacked him while he was pursuing a bear, and though he succeeded in killing four of his rascally pursuers, his canoe had been sadly mutilated, and he had received a wound which he feared would be the cause of his death. In due time the wound was revealed to the public eye, and the young women turned away with a shudder; and then the vagabond bachelor was conveyed to his lodge, and the medicine-man sent for to administer relief.

A day or two elapsed, and the poor hunter was evidently in a bad way. They asked him what individual in the village he would have to attend him. He expressed a preference for the father of Muck-o-wiss, who came and faithfully attended to his duties as a nurse; but the sick was not yet satisfied. "Whom will you have now?" asked the old man, and the name of Muck-o-wiss trembled on the lips of the sick lover. His chief desire was granted, and for three days did the maiden attend to the little wants of her unfortunate lover. Another day, and he was rapidly mending. He was now so nearly restored that the maiden began to talk of returning to her mother's wigwam. This intelligence roused the hunter from his bed of furs, and he once more avowed his undying attachment to the charming maiden. She repulsed him with a frown, and retired from the lodge; so the hunter was again sadly disappointed. The maiden hastened to tell the news to all the women of the village, and after they had enjoyed themselves for upwards of an hour, Muck-o-wiss returned to the wigwam of her lover, and told him that she would become his wife on one condition, which was, that on the day he should succeed in killing five bears, on that day would she enter his lodge and make it her permanent home. For an Indian to kill five bears on one day was considered a remarkable feat, and the roguish Muck-o-wiss thought herself secure.

Days passed on, and the vagabond bachelor was again restored to sound health and devoting himself to the chase. It was just the season when the black bear takes up its annual journey for the south, and the hunter had discovered a narrow place in the lake, where the animals were in the habit of coming. It was the last day of autumn, and early in the morning he had stationed himself in a good ambush. By the time the sun cast a short shadow, he had killed three fine specimens, and placed them before the lodge of his intended wife. The middle of the afternoon arrived, and he had deposited the fourth animal at the same place. The sunset hour was nigh at hand, and the hunter had killed and placed in his canoe the fifth and largest bear that he had ever seen. The happiest hour of the poor man's life was now surely nigh at hand. Impatiently did he paddle his way home. The villagers saw that the vagabond bachelor had been successful, and Muck-o-wiss and all her female companions were filled with consternation. But the truly heroic warriors, who had striven in vain to win the love of the village beauty, were not only astonished, but indignant, for they could not bear the idea of losing, in such a manner, the prize which had urged them on in the more noble deeds of war. But now has the canoe once more reached the shore. Upon his back has the hunter lifted his prize, and up the bank is he toiling and staggering along with the immense load, and now has he fixed his eyes upon the lodge where he is hoping to receive his promised bride. His heart flutters with tumultuous joy—his knees tremble from fatigue—a strange faintness passes over his brain—he reels from his upright position—the bear falls to the ground—and the vagabond bachelor is—dead.

ORIGIN OF THE WATER LILY.

MANY, many moons ago, an old and very celebrated hunter of the Pottowattomie nation was at the point of death, in a remote forest. He was alone on his bed of leaves, for he had been stricken by the hand of disease while returning from a hunting expedition. Among the treasures that he was to leave behind him was a beautiful hickory arrow, with which he had killed a great number of animals. The head thereof was made of a pure white flint, and the feathers which adorned it had been plucked from the wings of the scarlet birds. It had been the means of saving his life on many occasions, and its virtues were so peculiar, that it could pass entire through a buffalo without being tinged with the life-blood of the animal.

The greatest weight which rested upon the mind of the dying Indian, arose from the idea that he could not bequeath his arrow to his oldest son. He was alone in the wilderness, and it made him very unhappy to think that the treasure of his family might yet become the property of an enemy, who would be likely to cross his trail after the ravens or wolves had eaten his flesh. But this was a thought that he could not possibly endure, and as the pall of night settled upon the world, he fixed his eyes upon the northern star, which had guided him through many dangers, and prayed to the Master of Life that he would take his arrow and carry it safely to the smiling planet. A moment more and the unknown hunter buried his head among the dry leaves, and—died.

On the following night, a terrible gale of wind swept over the land, which took the arrow from the ground and hurled it into the upper air. A strange silence immediately followed, when the northern star was seen to tremble in the sky: another brief period elapsed, and there was a deafening noise heard in the firmament, when the evening star left its own quiet home, and fell upon the northern star for the purpose of winning, by single combat, the arrow of the great hunter. The conflict was a desperate one, and as the two stars fought for the earthly prize, sparks of white light shot from their sides, and in unnumbered particles fell upon the country now known as Michigan. A long rain storm soon followed, by which the particles of light were taken to the river, and by a decree of the Master of Life, were changed into the beautiful white lilies which adorn the numerous streams of the western country.

THE FAITHFUL COUSINS.

I NOW speak of two Chippeway hunters, who lived among the Porcupine mountains, near Lake Superior. They were the oldest sons of two brothers, and noted in their village for the warm friendship existing between them, and for their powers in hunting. They were very famous throughout the land, and into whatever village they happened to enter, the old men asked them to remain and marry their handsome women, but the hunters laughed at all such proposals, for they had pledged their words to each other that they would ever remain single and free.

It was when the leaves were fading, that the young cousins heard of a great hunt which was to take place in a distant village. It was got up by an old warrior, who was the father of a beautiful daughter, and he had determined that the most successful hunter should become his son-in-law. This intelligence had been conveyed to the cousins in a secret manner, and on departing from their own village, they spoke not a word of their determination. In due time the hunt took place, and an immense quantity of game was taken. Some of the hunters brought home two bears, some three and four deer, but the two cousins captured each five bears. As no one man had eclipsed his fellows, it was resolved by the old warrior that the man who should bring to his lodge the scalps of ten bears, should be the successful candidate for the hand of his daughter. Another hunt took place, and each of the cousins brought in, not only the scalps of ten full grown bears, but also a large quantity of choice meats, which they deposited at the tent door of the chief. The difficulty of making a selection was now even greater than before, but the truth was, the young friends had no desire to marry the beautiful girl, but were only anxious to manifest their bravery, or rather wonderful expertness in killing wild animals. Their singular conduct astonished everybody, but mostly the venerable warrior and his favorite daughter.

The important question must be decided, however, and the old man resorted to a number of expedients to decide upon a future son-in-law. The first was that the two cousins should enter upon a wrestling match—they did so, and the twain fell to the ground at the same moment. The next was that they should try their agility in leaping over a suspended stick, but in this trial they also came out exactly even. The third was, that they shoot their arrows at a pair of humming birds, and the maker of the best shot to be the lady's husband; the arrows were thrown, and the right wing of each bird was broken. The fourth expedient was that they should go upon a squirrel hunt—they did so, and each one returned with just exactly one hundred of those sprightly creatures. It now came to pass, and was whispered about the village, that one of the cousins had really become interested in the girl who was the innocent cause of so much contention, and when her father found this out, he resolved to make one more experiment. He therefore commanded the young men to kill each a specimen of the *ke necoh* or war-eagle, and the one who should present her with the greatest number of perfectly formed feathers, would be welcomed as a relative. The trial was made and the whole number of feathers obtained was twenty-one, the odd feather having been gained by the enamored cousin. The girl was of course awarded to him in due time, but what was the surprise of all the villagers, when it was proclaimed that he would not receive the prize unless the young men of the tribe should first build him a handsome lodge and furnish it with the choicest of meats and skins. At this suggestion the young men were greatly enraged, but they concluded, in consideration of their admiration for the Indian girl, to change their minds, and forthwith proceeded to erect the new lodge.

In the meanwhile, it was ascertained that the unlucky cousin had become somewhat offended at his companion, whereupon the accepted lover joined the other in a bear hunt for the purpose of effecting a reconciliation. It so happened, however, that the existing coldness between them could not be removed, and while the twain were toiling up a remote hill with the view of encamping for the night, the disappointed cousin was suddenly transformed into a large fire-fly, and having ascended into the air, immediately experienced another change, and became what is now known as the Northern Star. The remaining cousin felt himself severely punished by this abandonment for having broken his vow, and therefore became an exile from his native land and led a comfortless and solitary life; while the maiden whom he was to wed, it is said, is still waiting patiently, but in vain, for the return of her long lost lover.

THE OSAGE DAMSEL.

THERE once lived in the Osage country an Indian whose name was *Koo-zhe-ge-ne-cah*, or *The Distant Man.* He had been a famous warrior and hunter, but time had weakened his arm and lifted a mist before his eye. His wives were all dead, and the only one of his kindred left upon earth to minister to his wants was a little damsel, his grandchild, and the joy of his old age. The twain were much beloved by all their tribe, and when journeying across the broad prairies they were always supplied with the gentlest of horses, and they never had to ask the second time for their favorite food. Whenever the tribe came to a halt on the bank of a river, in a country abounding in game, the first tent-poles planted in the ground were those belonging to the Distant Man and his child, and their tent always stood next to that of the chief.

It was midsummer, and the entire Osage nation was encamped upon a plain at the foot of a mountain, covered to the very summit with rich grass and brilliant flowers. The last hunts had been successful, and in every lodge was to be found an abundance of buffalo and deer meat. Feasting and merrymaking, dancing and playing ball, were the chief employments of the hour throughout the entire village, while in every direction upon the prairies the horses, with their feet hobbled, were cropping their sweet food. The children and the dogs sported upon the green together, and many a laugh resounded long and loud. The sun was near his setting, when suddenly an unusual stillness pervaded the air. The people gathered together in haste and wondered what it could all mean. The strange silence caused them to listen with increased attention, when a distant whoop came stealing along the air. It seemed to come from the neighboring mountain, and as the multitude cast their eyes in that direction, they saw a single horseman coming towards their encampment with the speed of the wind. They waited in breathless expectation, and were astonished at the boldness of the stranger in riding with such fury directly into their midst.

He was mounted upon a black horse of gigantic size, with splendidly flowing mane and tail, and an eye of intense brilliancy, and was caparisoned in a most gorgeous manner. The stranger was clad from head to foot with a dress of many colors, and from his hair hung a great variety of the most curious plumes. He carried a lance, and to his side were fastened a bow and a quiver of arrows. He was in the prime of life, and his bearing was that of a warrior chief. He avowed himself the son of the Master of Life, and his home to be in the Spirit Land. He said that there was a woman in that land who had told him that the most beautiful maiden in the Osage nation was her daughter. From other lips also had he heard that she was good as well as beautiful, and that her only protector and friend was an old man named *Koo-ze-ghe-ne-cah.* He had asked for a dream that he might see this being of the earth. Having seen her, and being in want of a wife, he was now come to demand her of her venerable parent, and forthwith rode to the door of his tent to make a bargain. The stranger dismounted not from his horse, but talked with the old man leaning upon the neck of his noble animal, the maiden meanwhile sitting in pensive quietness within her tent door, working a pair of moccasins. The old man doubted the stranger's words, and desired him to prove that he was the son of the Master of Life. "What sign of my nature and power would you witness?" inquired the stranger. "That you would cover the heavens with thick darkness, picture it with lightning, and fill the air with loud thunder," replied the old man. "Do this, and my daughter shall be your bride." Suddenly a storm arose, and the sign was fulfilled to the utmost extent, so that the entire nation were stricken with fear. Night came on, the sky was without a cloud, but spangled with stars, and the air was perfectly serene, and when the stranger and his steed were sought for, it was found that they had disappeared. Peace rested upon the Osage village, and the oldest men of that tribe never enjoyed a more refreshing sleep than on that memorable night.

On the following day everything about the Osage encampment

wore its ordinary aspect, and the events of the previous day were talked over as people talk of their dreams. The old man and the maiden made an offering to the Master of Life, and while the former, before the assembled nation, promised to give up his child, she, in her turn, expressed her entire willingness to become the bride of the stranger, should he ever return. Not only was she prompted to do this by the honor conferred upon her, and also by the nobleness of the stranger, but she thought it would make her so happy to rejoin her long departed mother in the spirit land. She was only troubled about the feeble old man, whom she dearly loved; but when the whole nation promised, as with one voice, to make him the object of their peculiar care, she was satisfied.

Again was the sun in the western horizon. Again did the stranger appear mounted as before. But as he entered the village, there trotted by his side a white horse of exceeding beauty, decked from forelock to tail with the richest and rarest of ornaments. He had come for his bride, and was impatient to be gone. He led the white horse to the tent of the girl he loved, and throwing at her feet a dress of scarlet feathers, he motioned her to prepare for a long journey. When she was ready, he motioned to the white horse to fall upon his knees, and the maiden leaped upon his back. The twain then walked their horses to the outskirts of the village, and as they passed along the stranger took from his quiver and tossed into the hands of the Osage chief and each of his warriors and hunters, a charmed arrow, which, he said, would enable them not only to subdue their enemies, but also supply them with an abundance of game, as long as they roamed the prairies. The stranger now gave a whoop and the horses started upon the run. Their path lay over the mountain, where the stranger had been first seen. They flew more swiftly than the evening breeze, and just as the sun disappeared, they reached the summit of the mountain and also disappeared, as if received into the bosom of a golden cloud.

THE SPECTRE AND HUNTER.

The following legend was originally translated into English by an educated Choctaw, named *J. L. McDonald*, and subsequently embodied in a private letter to another Choctaw, named *Peter P. Pitchlyn*. The former of these very worthy Indian gentlemen has long been dead, and it is therefore with very great pleasure that I avail myself of the opportunity, kindly afforded me by the latter gentleman, of associating the legendary relic with my own. I have ventured, by the permission and advice of Mr. Pitchlyn, to alter an occasional expression in the text, but have not trespassed upon the spirit of the story.

KO-WAY-HOOM-MAH, or the Red Panther, once started out on a hunting expedition. He had an excellent bow, and carried with him some jerked venison. His only companion was a large white dog, which attended him in all his rambles. This dog was a cherished favorite, and shared in all his master's privations and successes. He was the social companion of the hunter by day, and his watchful guardian by night.

The hunter had traveled far, and as the evening approached, he encamped upon a spot that bore every indication of an excellent hunting-ground. Deer-tracks were seen in abundance, and turkeys were heard clucking in various directions, as they retired to their roosting places. Ko-way-hoom-mah kindled a fire, and having shared a portion of his provision with his dog, he spread his deer-skin and his blanket by the crackling fire, and mused on the adventures of the day already passed, and on the probable success of the ensuing one. It was a bright starlight night; the air was calm, and a slight frost which was falling, rendered the fire comfortable and cheering. His dog lay crouched and slumbering at his feet, and from his stifled cries, seemed dreaming of the chase. Everything tended to soothe the feelings of our hunter, and to prolong that pleasant train of associations, which the beauty of the night and the anticipations of the morrow were calculated to inspire. At length, when his musings were assuming that indefinite and dreamy state which precedes a sound slumber, he was startled by a distant cry, which thrilled on his ear, and roused him into instant watchfulness. He listened with breathless attention, and in a few minutes again heard the cry, keen, long, and piercing. The dog gave a plaintive and ominous howl. Ko-way-hoom-mah felt uneasy. Can it be a lost hunter? was the inquiry which suggested itself. Surely not, for a true hunter feels lost nowhere. What then can it be? With these reflections our hunter stepped forth, gathered more fuel, and again replenished his fire. Again came a cry, keen, long, and painfully thrilling, as before. The voice was evidently approaching, and again the dog raised a low and mournful howl. Ko-way-hoom-mah then felt the blood curdling to his heart, and folding his blanket around him, he seated himself by the fire and fixed his eyes intently in the direction from which he expected the approach of his startling visitor. In a few moments he heard the approach of his footsteps. In another minute, a ghastly shape made its appearance, and advanced towards the fire. It seemed to be the figure of a hunter, like himself. Its form was tall and gaunt, its features livid and unearthly. A tattered robe was girded round his waist, and covered his shoulders, and he bore an unstrung bow and a few broken arrows.

The spectre advanced to the fire, and seemed to shiver with cold. He stretched forth one hand, then the other to the fire, and as he did so, he fixed his hollow and ghastly eye on Ko-way-hoom-mah, and a slight smile lighted up his livid countenance, but not a word did he utter. Ko-way-hoom-mah felt his flesh and hair creep, and the blood freezing in his veins, yet with instinctive Indian courtesy he presented his deer-skin as a seat for his grim visitor. The spectre waved his hand, and shook his head in refusal. He stepped aside, plucked up a parcel of briers from an adjacent thicket, spread them by the fire, and on his thorny couch he stretched himself and seemed to court repose.

Our hunter was petrified with mingled fear and astonishment. His eyes continued long riveted on the strange and ghastly being stretched before him, and he was only awakened from his trance of horror by the voice of his faithful dog. "Arise," said the dog, suddenly and supernaturally gifted with speech, "Arise, and flee for your life! The spectre now slumbers: should you also slumber, you are lost. Arise and flee, while I stay and watch!" Ko-way-hoom-mah arose, and stole softly from the fire. Having advanced a few hundred paces, he stopped to listen; all was silent, and with a beating heart he continued his stealthy and rapid flight. Again he listened, and again, with renewed confidence, he pursued his rapid course, until he had gained several miles on his route homeward. Feeling at length a sense of safety, he paused to recover breath, on the brow of a lofty hill. The night was calm and serene, the stars shone with steady lustre, and as Ko-way-hoom-mah gazed upwards, he breathed freely and felt every apprehension vanish. Alas! on the instant, the distant baying of his dog struck on his ear; with a thrill of renewed apprehension, he bent his ear to listen, and the appalling cry of his dog, now more distinctly audible, convinced him that the spectre was in full pursuit. Again he fled with accelerated speed, over hill, over plain, through swamps and thickets, till once more he paused by the side of a deep and rapid river. The heavy baying of his dog told him too truly, that his fearful pursuer was close at hand. One minute he stood for breath, and he then plunged into the stream. But scarcely had he gained the centre, when the spectre appeared on the bank, and plunged in after him, closely followed by the panting dog. Ko-way-hoom-mah's apprehensions now amounted to agony. He fancied he saw the hollow and glassy eyeballs of his pursuer glaring above the water, and that his skeleton hand was already outstretched to grapple with him. With a cry of horror he was about to give up the struggle for life and sink beneath the waves, when his faithful dog, with a fierce yell, seized upon his master's enemy. After a short but severe struggle they both sunk; the waters settled over them forever. He became an altered man. He shunned the dance and the ball play, and his former hilarity gave place to a settled melancholy. In about a year after this strange adventure he joined a war party against a distant enemy and never returned.

THE END.

NEW AND VALUABLE PUBLICATIONS OF
LIPPINCOTT, GRAMBO & Co.,
SUCCESSORS TO GRIGG, ELLIOT & Co., PHILADELPHIA.

THE IRIS:
A SOUVENIR FOR 1851.

A super-royal 8vo. Illustrated with original Illuminations and Steel Engravings, executed in the best style of the Art.

EDITED BY

PROFESSOR JOHN S. HART, OF PHILADELPHIA.

The Contributions are from the first talent of the country, and entirely original, and the Publishers have made this the most attractive and valuable Gift-Book of the season.

A COMPLETE DICTIONARY
OF
POETICAL QUOTATIONS:
COMPRISING THE MOST EXCELLENT AND APPROPRIATE PASSAGES

IN THE

OLD BRITISH POETS:
BY JOSEPH ADDINGTON.

WITH CHOICE AND COPIOUS SELECTIONS

FROM THE BEST

MODERN BRITISH AND AMERICAN POETS.
EDITED BY

SARAH JOSEPHA HALE.

Beautifully illustrated with Engravings. In one super-royal 8vo. volume, in various bindings.

The publishers extract, from the many highly complimentary notices of the above valuable and beautiful work, the following :—

"We have at last a volume of Poetical Quotations worthy of the name. It contains nearly six hundred octavo pages, carefully and tastefully selected from all the home and foreign authors of celebrity. It is invaluable to a writer, while to the ordinary reader it presents every subject at a glance."—*Godey's Lady's Book.*

"The plan or idea of Mrs. Hale's work is felicitous. It is one for which her fine taste, her orderly habits of mind, and her long occupation with literature, has given her peculiar facilities; and thoroughly has she accomplished her task in the work before us."—*Sartain's Magazine.*

"It is a choice collection of poetical extracts from every English and American author worth perusing, from the days of Chaucer to the present time."—*Washington Union.*

"Its graceful editress, in her short preface, thus speaks, and most truly, of its contents: 'Whatever is loveliest in sentiment and loftiest in aspiration is here represented: specimens of the varied forms in which gifted minds have contributed to the polish of wit, the beauty of wisdom, the sweetness of love, the power of patriotism, the holiness of piety—all that has most deeply stirred the soul of the Anglo-Saxon race for the last three hundred years, is here embodied.' It contains copious selections from all the standard British and American Poets upon almost every subject within the range of thought. The subjects are arranged alphabetically, and a 'Table of Contents' at the commencement renders reference to them perfectly easy."—*New Hampshire Patriot.*

"There is nothing negative about this work; it is *positively* good."—*Evening Bulletin.*

SPLENDID LIBRARY EDITIONS.

ILLUSTRATED STANDARD POETS.

Elegantly Printed and Uniform in Size and Style.

The following editions of Standard British Poets are illustrated with numerous steel engravings, and may be had in all varieties of binding.

BYRON'S WORKS.

Complete in one vol. octavo.

INCLUDING ALL HIS SUPPRESSED AND ATTRIBUTED POEMS;

With Six beautiful Engravings.

☞This edition has been carefully compared with the recent London edition of Mr. Murray, and made complete by the addition of more than fifty pages of poems heretofore unpublished in England. Among these there are a number that have never appeared in any American edition; and the publishers believe they are warranted in saying, that this is the *most complete edition of Lord Byron's Poetical Works* ever published in the United States.

COWPER & THOMSON'S PROSE AND POETICAL WORKS.

Complete in one vol. octavo.

Including two hundred and fifty Letters, and sundry Poems of Cowper, never before published in this country; and of Thomson a new and interesting Memoir, and upwards of twenty new Poems, for the first time printed from his own Manuscripts, taken from a late edition of the Aldine Poets now publishing in London.

With Seven beautiful Engravings.

THE POETICAL WORKS OF MRS. HEMANS.

Only complete edition, in one vol. octavo.

WITH SEVEN BEAUTIFUL ENGRAVINGS.

☞ This is a new and complete edition, with a splendid engraved likeness of Mrs. Hemans on steel, and contains all the Poems in the last London and American editions.

THE POETICAL WORKS OF ROGERS, CAMPBELL, MONTGOMERY, LAMB, AND KIRK WHITE.

Complete in one volume, octavo; with Six beautiful Engravings.

☞ The beauty, correctness, and convenience of this favorite edition of these standard authors are so well known, that it is scarcely necessary to add a word in its favor. It is only necessary to say, that the publishers have now issued an illustrated edition, which greatly enhances its former value. The engravings are excellent and well selected. It is the best library edition extant.

MILTON, YOUNG, GRAY, BEATTIE, AND COLLINS' POETICAL WORKS.

Complete in one volume, octavo; with Six beautiful Engravings.

HEBER, POLLOK, AND CRABBE'S POETICAL WORKS.

Complete in one volume, octavo; with Six beautiful Engravings.

No library can be considered complete without a copy of the above beautiful and cheap editions of the English Poets.

VALUABLE AND POPULAR BOOKS,

Particularly Suitable for Family Libraries.

PUBLISHED BY LIPPINCOTT, GRAMBO & CO.,

SUCCESSORS TO GRIGG, ELLIOT & CO.

No. 14 North Fourth Street, Philadelphia.

AND FOR SALE BY BOOKSELLERS AND COUNTRY MERCHANTS GENERALLY IN THE UNITED STATES.

"EDUCATED MIND is *a Nation's wealth*, and promotes the happiness of mankind."

FARMERS, LOOK TO YOUR INTERESTS!

The following Books are particularly adapted for a Farmer's Library.

ONE DOLLAR

Once expended in useful precaution may save you

Hundreds of Dollars absolute Losses every Year.

It is a fact too clearly established to admit of doubt or disputation, that in the animal kingdom as in the human family, multitudes of lives and consequent losses of property, are occasioned by

Ignorance of those simple remedies which are within the reach of every one.

How important, therefore, that every

FARMER

should be possessed of that knowledge, without which

Neither Life nor Property is exempt from danger.

As Works of unparalleled value in this respect, the Publishers would respectfully call the attention of the

FARMING AND STOCK RAISING COMMUNITY

TO THE FOLLOWING BOOKS:

Mason's Farrier and Stud Book—New Edition.

THE GENTLEMAN'S NEW POCKET FARRIER:

COMPRISING A GENERAL DESCRIPTION OF THE NOBLE AND USEFUL ANIMAL,

THE HORSE;

With modes of management in all cases, and treatment in disease.

BY RICHARD MASON, M. D.,

Formerly of Surry County, Virginia.

TO WHICH IS ADDED, A PRIZE ESSAY ON MULES;

An Appendix, containing Recipes for Diseases of Horses, Oxen, Cows, Calves, Sheep, Dogs, Swine, etc. etc., with annals of the Turf, American Stud Book, Rules for Training, Racing, etc.

WITH A SUPPLEMENT:

Comprising an Essay on Domestic Animals, especially the Horse; with Remarks on Treatment and Breeding; together with Trotting and Racing Tables, showing the best time on record, at one, two, three and four mile heats; Pedigrees of Winning Horses, since 1839; and of the most celebrated Stallions and Mares; with Useful Calving and Lambing Tables, &c. &c. BY J. S. SKINNER, Editor now of the Farmer's Library, New York; Founder of the American Farmer, in 1819, and of the Turf Register and Sporting Magazine, in 1829; being the first Agricultural and the first Sporting Periodicals established in the United States.

Hinds' Farriery and Stud-Book—New Edition.

FARRIERY,

TAUGHT ON A NEW AND EASY PLAN,

BEING A TREATISE ON THE

DISEASES AND ACCIDENTS OF THE HORSE;

WITH

Instructions to the Shoeing Smith, Farrier, and Groom, preceded by a Popular Description of the Animal Functions in Health, and how these are to be restored when disordered.

BY JOHN HINDS, Veterinary Surgeon.

With considerable Additions and Improvements, particularly adapted to this Country

BY THOMAS M. SMITH,

Veterinary Surgeon, and Member of the London Veterinary Medical Society.

WITH A SUPPLEMENT:

COMPRISING

An Essay on Domestic Animals, especially the Horse; with Remarks on Treatment and Breeding; together with Trotting and Racing Tables, showing the best time on Record, at one, two, three, and four mile heats; pedigrees of Winning Horses, since 1839; and of the most celebrated Stallions and Mares: with Useful Calving and Lambing Tables, &c. &c.

BY J. S. SKINNER,

Editor now of the Farmer's Library, New York; Founder of the American Farmer, in 1819; and of the Turf Register and Sporting Magazine, in 1829: being the first Agricultural and the first Sporting Periodicals established in the United States.

THE PUBLISHERS HAVE RECEIVED NUMEROUS FLATTERING NOTICES of the great practical value of these works. The distinguished editor of the American Farmer, speaking of them, observes—"We cannot too highly recommend these books, and therefore advise every owner of a horse to obtain them."

"There are receipts in those books that show how FOUNDER may be cured, and the traveler pursue his journey the next day, by giving a *tablespoonful of alum.* This was got from Dr. P. Thornton, of Montpelier, Rappahannock County, Virginia, as founded on his own observation in several cases."

"The constant demand for MASON AND HINDS' FARRIER, has induced the publishers, Messrs. GRIGG, ELLIOT & Co., to put forth new editions with a 'SUPPLEMENT' of 100 pages, by J. S. SKINNER, Esq. We should have sought to render an acceptable service to our agricultural readers, by giving a chapter from the Supplement, 'On the relations between Man and the Domestic Animals—especially the Horse—and the obligations they impose;' or the one on 'The Form of Animals,'—but that either one of them would overrun the space here allotted to such subjects."

"LIST OF MEDICINES,

And other articles which ought to be at hand about every training and livery stable, and every Farmer's and Breeder's establishment, will be found in these valuable works."

RUSCHENBERGER'S NATURAL HISTORY.

IN TWO BEAUTIFUL VOLUMES WORTHY OF THE HIGHEST COMMENDATION.

They embrace elements of Anatomy and Physiology, Mammalogy, Ornithology, Herpetology, Conchology, Entomology, Botany and Geology, each of which Divisions of Science is treated of in the most masterly yet simple manner, on the basis of a set of works ordered and approved by the Royal Council of Public Instruction in France.

The author has done his work well, and is highly complimented by the most distinguished scholars in the country. The work is a text-book in the Philadelphia High School. It is splendidly illustrated, and parents could not do better than to present their children with this book in preference to those of a more trivial character, combining as it does amusement with important instruction. Any one of the works may be had separately.

BIGLAND'S NATURAL HISTORY

Of Animals, Birds, Fishes, Reptiles and Insects, illustrated with numerous and beautiful engravings. By JOHN BIGLAND, author of a "View of the World," "Letters on Universal History," &c. Complete in 1 vol. 12mo.

This work is particularly adapted for the use of Schools and Families, forming the most elegantly written and complete work on the subject of Natural History ever published, and is worthy of the special attention of the teachers of all our schools and academies.

GOLDSMITH'S ANIMATED NATURE.

IN TWO VOLS. OCTAVO.

Beautifully Illustrated with 385 *Plates.*

"Goldsmith can never be made obsolete while delicate genius, exquisite feeling, fine invention, the most harmonious metre, and the happiest diction are at all valued."

This is a work that should be in the library of every family, being written by one of the most talented authors in the English language.

McMAHON'S AMERICAN GARDENER.

NINTH EDITION, MUCH IMPROVED.

In one volume, octavo.

This is an invaluable work to all who wish to obtain any information on the subject of Gardening in all its various branches.

CHAMBERS' INFORMATION FOR THE PEOPLE;

OR,

POPULAR ENCYCLOPÆDIA:

EMBRACING ALL THE BRANCHES OF GENERAL KNOWLEDGE NECESSARY TO CONSTITUTE

A WELL INFORMED MAN.

Altogether, 1700 *Imperial Octavo Pages, Two Large Volumes of* 850 *Pages each.*

☞ This work should find a place in every Family Library.

SPLENDID LIBRARY EDITIONS.

ILLUSTRATED STANDARD POETS.

Elegantly Printed and Uniform in Size and Style.

The following editions of Standard British Poets are illustrated with numerous steel engravings, and may be had in all varieties of binding.

BYRON'S WORKS.

Complete in 1 Vol. Octavo.

Including all his Suppressed and Attributed Poems; with 6 beautiful engravings.

☞ This edition has been carefully compared with the recent London edition of Mr. Murray, and made complete by the addition of more than fifty pages of poems heretofore unpublished in England. Among these there are a number that have never appeared in any American edition; and the publishers believe they are warranted in saying, that this is the *most complete edition of Lord Byron's Poetical Works* ever published in the United States.

COWPER AND THOMSON'S PROSE AND POETICAL WORKS.

Complete in 1 Vol. Octavo,

Including two hundred and fifty Letters, and sundry Poems of Cowper, never before published in this country; and of Thomson a new and interesting Memoir, and upwards of twenty new Poems, for the first time printed from his own Manuscripts, taken from a late edition of the Aldine Poets now publishing in London.

WITH SEVEN BEAUTIFUL ENGRAVINGS.

The distinguished Professor Silliman, speaking of this edition, observes, "I am as much gratified by the elegance and fine taste of your edition as by the noble tribute of genius and moral excellence which these delightful authors have left for all future generations; and Cowper, especially, is not less conspicuous as a true Christian, moralist and teacher, than as a poet of great power and exquisite taste."

THE POETICAL WORKS OF MRS. HEMANS.

Complete in 1 Vol. 8vo.; with 7 beautiful Engravings.

☞ This is a new and complete edition, with a splendid engraved likeness of Mrs. Hemans on steel, and contains all the poems in the last London and American editions. With a Critical Preface by Mr. Thatcher, of Boston.

"As no work in the English language can be commended with more confidence, it will argue bad taste in a female in this country to be without a complete edition of the writings of one who was an honor to her sex and to humanity, and whose productions, from first to last, contain no syllable calculated to call a blush to the cheek of modesty and virtue. There is, moreover, in Mrs. Hemans' poetry a moral purity, and a religious feeling, which commend it, in an especial manner, to the discriminating reader. No parent or guardian will be under the necessity of imposing restrictions with regard to the free perusal of every production emanating from this gifted woman. There breathes throughout the whole a most eminent exemption from impropriety of thought or diction; and there is at times a pensiveness of tone, a winning sadness in her more serious compositions, which tells of a soul which has been lifted from the contemplation of terrestrial things, to divine communings with beings of a purer world."

THE POETICAL WORKS OF ROGERS, CAMPBELL, MONTGOMERY, LAMB, AND KIRK WHITE.

Complete in 1 Vol. 8vo.; with 6 beautiful engravings.

☞ The beauty, correctness and convenience of this favorite edition of these standard authors are so well known, that it is scarcely necessary to add a word in its favor. It is only necessary to say, that the publishers have now issued an illustrated edition, which greatly enhances its former value. The engravings are excellent and well selected. It is the best library edition extant.

MILTON, YOUNG, GRAY, BEATTIE, AND COLLINS' POETICAL WORKS.

Complete in 1 Vol. 8vo.; with 6 beautiful engravings.

HEBER, POLLOK, AND CRABBE'S POETICAL WORKS.

Complete in 1 Vol. 8vo.; with 6 beautiful engravings.

A writer in the Boston Traveller holds the following language with reference to these valuable editions:—

Mr. Editor—I wish, without any idea of puffing, to say a word or two upon the "Library of English Poets" that is now published at Philadelphia, by Grigg & Elliot; it is certainly, taking into consideration the elegant manner in which it is printed, and the reasonable price at which it is afforded to purchasers, the best edition of the modern British Poets that has ever been published in this country. Each volume is an octavo of about 500 pages, double columns, stereotyped, and accompanied with fine engravings, and biographical sketches, and most of them are reprinted from Galignani's French edition. As to its value we need only mention that it contains the entire works of Montgomery, Gray, Beattie, Collins, Byron, Cowper, Thomson, Milton, Young, Rogers, Campbell, Lamb, Hemans, Heber, Kirk White, Crabbe, the Miscellaneous Works of Goldsmith, and other martyrs of the lyre. The publishers are doing a great service by their publication, and their volumes are almost in as great demand as the fashionable novels of the day, and they deserve to be so, for they are certainly printed in a style superior to that in which we have before had the works of the English Poets."

No library can be considered complete without a copy of the above beautiful and cheap editions of the English Poets, and persons ordering all or any of them will please say Grigg, Elliot & Co.'s illustrated editions.

JOSEPHUS'S (FLAVIUS) WORKS.

GRIGG, ELLIOT & CO.'S FAMILY EDITION.

BY THE LATE WILLIAM WHISTON, A. M.

FROM THE LAST LONDON EDITION, COMPLETE.

One Vol., Beautifully Illustrated with Steel Plates,

And the only readable edition published in this country.

As a matter of course, every family in our country has a copy of the Holy Bible—and as the presumption is, the greater portion often consult its pages, we take the liberty of saying to all those that do, that the perusal of the writings of Josephus will be found very interesting and instructive.

All those who wish to possess a beautiful and correct copy of this valuable work, would do well to purchase this edition. It is for sale at all the principal bookstores in the United States, by country merchants generally in the Southern and Western States.

Say's Political Economy.

A TREATISE ON POLITICAL ECONOMY,

OR THE

Production, Distribution, and Consumption of Wealth.

BY JEAN BAPTISTE SAY.

FIFTH AMERICAN EDITION, WITH ADDITIONAL NOTES,

BY C. C. BIDDLE, ESQ.,

In One Volume, Octavo.

It would be beneficial to our country if all those who are aspiring to office, were required by their constituents to be conversant with the pages of Say.

The distinguished biographer of the author, in noticing this work, observes, "Happily for science he commenced that study which forms the basis of his admirable treatise on *Political Economy*, a work which not only improved under his hand with every successive edition, but has been translated into most of the European languages."

The editor of the North American Review, speaking of Say, observes, that "he is the most popular, and perhaps the most able writer on Political Economy, since the time of Smith."

BENNETT'S (Rev. John)

LETTERS TO A YOUNG LADY,

ON A VARIETY OF SUBJECTS CALCULATED TO IMPROVE THE HEART, TO FORM THE MANNERS, AND ENLIGHTEN THE UNDERSTANDING.

"That our Daughters may be as polished corners of the Temple."

The publishers sincerely hope, (*for the happiness of mankind,*) that a copy of this valuable little work will be found the companion of every young lady, as much of the happiness of every family depends on the proper cultivation of the female mind.

THE DAUGHTER'S OWN BOOK.

OR, PRACTICAL HINTS FROM A FATHER TO HIS DAUGHTER.

ONE VOLUME 18MO.

This is one of the most practical and truly valuable treatises on the culture and discipline of the female mind, which has hitherto been published in this country, and the publishers are very confident, from the great demand for this invaluable little work, that ere long it will be found in the library of every young lady.

LAURENCE STERNE'S WORKS,

WITH A LIFE OF THE AUTHOR, WRITTEN BY HIMSELF,

With 7 Beautiful Illustrations, engraved by Gilbert and Gihon, from Designs by Darley.

ONE VOLUME OCTAVO, CLOTH GILT.

To commend, or to criticise Sterne's works, in this age of the world, would be all "wasteful and extravagant excess." Uncle Toby—Corporal Trim—The Widow—Le Fevre—Poor Maria—The Captive—even the Dead Ass,—this is all we have to say of Sterne; and in the memory of these characters, histories and sketches, a thousand follies and worse than follies are forgotten. The volume is a very handsome one.

BOOK OF POLITENESS.

THE GENTLEMAN AND LADY'S

BOOK OF POLITENESS AND PROPRIETY OF DEPORTMENT.

DEDICATED TO THE YOUTH OF BOTH SEXES.

BY MADAME CELNART.

Translated from the Sixth Paris edition, enlarged and improved.

Fifth American Edition. 1 Vol. 18mo.

A Dictionary of

SELECT AND POPULAR QUOTATIONS,

WHICH ARE IN DAILY USE:

TAKEN FROM THE LATIN, FRENCH, GREEK, SPANISH AND ITALIAN LANGUAGES;

TOGETHER WITH A COPIOUS COLLECTION OF LAW MAXIMS AND LAW TERMS

Translated into English, with illustrations, Historical and Idiomatic.

New American edition, corrected with additions.

One Vol. 12mo.

This volume comprises a copious collection of legal and other terms, which are in common use, with English translations and Historical Illustrations, and we should judge its author had surely been to a great "Feast of Languages," and stole all the scraps. A work of this character should have an extensive sale, as it entirely obviates a serious difficulty in which most readers are involved by the frequent occurrence of Latin, Greek, and French passages, which we suppose are introduced by authors for a mere show of learning—a difficulty very perplexing to readers in general. This "Dictionary of Quotations," concerning which too much cannot be said in its favor, effectually removes the difficulty, and gives the reader an advantage over the author, for we believe a majority are themselves ignorant of the meaning of the terms they employ—very few truly learned authors will insult their readers by introducing Latin or French quotations in their writings when "Plain English" is just as good; but we will not enlarge on this point.

If the book is useful to those unacquainted with other languages, it is no less valuable to the classically educated as a book of reference, and answers all the purposes of a Lexicon—indeed, on many accounts, it is better. It saves the trouble of tumbling over the larger volumes, to which every one, and especially those engaged in the Legal Profession, are very often subjected. It should have a place in every library in the country.

THE AMERICAN CHESTERFIELD;

Or, "Youth's Guide to the Way to Wealth, Honor, and Distinction," &c. 18mo.

CONTAINING ALSO A COMPLETE TREATISE ON THE ART OF CARVING.

"We most cordially recommend the American Chesterfield to general attention; but to young persons particularly, as one of the best works of the kind that has ever been published in this country. It cannot be too highly appreciated, nor its perusal be unproductive of satisfaction and usefulness."

SENECA'S MORALS.

BY WAY OF ABSTRACT TO WHICH IS ADDED, A DISCOURSE UNDER THE TITLE OF AN AFTER-THOUGHT.

By Sir Roger L'Estrange, Knt.

A NEW FINE EDITION, ONE VOLUME, 18MO.

A copy of this valuable little work should be found in every family library.

BURDER'S VILLAGE SERMONS.

Or, 101

PLAIN AND SHORT DISCOURSES ON THE PRINCIPAL DOCTRINES OF THE GOSPEL;

INTENDED FOR THE USE OF FAMILIES, SUNDAY SCHOOLS, OR COMPANIES ASSEMBLED FOR RELIGIOUS INSTRUCTION IN COUNTRY VILLAGES.

BY GEORGE BURDER.

To which is added to each Sermon, a Short Prayer, with some General Prayers for Families, Schools, &c., at the end of the work.

Complete in One Volume, Octavo.

These sermons, which are characterized by a beautiful simplicity, the entire absence of controversy, and a true evangelical spirit, have gone through many and large editions, and been translated into several of the continental languages. "They have also been the honored means not only of converting many individuals, but also of introducing the Gospel into districts, and even into parish churches, where before it was comparatively unknown."

"This work fully deserves the immortality it has attained."

This is a fine library edition of this invaluable work, and when we say that it should be found in the possession of every family, we only reiterate the sentiments and sincere wishes of all who take a deep interest in the eternal welfare of mankind.

New Song Book.

Grigg's Southern and Western Songster;

BEING A

CHOICE COLLECTION OF THE MOST FASHIONABLE SONGS, MANY OF WHICH ARE ORIGINAL.

In One Vol. 18mo.

Great care was taken in the selection, to admit no song that contained, in the slightest degree, any indelicate or improper allusions, and with great propriety it may claim the title of "The Parlor Song Book or Songster." The immortal Shakspeare observes—

"The man that hath not music in himself,
Nor is not moved with concord of sweet sounds,
Is fit for treasons, stratagems, and spoils."

Family Prayers and Hymns

ADAPTED TO FAMILY WORSHIP, AND TABLES FOR THE REGULAR READING OF THE SCRIPTURES.

BY REV. S. C. WINCHESTER, A. M.,

Late Pastor of the Sixth Presbyterian Church, Philadelphia; and the Presbyterian Church at Natchez, Miss.

One Volume, 12mo.

THE WESTERN MERCHANT.

A NARRATIVE

CONTAINING USEFUL INSTRUCTION FOR THE WESTERN MAN OF BUSINESS, WHO MAKES HIS PURCHASES IN THE EAST;

ALSO,

INFORMATION FOR THE EASTERN MAN WHOSE CUSTOMERS ARE IN THE WEST: LIKEWISE HINTS FOR THOSE WHO DESIGN EMIGRATING TO THE WEST: DEDUCED FROM ACTUAL EXPERIENCE.

BY LUKE SHORTFIELD, A Western Merchant.

In One Volume, 12mo.

This is a new work and will be found very interesting to the Country Merchant, &c. &c.

A sprightly, pleasant book, with a vast amount of information in a very agreeable shape. Business, Love and Religion are all discussed, and many proper sentiments expressed in regard to each. The "moral" of the work is summed up in the following concluding sentences: "Adhere steadfastly to your business; adhere steadfastly to your first love; adhere steadfastly to the church."

To Carpenters and Mechanics.

Just Published.

A NEW AND IMPROVED EDITION OF THE

CARPENTER'S NEW GUIDE,

BEING A COMPLETE BOOK OF LINES FOR

CARPENTRY AND JOINERY,

Treating fully on Practical Geometry, Saffit's Brick and Plaster Groins, Niches of every description, Sky-Lights, Lines for Roofs and Domes, with a great variety of Designs for Roofs, Trussed Girders, Floors, Domes, Bridges, &c., Angle Bars for Shop Fronts, &c., and Raking Mouldings.

ALSO,

Additional Plans for various Stair-Cases, with the Lines for producing the Face and Falling Moulds, never before published, and greatly superior to those given in a former edition of this work.

BY WILLIAM JOHNSON,

ARCHITECT, OF PHILADELPHIA.

THE WHOLE FOUNDED ON TRUE GEOMETRICAL PRINCIPLES;

THE THEORY AND PRACTICE

Well explained and fully exemplified, on eighty-three Copper Plates, including some Observations and Calculations on the Strength of Timber.

BY PETER NICHOLSON,

Author of "The Carpenter and Joiners' Assistant," "The Student's Instructor to the Five Orders," &c.

Thirteenth Edition. 1 Vol. 4to.

THE ERRORS OF MODERN INFIDELITY,

ILLUSTRATED AND REFUTED,

BY S. M. SCHMUCKER, A. M.,

In One Volume 12mo., cloth. ***Just Published.***

We cannot but regard this work, in whatever light we view it in reference to its design, as one of the most masterly productions of the age, and fitted to unroot one of the most fondly cherished and dangerous of all ancient or modern errors. God must bless such a work, armed with his own truth, and doing fierce and successful battle against black infidelity, which would bring His Majesty and Word down to the tribunal of human reason, for condemnation and annihilation.—*Albany Spectator.*

The Child's First Book in Geography.

BY A DISTINGUISHED PRACTICAL TEACHER.

A Small Quarto, illustrated by numerous Maps, on a new and improved plan, and over one hundred Beautiful and Original Cuts, forming the most complete and attractive Primary Geography, yet published in this country. This elementary work, as also the larger School Geography named below, contains as much or more Geographical information and better arranged, than any other Geographies now used in the schools of this country, for the truth of which the publishers particularly request all teachers to examine for themselves. Copies for examination will be furnished gratis.

SMITH'S NEW COMMON SCHOOL GEOGRAPHY,

Illustrated with numerous engravings, and particularly adapted for all Common Schools, Academies, &c. This is a new work, and all persons ordering, will please say, Grigg, Elliot & Co.'s Edition of Smith's Geography.

There is no *School Book* ever issued from the American press, that is more highly recommended than this invaluable elementary work; and it will be universally introduced into all the Private and Public Schools in the United States, if real merit is taken into consideration, and all Teachers are particularly requested to give it a candid examination.

WALKER'S SCHOOL DICTIONARY,

New Edition, well bound. The above is a popular Philadelphia School Edition, printed from New Stereotype Plates, on Fine White Paper, and well bound, and has been adopted and introduced into the Public Schools of Philadelphia.

Chamber of the Controllers of Public Schools,
First School District of Pennsylvania,
Philadelphia, March 15, 1848.

At a meeting of the Controllers of Public Schools, First School District of Pennsylvania, held at the Controllers' Chamber, on Tuesday, March 14th, the following resolution was adopted:

Resolved, That "*Walker's Critical Pronouncing Dictionary,*" published by Grigg, Elliot & Co., be adopted for use in the Public Schools.

Certified from the Minutes.

THOMAS B. FLORENCE, *Secretary.*

Messrs. Grigg, Elliot & Co.

THE AMERICAN MANUAL:

Containing a Brief Outline of the Origin and Progress of Political Power, and the Laws of Nations; a Commentary on the Constitution of the United States of North America, and a lucid Exposition of the Duties and Responsibilities of Voters, Jurors, and Civil Magistrates; with Questions, Definitions, and Marginal Exercises; designed to develope and strengthen the Moral and Intellectual Powers of Youth, and impart an accurate knowledge of the nature and necessity of Political Wisdom. Adapted to the use of Schools, Academies, and the Public. By Joseph Bartlett Burleigh, A. M., a Member of the Baltimore Bar, and President of Newton University.—"Regnant Populi." This invaluable work has received the highest recommendations from many of the most distinguished and practical Teachers in this country. Teachers who study the welfare and improvement of their pupils will examine and use this book.

AN ETYMOLOGICAL
DICTIONARY OF THE ENGLISH LANGUAGE,

Containing the Radicals and Definitions of Words derived from the Greek, Latin, and French Languages; and all the generally used Technical and Polite Phrases adopted from the French and Latin. Designed chiefly as a Book of Reference for professional men, and the curious in Literature, in explaining Words and Phrases, the origin of which requires much Historical and Philosophical Research; and adapted also to be used as an Academical Class Book. By WILLIAM GRIMSHAW, author of a History of the United States, History of England, France, &c. Third edition, carefully Revised and Enlarged. In 1 vol. 12mo.

The Life of
GENERAL ZACHARY TAYLOR,

COMPRISING A NARRATIVE OF EVENTS CONNECTED WITH HIS PROFESSIONAL CAREER, AND AUTHENTIC INCIDENTS OF HIS EARLY YEARS.

BY J. REESE FRY AND R. T. CONRAD.

WITH AN ORIGINAL AND ACCURATE PORTRAIT, AND ELEVEN ELEGANT ILLUSTRATIONS, BY DARLEY.

In one handsome 12mo. volume.

It is by far the fullest and most interesting biography of General Taylor that we have ever seen.—*Richmond (Whig) Chronicle.*

On the whole, we are satisfied that this volume is the most correct and comprehensive one yet published.—*Hunt's Merchants' Magazine.*

"The superiority of this edition over the ephemeral publications of the day consists in fuller and more authentic accounts of his family; his early life and Indian wars. The narrative of his proceedings in Mexico is drawn partly from reliable private letters, but chiefly from his own official correspondence.

"It forms a cheap, substantial and attractive volume, and one which should be read at the fireside of every family who desire a faithful and true life of the Old General."

N. B. Be careful to order *Grigg, Elliot & Co.'s Illustrated Editions* of those works.

JUST PUBLISHED,

Illustrated Editions of the following Works:

GENERAL TAYLOR AND HIS STAFF;

COMPRISING MEMOIRS OF GENERALS

TAYLOR, WORTH, WOOL AND BUTLER:

COLS. MAY, CROSS, CLAY, HARDIN, YELL, HAYS,

AND

OTHER DISTINGUISHED OFFICERS ATTACHED TO GENERAL TAYLOR'S ARMY.

INTERSPERSED WITH

NUMEROUS ANECDOTES OF THE MEXICAN WAR,

AND

PERSONAL ADVENTURES OF THE OFFICERS.

Compiled from Public Documents and Private Correspondence.

WITH

ACCURATE PORTRAITS, AND OTHER BEAUTIFUL ILLUSTRATIONS.

In One Volume, 12mo.

GENERAL SCOTT AND HIS STAFF;

COMPRISING MEMOIRS OF GENERALS

SCOTT, TWIGGS, SMITH, QUITMAN, SHIELDS,

PILLOW, LANE, CADWALADER, PATTERSON AND PIERCE;

COLS. CHILDS, RILEY, HARNEY AND BUTLER,

AND OTHER

DISTINGUISHED OFFICERS ATTACHED TO GENERAL SCOTT'S ARMY;

TOGETHER WITH

Notices of General Kearney, Colonel Doniphan, Colonel Fremont, and other Officers distinguished in the Conquest of California and New Mexico.

AND PERSONAL ADVENTURES OF THE OFFICERS.

Compiled from Public Documents and Private Correspondence.

WITH

ACCURATE PORTRAITS, AND OTHER BEAUTIFUL ILLUSTRATIONS.

In one volume, 12mo.

CAMP LIFE OF A VOLUNTEER.

A CAMPAIGN IN MEXICO;

OR, A GLIMPSE AT LIFE IN CAMP.

BY "ONE WHO HAS SEEN THE ELEPHANT."

SONGS FOR THE PEOPLE.

Edited by ALBERT G. EMERICK, Professor of Music.

Illustrated with NUMEROUS ENGRAVINGS, from Original Designs, BY W. CROOME & CO. 1 vol. 8vo., scarlet cloth.

LIFE OF PAUL JONES.

In One Volume 12mo., with One Hundred Illustrations.

"Life of Rear Admiral John Paul Jones," &c. &c., by James Hamilton. The work is compiled from his original journals and correspondence; and includes an account of his services in the American Revolution, and in the war between the Russians and Turks in the Black Sea. There is scarcely any Naval Hero of any age who combined in his character so much of the adventurous, skilful and daring, as Paul Jones. The incidents of his life are almost as startling and absorbing as those of romance. His achievements during the American Revolution—the fight between the *Bon Homme Richard* and *Serapis*, the most desperate naval action on record, and the alarm into which, with so small a force, he threw the coasts of England and Scotland, are matters comparatively well known to Americans; but the incidents of his subsequent career have been veiled in obscurity, which is dissipated by this Biography. A book like this, narrating the actions of such a man, ought to meet with an extensive sale, and become as popular as *Robinson Crusoe* in fiction, or *Weems' Life of Marion and Washington*, and similar books in fact. It contains 400 pages—has a handsome portrait and medallion likeness of Jones, and is illustrated with numerous original wood engravings of naval scenes and distinguished men with whom he was familiar.

L. G. Curtis, Esq., editor of the Commercial, Cincinnati, Ohio, speaking of this work' &c., observes:—"'Life of Rear Admiral Paul Jones, illustrated with numerous engravings from original drawings.' This book we prize above any in our possession. John Paul Jones was truly an extraordinary man. He had the honor to hoist with his own hands the flag of freedom, the first time it was displayed in the Delaware, and in after life declared that he attended it with veneration ever after. To Paul Jones the honor of raising up an American navy belongs. He was the first commander in the world who made the proud flag of England 'come down.' His life, as printed by Messrs. Grigg, Elliot & Co., should be in the hands of every intelligent American."

The Life and Opinions of Tristram Shandy, Gentleman.

COMPRISING THE HUMOROUS ADVENTURES OF

UNCLE TOBY AND CORPORAL TRIM.

BY L. STERNE.

Beautifully illustrated by Darley, stitched.

A SENTIMENTAL JOURNEY, BY L. STERNE.

Illustrated as above, by Darley, stitched.

The beauties of this author are so well known, and his errors in style and expression so few and far between, that one reads with renewed delight his delicate turns, &c.

THE LIFE OF GENERAL JACKSON,

WITH A LIKENESS OF THE OLD HERO. 1 Volume 18mo.

A COMPLETE DICTIONARY

OF

POETICAL QUOTATIONS:

COMPRISING THE MOST EXCELLENT AND APPROPRIATE PASSAGES

IN THE

OLD BRITISH POETS:

WITH CHOICE AND COPIOUS SELECTIONS

FROM THE BEST

MODERN BRITISH AND AMERICAN POETS.

EDITED BY

SARAH JOSEPHA HALE.

As nightingales do upon glow-worms feed,
So poets live upon the living light
Of Nature and of Beauty.

Bailey's Festus.

Beautifully illustrated with engravings. In one super-royal 8vo. volume, in various bindings.

The publishers extract, from the many highly complimentary notices of the above valuable and beautiful work, the following:

"We have at last a volume of Poetical Quotations worthy of the name. It contains nearly six hundred octavo pages, carefully and tastefully selected from all the home and foreign authors of celebrity. It is invaluable to a writer, while to the ordinary reader it presents every subject at a glance."—*Godey's Lady's Book.*

"The plan or idea of Mrs. Hale's work is felicitous. It is one for which her fine taste, her orderly habits of mind, and her long occupation with literature, has given her peculiar facilities; and thoroughly has she accomplished her task in the work before us."—*Sartain's Magazine.*

"It is a choice collection of poetical extracts from every English and American author, worth perusing, from the days of Chaucer to the present time."—*Washington Union.*

"Its graceful editress, in her short preface, thus speaks, and most truly, of its contents: "Whatever is loveliest in sentiment and loftiest in aspiration is here represented: specimens of the varied forms in which gifted minds have contributed to the polish of wit, the beauty of wisdom, the sweetness of love, the power of patriotism, the holiness of piety—all that has most deeply stirred the soul of the Anglo-Saxon race for the last three hundred years, is here embodied." It contains copious selections from all the standard British and American Poets upon almost every subject within the range of thought. The subjects are arranged alphabetically, and a "Table of Contents" at the commencement renders reference to them perfectly easy."—*New Hampshire Patriot.*

"There is nothing negative about this work; it is *positively* good."—*Evening Bulletin.*

***** Public, private and social libraries, and all who purchase to sell again, supplied on the most reasonable terms with every article in the Book and Stationery line; including new novels, and all new works in every department of literature and science.**

☞ **Particular attention will also be paid to all orders, through country merchants, or by mail, for Law, Medical and Miscellaneous Books, for public and private libraries, and no effort will be spared to complete all such orders on the most reasonable terms.**

www.ingramcontent.com/pod-product-compliance
Lightning Source LLC
LaVergne TN
LVHW010231110826
845151LV00004B/1257
9781425524814